HIGHER LEARNING

READING AND WRITING ABOUT COLLEGE

SECOND EDITION

EDITED BY

Patti See

UNIVERSITY OF WISCONSIN–EAU CLAIRE

Bruce Taylor

UNIVERSITY OF WISCONSIN–EAU CLAIRE

PEARSON

Prentice
Hall

Upper Saddle River, New Jersey
Columbus, Ohio

Library of Congress Cataloging-in-Publication Data

Higher learning: reading and writing about college/edited by Patti See,
Bruce Taylor.—2nd ed.
     p.cm.
   ISBN 0-13-114163-5
   1. Readers—Education, Higher.   2. Universities and colleges—Problems, exercises,
etc.   3. Education, Higher—Problems, exercises, etc.   4. Readers—Universities and
colleges.   5. English language—Rhetoric.   6. Academic writing.   7. College readers.
I. See, Patti. II. Taylor, Bruce.

PE1127.E37H54 2006
428.6—dc22

                                                                          2005006365

Credits and Permissions are listed on pages xiii–xv, constituting an extension
of the copyright page.

Vice President and Publisher: Jeffery W. Johnston
Senior Acquisitions Editor: Sande Johnson
Assistant Editor: Susan Kauffman
Production Editor: Holcomb Hathaway
Design Coordinator: Diane C. Lorenzo
Cover Designer: Jeff Vanik
Cover Photos: See p. xiii
Production Manager: Susan Hannahs
Director of Marketing: Ann Castel Davis
Marketing Manager: Amy Judd
Compositor: Integra–Pondicherry, India
Cover Printer: Courier Stoughton, Inc.
Printer/Binder: Courier Stoughton, Inc.

Pearson Education Ltd.   Pearson Education Canada, Ltd.
Pearson Education Australia Pty. Limited   Pearson Educación de Mexico, S.A. de C.V.
Pearson Education Singapore Pte. Ltd.   Pearson Education–Japan
Pearson Education North Asia Ltd.   Pearson Education Malaysia Pte. Ltd.

10 9 8 7 6 5 4 3 2
ISBN 0-13-114163-5

Contents

CHAPTER ONE

Where We're Coming From   1

LEAVING OTHER LIVES

From *Up from Slavery* • *Booker T. Washington*   *2*

MEMOIR (1901)   Prejudices in 1872 force the author to sleep outside during his journey to college, but when he finally reaches what he calls his "promised land," he must pass an unconventional test before he is admitted.

Incurring My Mother's Displeasure • *Zitkala-Sa*   *7*

MEMOIR (1900)   Recounts the author's difficulty balancing her Native American childhood with learning the "white man's ways" at college and living with the pain of disobeying her mother by continuing her education.

From *One Writer's Beginnings* • *Eudora Welty*   *10*

MEMOIR (1983)   Chronicles the author's earliest memories in a household that valued books.

Saved • *Malcolm X*   *15*

MEMOIR (1965)   Malcolm X uses his time in jail to hone his reading and writing skills.

Miss Rinehart's Paddle • *Jeri McCormick*   *19*

POEM (1991)   Depicts the loss of power for students who always follow the rules and those who can't help themselves.

50% Chance of Lightning • *Cristina Salat*   *21*

FICTION (1994)   Best friends and high school seniors decide their futures much differently: Robin has the guts to "come out" in a column in her school newspaper, but she is unsure that she will find her life's plan in a college catalogue.

Somewhere in Minnesota • *Peter Klein*   *30*

POEM / STUDENT WRITTEN (1979)   The "brilliant future" that awaits many high school graduates is especially bright as portrayed in their senior photos.

CHAPTER TWO

School Daze   55

LIFE IN THE FIRST YEAR

CHAPTER THREE

Student Relations   111

FAMILY, FRIENDS, AND LOVERS

CHAPTER FOUR

Teacher, Teacher   181

WILL THIS BE ON THE TEST?

CHAPTER FIVE

Been There, Done That   231

LOOKING FORWARD, LOOKING BACK

Appendix   281

Preface

I magine entering a foreign country where you understand just enough of the language to communicate but cannot quite grasp the customs or the etiquette of the land. Imagine you have to learn the culture of that country without anyone showing or telling you how. This is what going to college is like for many first-year students. *Higher Learning: Reading and Writing About College, Second Edition,* appeals to students and teachers because it is written from their point of view. The fiction, poetry, essays, creative nonfiction, lists, journal entries, articles, and a play included here allow students to see how their individual experiences fit into the culturally and historically diverse traditions and perspectives of university life.

Avid readers—students, teachers, and lifelong learners—know literature is the one place a person is never alone. This collection allows readers to discover people just like them, as well as people sometimes so different from them to be almost, at least at first, unimaginable. Students can watch these people struggle with problems and challenges, most of which never appear in any college catalogue or on any class syllabus. Although universities provide an array of student support systems, new students must work through some aspects of university life mostly on their own. Character, maturity, and experience will be as essential to success as high school class rank or SAT scores. Alienation, isolation, and loneliness will be as much of a challenge as English Composition or Calculus.

Many college texts for first-year students focus on time management, critical thinking, active reading, and lecture and text note taking. These survival skills are the nuts and bolts of college success. This collection displays the whole machine chugging along in all its imperfect glory. These readings provide good and bad examples, some broader views and alternative takes of individual experiences, parables of the admirable, cautionary tales, and funny stories.

College students, especially first-year students, often feel isolated. The degree to which they feel a sense of place and a way of fitting in, which many teachers and administrators by now take too much for granted, leads to how well the students perform and in fact to whether or not they complete a degree. *Higher Learning* offers some of the "inside" stories of college life and university culture, addressing the difficult issues that students face in their transition to college. It also provides students and teachers a vehicle to explore, reflect on, and perhaps even discover issues about ethnicity, class, age, gender, and sexual diversity.

Where to Use This Book

As editors, our first instinct would be to say this book should be used everywhere. Or at least everywhere there are people who ought to be paying attention to college, to university culture, to what an education is and how you get one, and to what all of it means. More specifically, natural venues may include transition to college/student success courses, composition courses, creative writing courses, critical thinking courses, and high school college prep courses.

How to Use This Book: A Primer for Careful Reading

Critical Thinking Points—arranged in the categories of *As You Read, After You've Read,* and *Some Possibilities for Writing*—accompany each selection, challenging students with the kinds of close and active critical reading and thinking required at the college level and providing prompts for contemplation, class discussion, and writing.

The *As You Read* questions will lend focus to a reading, help readers formulate their own questions, establish a historical and/or cultural context, or promote connections to students' lives. The *After You've Read* questions often require the kinds of debate, perspective, and points of view that make for lively and productive small-group or full-class discussion. *Some Possibilities for Writing* at the end of each reading are an opportunity to respond in writing in the broadest possible ways suitable for short assignments or journal entries.

The *Further Suggestions for Writing* at the end of each chapter offer a menu of varied prompts and assignments for longer, more fully developed, and perhaps more formal assignments that build the skills necessary for writing well in college. These writing prompts range from class reports to interviews, from essays to fully developed research papers that employ the traditional rhetorical strategies such as simple exposition, comparative and causal analyses, or argument and persuasion. The point, in some way or another, is to foster the attention and perspective, the self-awareness and self-assessment that are indeed *higher learning.*

These categories of questions may be necessary and helpful, but any questions from anywhere in the book might be used at any time in any way. Although each chapter of *Higher Learning* focuses on a particular stage of college life, this book is not necessarily meant to be read sequentially from page one to the end.

A Note on the Second Edition

Significant changes have been made to the literature gathered here and to the apparatus. Some pieces have been cut and some pieces added by established writers—such as Eudora Welty, Malcolm X, and Alice Walker—as well as by younger writers scrambling to be established, like Jill Wolfson, Richard Terrill, and Taylor Mali. Chapter Three has been expanded to include "Family and Friends" so that a fuller range of the kinds of relationships that assist or impede a student's experience is explored. Some questions have been deleted, and some new ones added to ask students to dig deeper and look further. The writing prompts have been rescaled so that smaller, more informal ones appear at the end of each selection while longer and more formal ones are at the end of each chapter. The annotated filmographies for each chapter have been expanded and revised.

Our goal in providing this book continues to be that students will not only be motivated to read, but they also will be moved to reflect and write about their own experiences, their campus, their college life in general, and the world around them.

Acknowledgments

We wish to thank the Network for Excellence in Teaching and the Office of Research and Sponsored Programs at the University of Wisconsin–Eau Claire for their grant funding for travel to share our research at professional conferences, as well as the Academic Skills Center and the Department of English for their support. Thank you to our editor, Sande Johnson, who has provided us with encouragement and guidance. Thank you to our reviewers who saw and commented on our book in various stages: Amy D'Antonio, Arizona State University; Christine Helfers, Arizona State University; Jennifer Rosti, Roanoke College; and Sherry Wynn, Oakland University.

Finally, thanks to our students in UW–Eau Claire's Developmental Education, Introduction to College Writing, and Creative Writing courses, who were our first and ongoing audience.

For additional information, activities, and resources intended to enhance the readings in this book, be sure to visit our website:

www.uwec.edu/taylorb/

About the Authors

Patti See teaches courses in critical thinking, learning strategies, transitions to college, and third-wave feminism. She also supervises tutoring programs for students of color; students with disabilities; and first-generation, low-income students.

Her stories, poems, and essays have appeared in *Salon Magazine, Women's Studies Quarterly, Journal of Development Education, The Wisconsin Academy Review, The Southwest Review,* as well as other magazines and anthologies. She speaks at universities and conferences on a variety of topics, including the First-Year Experience, Third-Wave feminism, women in popular films, critical thinking, and creative writing. She was the recipient of the 2004 Academic Staff Excellence in Performance Award from the University of Wisconsin–Eau Claire.

Bruce Taylor teaches courses in First-Year Experience, Introduction to College Writing, Creative Writing, and American Literature and in the Honors Program. He is the author of five chapbooks of poetry, including *This Day* (Juniper Press); he is the editor of seven anthologies, including the UPRIVER series of Wisconsin Poetry and Prose, and *Wisconsin Poetry,* published by the Wisconsin Academy of Sciences, Arts, and Letters. His poetry, prose, and translations have appeared in such places as *Carve Magazine, The Chicago Review, The Exquisite Corpse, The Nation, Nerve, The New York Quarterly, The Northwest Review, Poetry,* and *E2ink-1: the Best of the Online Journals 2002.*

He has also served as a member of the Literature Panel of the Wisconsin Arts Board and host of The Writer's Workshop: Wisconsin ETN, and he has served as program scholar and consultant for the Wisconsin Humanities Council, the Lila Wallace Foundation, the L.E. Phillips Library, and the Annenberg/CPB Project. He has won awards and fellowships from the Wisconsin Arts Board, Fulbright-Hayes, the National Endowment for the Arts, the National Endowment for the Humanities, and the Bush Artist Foundation, and he was the recipient of the 2004 Excellence in Scholarship Award from the University of Wisconsin–Eau Claire.

We would love to hear from you. Please email the authors with any feedback or suggestions at

seepk@uwec.edu   or   taylorb@uwec.edu

Credits and Permissions

Cover Photos

Left: Howard University class/Crampton Photo, Howard University, Call Number X-22353. Graduating class, Indian Industrial School, Carlisle, Pa., Call Number X-32087. Used with permission from Denver Public Library, Western History Collection.

Right: First Class at Eau Claire State Normal School (now University of Wisconsin–Eau Claire), 1916–1917. Professor George L. Simpson's Geography Class at Eau Claire State Normal School (now University of Wisconsin–Eau Claire), 1921. Both photos used with permission from Special Collections, McIntyre Library, University of Wisconsin–Eau Claire.

Chapter One

An excerpt from *One Writer's Beginnings* by Eudora Welty, pp. 3–10, Cambridge, Mass.: Harvard University Press, Copyright © 1983, 1984 by Eudora Welty. Reprinted by permission of the publisher.

"Saved" is from *The Autobiography of Malcolm X* (1964) by Alex Haley and Malcolm X. Used by permission of Random House, Inc.

"Miss Rinehart's Paddle" by Jeri McCormick. Reprinted by permission of the author.

"50% Chance of Lightning" by Cristina Salat from *Am I Blue? Coming Out from the Silence,* text copyright © 1994 by Cristina Salat. Used with permission of the author and Bookstop Literary Agency. All rights reserved.

"Somewhere in Minnesota" by Peter Klein. Reprinted by permission of the author.

"LD" by Jeff Richards originally appeared in *Tales Out of School* (Beacon Press Books, 2000). Copyright © 2000 by Jeff Richards. Reprinted by the permission of Russell and Volkening as agents for the author.

"School's Out: One Young Man Puzzles Over His Future Without College" by Laura Sessions Stepp originally appeared in *The Washington Post* on October 27, 2002. Reprinted by permission of *The Washington Post.*

Chapter Two

"A Day in the Life Of . . ." by Greg Adams. Reprinted by permission of the author.

"My First Week at Mizzou" by Andrew Hicks from *Another Year in the Life of a Nerd* by Andrew Hicks. Reprinted by permission of the author.

"Hunters and Gatherers" by Jennifer Hale. Reprinted by permission of the author.

"Theme for English B" from *Collected Poems* by Langston Hughes, copyright © 1994 by the estate of Langston Hughes. Reprinted by permission of Alfred A. Knopf Inc.

Chapter Three

Chapter Four

"Did I Miss Anything" by Tom Wayman originally appeared in *I'll Be Right Back*. Copyright © 1997 by Tom Wayman. Reprinted with permission of the author and Ontario Review Press.

"Grading Your Professors" by Jacob Neusner from *Grading Your Professors and Other Unexpected Advice* by Jacob Neusner, Beacon Press, 1984. Reprinted by permission of the author.

"Tales Out of School" by Susan Richards Shreve originally appeared as the introduction to *Tales Out of School* (Beacon Press Books, 2000). Copyright © 2000 by Susan Richards Shreve. Reprinted by the permission of Russell and Volkening as agents for the author.

"No Immediate Danger" by Mary McLaughlin Slèchta. Reprinted by permission of the author.

"Teachers: A Primer" by Ronald Wallace from *Time's Fancy* by Ronald Wallace, copyright © 1994. Reprinted by permission of the University of Pittsburgh Press.

"Open Admissions," copyright © 1983 by Shirley Lauro. Reprinted by permission of the William Morris Agency on behalf of the author.

"What Teachers Make" by Taylor Mali. Reprinted by permission of the author.

Chapter Five

"The Art of Regret" by Jonathon Ritz originally appeared in *American Literary Review,* Spring 1999. Reprinted by permission of the author.

"Raising My Hand" by Antler from *Last Words* by Antler (Ballantine Books / Available Press). Reprinted by permission of the author.

"The Eighty-Yard Run" by Irwin Shaw originally published in *Short Stories: Five Decades,* copyright © Irwin Shaw. Reprinted with permission of the estate of Irwin Shaw.

"Reunion" by Dawn Karima Pettigrew. Reprinted by permission of the author.

"Scarlet Ribbons" by Michael Perry. Reprinted by permission of the author.

"Signed, Grateful" by Kate Boyes. Reprinted by permission of the author.

"Passion" by Monica Coleman. Reprinted by permission of the author.

"On the Radio" by Richard Terrill originally appeared in *Coming Late to Rachmaninoff* (2003). Reprinted with permission of University of Tampa Press.

One

Where We're Coming From

LEAVING OTHER LIVES

The selections here examine how different people, places, times, and cultures affect who and what any individual becomes. This chapter explores reasons for going (or not going) to college, how formal education may or may not prepare students for adult life, the values of learning on one's own, and personal experiences of overcoming stereotypes and prejudices.

READING SELECTIONS

from *Up from Slavery*

Incurring My Mother's Displeasure

from *One Writer's Beginnings*

Saved

Miss Rinehart's Paddle

50% Chance of Lightning

Somewhere in Minnesota

LD

School's Out: One Young Man Puzzles Over His Future Without College

8th Grade Final Exam: Salina, Kansas, 1895

Up from Slavery

AN EXCERPT   **Booker T. Washington**

Booker T. Washington (1856–1915) was an American educator who urged blacks to attempt to uplift themselves through education and economic advancement. He was born in Franklin County, Virginia, the son of a slave. From 1872 to 1875, Washington attended a newly founded school for blacks, Hampton Normal and Agricultural Institute (now Hampton University). In 1879 he became an instructor at Hampton. The school was so successful that in 1881 Washington was appointed principal of a black school in Tuskegee, Alabama (now Tuskegee University).

The sight of it seemed to give me a new life. I felt that a new kind of existence had now begun—that life would now have a new meaning.

CRITICAL THINKING POINTS: *As you read*

1. What are some clues to the time and place?
2. The author had no idea where Hampton was or how much tuition cost. What circumstances might have led the author to have such a desire to go to college?
3. Recall a time when you felt proud of yourself for learning, simply for the sake of acquiring knowledge. What led to this?

Notwithstanding my success at Mrs. Ruffner's I did not give up the idea of going to the Hampton Institute. In the fall of 1872 I determined to make an effort to get there, although, as I have stated, I had no definite idea of the direction in which Hampton was, or of what it would cost to go there. I do not think that any one thoroughly sympathized with me in my ambition to go to Hampton unless it was my mother, and she was troubled with a grave fear that I was starting out on a 'wild-goose chase.' At any rate, I got only a half-hearted consent from her that I might start. The small amount of money that I had earned had been consumed by my stepfather and the remainder of the family, with the exception of a very few dollars, and so I had very little with which to buy clothes and pay my traveling expenses. My brother John helped me all that he could, but of course that was not a great deal, for his work was in the coal-mine, where he did not earn much, and most of what he did earn went in the direction of paying the household expenses.

Perhaps the thing that touched and pleased me most in connection with my starting for Hampton was the interest that many of the older coloured people took in

the matter. They had spent the best days of their lives in slavery, and hardly expected to live to see the time when they would see a member of their race leave home to
attend a boarding school. Some of these older people would give me a nickel, others
a quarter, or a handkerchief.

Finally the great day came, and I started for Hampton. I had only a small, cheap
satchel that contained what few articles of clothing I could get. My mother at the
time was rather weak and broken in health. I hardly expected to see her again, and
thus our parting was all the more sad. She, however, was very brave through it all.
At that time there were no through trains connecting that part of West Virginia with
eastern Virginia. Trains ran only a portion of the way, and the remainder of the distance was traveled by stage-coaches.

The distance from Malden to Hampton is about five hundred miles. I had not
been away from home many hours before it began to grow painfully evident that
I did not have enough money to pay my fare to Hampton. One experience I shall
long remember. I had been traveling over the mountains most of the afternoon in
an old-fashioned stage-coach, when, late in the evening, the coach stopped for the
night at a common, unpainted house called a hotel. All the other passengers except
myself were whites. In my ignorance I supposed that the little hotel existed for the
purpose of accommodating the passengers who traveled on the stage-coach. The
difference that the colour of one's skin would make I had not thought anything
about. After all the other passengers had been shown rooms and were getting ready
for supper, I shyly presented myself before the man at the desk. It is true I had practically no money in my pocket with which to pay for bed or food, but I had hoped
in some way to beg my way into the good graces of the landlord, for at that season
in the mountains of Virginia the weather was cold, and I wanted to get indoors for
the night. Without asking as to whether I had any money, the man at the desk firmly refused to even consider the matter of providing me with food or lodging. This
was my first experience in finding out what the colour of my skin meant. In some
way I managed to keep warm by walking about, and so got through the night. My
whole soul was so bent upon reaching Hampton that I did not have time to cherish
any bitterness toward the hotelkeeper.

By walking, begging rides both in wagons and in the cars, in some way, after a
number of days, I reached the city of Richmond, Virginia, about eighty-two miles
from Hampton. When I reached there, tired, hungry, and dirty, it was late in the
night. I had never been in a large city, and this rather added to my misery. When
I reached Richmond, I was completely out of money. I had not a single acquaintance
in the place, and, being unused to city ways, I did not know where to go. I applied
at several places for lodging, but they all wanted money, and that was what I did not
have. Knowing nothing else better to do, I walked the streets. In doing this I passed
by many food-stands where fried chicken and half-moon apple pies were piled high
and made to present a most tempting appearance. At that time it seemed to me that
I would have promised all that I expected to possess in the future to have gotten
hold of one of those chicken legs or one of those pies. But I could not get either of
these, nor anything else to eat.

I must have walked the streets till after midnight. At last I became so exhausted that I could walk no longer. I was tired, I was hungry, I was everything but discouraged. Just about the time when I reached extreme physical exhaustion, I came upon a portion of a street where the board sidewalk was considerably elevated. I waited for a few minutes, till I was sure that no passers-by could see me, and then crept under the sidewalk and lay for the night upon the ground, with my satchel of clothing for a pillow. Nearly all night I could hear the tramp of feet over my head. The next morning I found myself somewhat refreshed, but I was extremely hungry, because it had been a long time since I had had sufficient food.

As soon as it became light enough for me to see my surroundings I noticed that I was near a large ship, and that this ship seemed to be unloading a cargo of pig iron. I went at once to the vessel and asked the captain to permit me to help unload the vessel in order to get money for food. The captain, a white man, who seemed to be kindhearted, consented. I worked long enough to earn money for my breakfast, and it seems to me, as I remember it now, to have been about the best breakfast that I have ever eaten. My work pleased the captain so well that he told me if I desired I could continue working for a small amount per day. This I was very glad to do. I continued working on this vessel for a number of days. After buying food with the small wages I received there was not much left to add to the amount I must get to pay my way to Hampton. In order to economize in every way possible, so as to be sure to reach Hampton in a reasonable time, I continued to sleep under the same sidewalk that gave me shelter the first night I was in Richmond. Many years after that the coloured citizens of Richmond very kindly tendered me a reception at which there must have been two thousand people present. This reception was held not far from the spot where I slept the first night I spent in that city, and I must confess that my mind was more upon the sidewalk that first gave me shelter than upon the reception, agreeable and cordial as it was.

When I had saved what I considered enough money with which to reach Hampton, I thanked the captain of the vessel for his kindness, and started again.

Without any unusual occurrence I reached Hampton, with a surplus of exactly fifty cents with which to begin my education. To me it had been a long, eventful journey; but the first sight of the large, three-story, brick school building seemed to have rewarded me for all that I had undergone in order to reach the place. If the people who gave the money to provide that building could appreciate the influence the sight of it had upon me, as well as upon thousands of other youths, they would feel all the more encouraged to make such gifts. It seemed to me to be the largest and most beautiful building I had ever seen. The sight of it seemed to give me a new life. I felt that a new kind of existence had now begun—that life would now have a new meaning. I felt that I had reached the promised land, and I resolved to let no obstacle prevent me from putting forth the highest effort to fit myself to accomplish the most good in the world.

As soon as possible after reaching the grounds of the Hampton Institute, I presented myself before the head teacher for assignment to a class. Having been so long without proper food, a bath and change of clothing, I did not, of course, make a very favourable impression upon her, and I could see at once that there were doubts in her mind about the wisdom of admitting me as a student. I felt that I could hardly blame her if she got the idea that I was a worthless loafer or tramp. For some time she did not refuse to admit me, neither did she decide in my favour, and I continued to linger about her, and to impress her in all the ways I could with my worthiness. In the meantime I saw her admitting other students, and that added greatly to my discomfort, for I felt, deep down in my heart, that I could do as well as they, if I could only get a chance to show what was in me.

After some hours had passed, the head teacher said to me: "The adjoining recitation-room needs sweeping. Take the broom and sweep it." It occurred to me at once that here was my chance. Never did I receive an order with more delight. I knew that I could sweep, for Mrs. Ruffner had thoroughly taught me how to do that when I lived with her.

I swept the recitation-room three times. Then I got a dusting-cloth and I dusted it four times. All the woodwork around the walls, every bench, table, and desk, I went over four times with my dusting-cloth. Besides, every piece of furniture had been moved and every closet and corner in the room had been thoroughly cleaned. I had the feeling that in a large measure my future depended upon the impression I made upon the teacher in the cleaning of that room. When I was through, I reported to the head teacher.

She was a 'Yankee' woman who knew just where to look for dirt. She went into the room and inspected the floor and closets; then she took her handkerchief and rubbed it on the woodwork about the walls, and over the table and benches. When she was unable to find one bit of dirt on the floor, or a particle of dust on any of the furniture, she quietly remarked, "I guess you will do to enter this institution." I was one of the happiest souls on earth. The sweeping of that room was my college examination, and never did any youth pass an examination for entrance into Harvard or Yale that gave him more genuine satisfaction. I have passed several examinations since then, but I have always felt that this was the best one I ever passed.

I have spoken of my own experience in entering the Hampton Institute. Perhaps few, if any, had anything like the same experience that I had, but about that same period there were hundreds who found their way to Hampton and other institutions after experiencing something of the same difficulties that I went through. The young men and women were determined to secure an education at any cost.

1901

CRITICAL THINKING POINTS: *After you've read*

1. Washington learns several important lessons on his journey to Hampton. What are some of them?
2. Washington says about a reception for him in Richmond, "This reception was held not far from the spot where I slept the first night I spent in that city, and I must confess that my mind was more upon the sidewalk that first gave me

shelter than upon the reception, agreeable and cordial as it was." What might such a statement say about Washington?

3. Washington says of his first assignment from the head teacher, "The sweeping of that room was my college examination, and never did any youth pass an examination for entrance into Harvard or Yale that gave him more genuine satisfaction. I have passed several examinations since then, but I have always felt that this was the best one I ever passed." What were some of the reasons this was so important to him?

SOME POSSIBILITIES FOR WRITING

1. Write a scene in which Washington, who is sleeping under the boardwalk on his way to Hampton, meets a man who attends college. Or, write a scene between Washington and another African-American man who has no aspirations for college.

2. Washington says of first seeing Hampton, "I felt that I had reached the promised land." Why was education so important to him? Do you feel it is as important for you?

3. Find *Up from Slavery* and read Chapter 8, "Teaching School in a Stable and a Hen-House." After reading the piece, compare/contrast Washington as a student and a teacher. What insights about education arise from your writing?

Incurring My Mother's Displeasure

FROM *THE SCHOOL DAYS OF AN INDIAN GIRL*   Zitkala-Sa

Zitkala-Sa (1876–1938) was a Sioux Indian. "Incurring My Mother's Displeasure" appeared in the *Atlantic Monthly* in 1900. It is a part of her larger work, *The School Days of an Indian Girl.*

Thus, homeless and heavy-hearted, I began anew my life among strangers.

CRITICAL THINKING POINTS: *As you read*

1. What are some clues to the era?
2. The language and tone of this essay are very formal. Why might that be so?
3. Speculate on what causes prejudice among ethnic groups. What are some stereotypes, past or present, of Native Americans?

In the second journey to the East I had not come without some precautions. I had a secret interview with one of our best medicine men, and when I left his wigwam I carried securely in my sleeve a tiny bunch of magic roots. This possession assured me of friends wherever I should go. So absolutely did I believe in its charms that I wore it through all the school routine for more than a year. Then, before I lost my faith in the dead roots, I lost the little buckskin bag containing all my good luck.

At the close of this second term of three years I was the proud owner of my first diploma. The following autumn I ventured upon a college career against my mother's will. I had written for her approval, but in her reply I found no encouragement. She called my notice to her neighbors' children, who had completed their education in three years. They had returned to their homes, and were then talking English with the frontier settlers. Her few words hinted that I had better give up my slow attempt to learn the white man's ways, and be content to roam over the prairies and find my living upon wild roots. I silenced her by deliberate disobedience.

Thus, homeless and heavy-hearted, I began anew my life among strangers.

As I hid myself in my little room in the college dormitory, away from the scornful and yet curious eyes of the students, I pined for sympathy. Often I wept in secret, wishing I had gone West, to be nourished by my mother's love, instead of remaining among a cold race whose hearts were frozen hard with prejudice.

During the fall and winter seasons I scarcely had a real friend, though by that time several of my classmates were courteous to me at a safe distance. My mother had not yet forgiven my rudeness to her, and I had no moment for letter-writing.

By daylight and lamplight, I spun with reeds and thistles, until my hands were tired from their weaving, the magic design which promised me the white man's respect.

At length, in the spring term, I entered an oratorical contest among the various classes. As the day of competition approached, it did not seem possible that the event was so near at hand, but it came. In the chapel the classes assembled together, with their invited guests. The high platform was carpeted, and gaily festooned with college colors. A bright white light illumined the room and outlined clearly the great polished beams that arched the domed ceiling. The assembled crowds filled the air with pulsating murmurs. When the hour for speaking arrived all were hushed. But on the wall the old clock which pointed out the trying moment ticked calmly on.

One after another I saw and heard the orators. Still, I could not realize that they longed for the favorable decision of the judges as much as I did. Each contestant received a loud burst of applause, and some were cheered heartily. Too soon my turn came, and I paused a moment behind the curtains for a deep breath. After my concluding words, I heard the same applause that the others had called out.

Upon my retreating steps, I was astounded to receive from my fellow students a large bouquet of roses tied with flowing ribbons. With the lovely flowers I fled from the stage. This friendly token was a rebuke to me for the hard feelings I had borne them.

Later, the decision of the judges awarded me the first place. Then there was a mad uproar in the hall, where my classmates sang and shouted my name at the top of their lungs; and the disappointed students howled and brayed in fearfully dissonant tin trumpets. In this excitement, happy students rushed forward to offer their congratulations. And I could not conceal a smile when they wished to escort me in a procession to the students' parlor, where all were going to calm themselves. Thanking them for the kind spirit which prompted them to make such a proposition, I walked alone with the night to my own little room.

A few weeks afterward, I appeared as the college representative in another contest. This time the competition was among orators from different colleges in our state. It was held at the state capital, in one of the largest opera houses.

Here again was a strong prejudice against my people. In the evening, as the great audience filled the house, the student bodies began warring among themselves. Fortunately, I was spared witnessing any of the noisy wrangling before the contest began. The slurs against the Indian that stained the lips of our opponents were already burning like a dry fever within my breast.

But after the orations were delivered a deeper burn awaited me. There, before that vast ocean of eyes, some college rowdies threw out a large white flag, with a drawing of a most forlorn Indian girl on it. Under this they had printed in bold black letters words that ridiculed the college which was represented by a "squaw." Such worse than barbarian rudeness embittered me. While we waited for the verdict of the judges, I gleamed fiercely upon the throngs of palefaces. My teeth were hard set, as I saw the white flag still floating insolently in the air. Then anxiously we watched the man carry toward the stage the envelope containing the final decision.

There were two prizes given, that night, and one of them was mine!

The evil spirit laughed within me when the white flag dropped out of sight, and the hands which furled it hung limp in defeat.

Leaving the crowd as quickly as possible, I was soon in my room. The rest of the night I sat in an armchair and gazed into the crackling fire. I laughed no more in triumph when thus alone. The little taste of victory did not satisfy a hunger in my heart. In my mind I saw my mother far away on the Western plains, and she was holding a charge against me.

1900

CRITICAL THINKING POINTS: *After you've read*

1. In what ways is Zitkala-Sa "homeless"?
2. Why would the narrator physically and spiritually separate herself from her people in order to go to college? What are some details from the story that support your opinion?
3. Read or reread the selection from Booker T. Washington's *Up from Slavery*. How is Zitkala-Sa's experience at college similar to Washington's? How is it different?

SOME POSSIBILITIES FOR WRITING

1. Imagine what happens when the narrator finally returns to her tribe. Write a reunion scene between Zitkala-Sa and her mother.
2. Recall a time when you purposely disobeyed your parents. What circumstances led to this? Write about the moment when you knew you would go against their wishes. What was the outcome?
3. The narrator feels isolated from her classmates because of their prejudice. Have you ever felt isolated from classmates, friends, or family? Write a scene describing your isolation or someone else's.

One Writer's Beginnings

AN EXCERPT   Eudora Welty

Eudora Welty (1909–2001) received her bachelor of arts degree from the University of Wisconsin–Madison in 1929. She won the Pulitzer Prize for fiction with *Optimist's Daughter* in 1969. *One Writer's Beginnings* was nominated for the 1983 National Book Critics Circle Award.

I learned from the age of two or three that any room in our house, at any time of day, was there to read in, or to be read to.

CRITICAL THINKING POINTS: *As you read*

1. Pay attention to the things that are detailed in this essay. Why do you think the author chose the objects she did?
2. Pay attention to all the action in this essay. Why do you think she chose the actions she did?
3. Pay attention to the different ways in which the boys and girls are educated. How is this a sign of the times?

I n our house on North Congress Street in Jackson, Mississippi, where I was born, the oldest of three children, in 1909, we grew up to the striking of clocks. There was a mission-style oak grandfather clock standing in the hall, which sent its gong-like strokes through the living room, dining room, kitchen, and pantry, and up the sounding board of the stairwell. Through the night, it could find its way into our ears; sometimes, even on the sleeping porch, midnight could wake us up. My parents' bedroom had a smaller striking clock that answered it. Though the kitchen clock did nothing but show the time, the dining room clock was a cuckoo clock with weights on long chains, on one of which my baby brother, after climbing on a chair to the top of the china closet, once succeeded in suspending the cat for a moment. I don't know whether or not my father's Ohio family, in having been Swiss back in the 1700s before the first three Welty brothers came to America, had anything to do with this; but we all of us have been time-minded all our lives. This was good at least for a future fiction writer, being able to learn so penetratingly, and almost first of all, about chronology. It was one of a good many things I learned almost without knowing it; it would be there when I needed it.

My father loved all instruments that would instruct and fascinate. His place to keep things was the drawer in the "library table" where lying on top of his folded maps was a telescope with brass extensions, to find the moon and the Big Dipper after supper in our front yard, and to keep appointments with eclipses. There was a folding Kodak that was brought out for Christmas, birthdays, and trips. In the back of the drawer you could find a magnifying glass, a kaleidoscope, and a gyroscope kept in a black buckram box, which he would set dancing for us on a string pulled tight. He had also supplied himself with an assortment of puzzles composed of metal rings and intersecting links and keys chained together, impossible for the rest of us, however patiently shown, to take apart; he had an almost childlike love of the ingenious.

In time, a barometer was added to our dining room wall; but we didn't really need it. My father had the country boy's accurate knowledge of the weather and its skies. He went out and stood on our front steps first thing in the morning and took a look at it and a sniff. He was a pretty good weather prophet.

"Well, I'm not," my mother would say with enormous self-satisfaction.

He told us children what to do if we were lost in a strange country. "Look for where the sky is brightest along the horizon," he said. "That reflects the nearest river. Strike out for a river and you will find habitation." Eventualities were much on his mind. In his care for us children he cautioned us to take measures against such things as being struck by lightning. He drew us all away from the windows during the severe electrical storms that are common where we live. My mother stood apart, scoffing at caution as a character failing. "Why, I always loved a storm! High winds never bothered me in West Virginia! Just listen at that! I wasn't a bit afraid of a little lightning and thunder! I'd go out on the mountain and spread my arms wide and run in a good big storm!"

So I developed a strong meteorological sensibility. In the years ahead when I wrote stories, atmosphere took its influential role from the start. Commotion in the weather and the inner feelings aroused by such a hovering disturbance emerged connected in dramatic form. (I tried a tornado first, in a story called "The Winds.")

From our earliest Christmas times, Santa Claus brought us toys that instruct boys and girls (separately) how to build things—stone blocks cut to the castle-building style, Tinker Toys, and Erector sets. Daddy made for us himself elaborate kites that needed to be taken miles out of town to a pasture long enough (and my father was not afraid of horses and cows watching) for him to run with and get up on a long cord to which my mother held the spindle, and then we children were given it to hold, tugging like something alive at our hands. They were beautiful, sound, shapely box kites, smelling delicately of office glue for their entire short lives. And of course, as soon as the boys attained anywhere near the right age, there was an electric train, the engine with its pea-sized working headlight, its line of cars, tracks equipped with switches, semaphores, its station, its bridges, and its tunnel, which blocked off all other traffic in the upstairs hall. Even from downstairs, and through the cries of excited children, the elegant rush and click of the train could be heard through the ceiling, running around and around its figure eight.

All of this, but especially the train, represents my father's fondest beliefs—in progress, in the future. With these gifts, he was preparing his children.

And so was my mother with her different gifts.

I learned from the age of two or three that any room in our house, at any time of day, was there to read in, or to be read to. My mother read to me. She'd read to me in the big bedroom in the mornings, when we were in her rocker together, which ticked in rhythm as we rocked, as though we had a cricket accompanying the story. She'd read to me in the dining room on winter afternoons in front of the coal fire, with our cuckoo clock ending the story with "Cuckoo," and at night when I'd got in my own bed. I must have given her no peace. Sometimes she read to me in the kitchen while she sat churning, and the churning sobbed along with any story. It was my ambition to have her read to me while I churned; once she granted my wish, but she read off my story before I brought her butter. She was an expressive reader. When she was reading "Puss in Boots," for instance, it was impossible not to know that she distrusted all cats.

It had been startling and disappointing to me to find out that story books had been written by people, that books were not natural wonders, coming up of themselves like grass. Yet regardless of where they came from, I cannot remember a time when I was not in love with them—with the books themselves, cover and binding and the paper they were printed on, with their smell and their weight and with their possession in my arms, captured and carried off to myself. Still illiterate, I was ready for them, committed to all the reading I could give them.

Neither of my parents had come from homes that could afford to buy many books, but though it must have been something of a strain on his salary, as the youngest officer in a young insurance company, my father was all the while carefully selecting and ordering away for what he and mother thought we children should grow up with. They bought first for the future.

Besides the bookcase in the living room, which was always called "the library," there were the encyclopedia tables and dictionary stand under windows in our dining room. Here to help us grow up arguing around the dining room table were the *Unabridged Webster*, the *Columbia Encyclopedia*, *Compton's Pictured Encyclopedia*, the *Lincoln Library of Information*, and later the *Book of Knowledge*. And the year we moved into our new house, there was room to celebrate it with the new 1925 edition of the Britannica, which my father, his face always deliberately turned toward the future, was of course disposed to think better than any previous edition.

In "the library," inside the mission-style bookcase with its three diamond-latticed glass doors, with my father's Morris chair and the glass-shaded lamp on its table beside it, were books I could soon begin on—and I did, reading them all alike and as they came, straight down their rows, top shelf to bottom. There was the set of Stoddard's Lectures, in all its late nineteenth-century vocabulary and vignettes of peasant life and quaint beliefs and customs, with matching halftone illustrations: Vesuvius erupting, Venice by moonlight, gypsies glimpsed by their campfires. I didn't know then the clue they were to my father's longing to see the rest of the world. I read straight through his other love-from-afar: the Victrola Book of the Opera, with opera after opera in synopsis, with portraits in costume of Melba, Caruso, Galli-Curci, and Geraldine Farrar, some of whose voices we could listen to on our Read Seal records.

My mother read secondarily for information; she sank as a hedonist into novels. She read Dickens in the spirit in which she would have eloped with him.

The novels of her girlhood that had stayed on in her imagination, besides those of Dickens and Scott and Robert Louis Stevenson, were *Jane Eyre, Trilby, The Woman in White, Green Mansions, King Solomon's Mines*. Marie Corelli's name would crop up but I understood she had gone out of favor with my mother, who had only kept Ardath out of loyalty. In time she absorbed herself in Galsworthy, Edith Wharton, above all in Thomas Mann of the Joseph volumes.

St. Elmo was not in our house; I saw it often in other houses. This wildly popular Southern novel is where all the Edna Earles in our population started coming from. They're all named for the heroine, who succeeded in bringing a dissolute, sinning roué and atheist of a lover (St. Elmo) to his knees. My mother was able to forgo it. But she remembered the classic advice given to rose growers on how to water their bushes long enough: "Take a chair and St. Elmo."

To both my parents I owe my early acquaintance with a beloved Mark Twain. There was a full set of Mark Twain and a short set of Ring Lardner in our bookcase, and they were the volumes that in time united us all, parents and children.

Reading everything that stood before me was how I became upon a worn old book without a back that had belonged to my father as a child. It was called *Sanford and Merton*. Is there anyone left who recognizes it, I wonder? It is the famous moral tale written by Thomas Day in the 1780s, but of him no mention is made on the title page of this book; here it is *Sanford and Merton in Words of One Syllable* by Mary Godolphin. Here are the rich boy and the poor boy and Mr. Barlow, their teacher and interlocutor, in long discourses alternating with dramatic scenes— danger and rescue allotted to the rich and the poor respectively. It may have only words of one syllable, but one of them is "quoth." It ends with not one but two morals, both engraved on rings: "Do what you ought, come what may," and "If we would be great, we must first learn to be good."

This book was lacking its front cover, the back held on by strips of pasted paper, now turned golden, in several layers, and the pages stained, flecked, and tattered around the edges; its garish illustrations had come unattached but were preserved, laid in. I had the feeling even in my heedless childhood that this was the only book my father as a little boy had had of his own. He had held onto it, and might have gone to sleep on its coverless face: he had lost his mother when he was seven. My father had never made any mention to his own children of the book, but he had brought it along with him from Ohio to our house and shelved it in our bookcase.

My mother had brought from West Virginia that set of Dickens; those books looked sad, too—they had been through fire and water before I was born, she told me, and there they were, lined up—as I later realized, waiting for me.

I was presented, from as early as I can remember, with books of my own, which appeared on my birthday and Christmas morning. Indeed, my parents could not give me books enough. They must have sacrificed to give me on my sixth or seventh birthday—it was after I became a reader for myself—the ten-volume set of *Our Wonder World*. These were beautifully made, heavy books I would lie down with on the floor in front of the dining room hearth, and more often than the rest volume 5, *Every Child's Story Book*, was under my eyes. There were the fairy tales—Grimm, Andersen, the

English, the French, "Ali Baba and the Forty Thieves"; and there was Aesop and Reynard the Fox; there were the myths and legends, Robin Hood, King Arthur, and St. George and the Dragon, even the history of Joan of Arc; a whack of *Pilgrim's Progress* and a long piece of Gulliver. They all carried their classic illustrations. I located myself in these pages and could go straight to the stories and pictures I loved; very often "The Yellow Dwarf" was the first choice, with Walter Crane's Yellow Dwarf in full color making his terrifying appearance flanked by turkeys. Now that volume is as worn and backless and hanging apart as my father's poor *Sanford and Merton*. The precious page with Edward Lear's "Jumblies" on it has been in danger of slipping out for all these years. One measure of my love for Our Wonder World was that for a long time I wondered if I would go through fire and water for it as my mother had done for Charles Dickens; and the only comfort was to think I could ask my mother to do it for me.

I believe I'm the only child I know of who grew up with this treasure in the house. I used to ask others, "Did you have *Our Wonder World?*" I'd have to tell them *The Book of Knowledge* could not hold a candle to it.

I live in gratitude to my parents for initiating me—and as early as I begged for it, without keeping me waiting—into knowledge of the word, into reading and spelling, by way of the alphabet. They taught it to me at home in time for me to begin to read before starting to school. I believe the alphabet is no longer considered an essential piece of equipment for traveling through life. In my day it was the keystone to knowledge. You learned the alphabet as you learned to count to ten, as you learned "Now I lay me" and the Lord's Prayer and your father's and mother's name and address and telephone number, all in case you were lost.

1983

CRITICAL THINKING POINTS: *After you've read*

1. What kinds of people are the narrator's father and mother? How do you know that?

2. Compare and contrast what the father and the mother feel is important in an education.

3. What kinds of skills does Welty believe were important for her to learn as a writer?

SOME POSSIBILITIES FOR WRITING

1. Fill in the blank and write your own essay: "One _____'s Beginnings."

2. Use Welty's essay as a model to write your own description of the house in which you grew up.

3. Welty says, "It had been startling and disappointing to me to find out that story books had been written by people." What in your life has held that kind of power over you? Why?

Saved

FROM *THE AUTOBIOGRAPHY OF MALCOLM X*   **Malcolm X**

While serving seven years in prison on a burglary charge, Malcolm X (born Malcolm Little; 1925–1965) experienced a life-changing conversion to Islam, honed his reading and writing skills, and emerged as a dynamic political leader of Black Muslims. He was assassinated in 1965.

. . . months passed without my even thinking about being imprisoned. In fact, up to then, I never had been so truly free in my life.

CRITICAL THINKING POINTS: *As you read*

1. What do you know about Malcolm X? How does that "back story" influence your reading of this excerpt?
2. List some of the various motivations Malcolm X has for learning.
3. Malcolm X says, "Anyone who has read a great deal can imagine the new world that opened." What are some of the elements of that world?

I became increasingly frustrated at not being able to express what I wanted to convey in letters that I wrote, especially those to Mr. Elijah Muhammad. In the street, I had been the most articulate hustler out there—I had commanded attention when I said something. But now, trying to write simple English, I not only wasn't articulate, I wasn't even functional. How would I sound writing in slang, the way I would *say* it, something such as "Look, daddy, let me pull your coat about a cat, Elijah Muhammad."

Many who today hear me somewhere in person, or on television, or those who read something I've said, will think I went to school far beyond the eighth grade. This impression is due entirely to my prison studies.

It had really begun back in the Charlestown Prison, when Bimbi first made me feel envy of his stock of knowledge. Bimbi had always taken charge of any conversation he was in, and I tried to emulate him. But every book I picked up had few sentences which didn't contain anywhere from one to nearly all of the words that might as well have been Chinese. When I just skipped those words, of course, I really ended up with little idea of what the book said. So I had come to the Norfolk Prison Colony still going through only book-reading motions. Pretty soon, I would have quit even these motions, unless I had received the motivation that I did.

I saw that the best thing I could do was get hold of a dictionary—to study, to learn some words. I was lucky enough to reason also that I should try to improve my penmanship. It was sad. I couldn't even write in a straight line. It was both ideas together that moved me to request a dictionary along with some tablets and pencils from the Norfolk Prison Colony school.

I spent two days just riffling uncertainly through the dictionary's pages. I'd never realized so many words existed! I didn't know *which* words I needed to learn. Finally, just to start some kind of action, I began copying.

In my slow, painstaking, ragged handwriting, I copied into my tablet everything printed on that first page, down to the punctuation marks.

I believe it took me a day. Then, aloud, I read back, to myself, everything I'd written on the tablet. Over and over, aloud, to myself, I read my own handwriting.

I woke up the next morning, thinking about those words—immensely proud to realize that not only had I written so much at one time, but I'd written words that I never knew were in the world. Moreover, with a little effort, I also could remember what many of these words meant. I reviewed the words whose meanings I didn't remember. Funny thing, from the dictionary's first page right now, that "aardvark" springs into my head. The dictionary had a picture of it, a long-tailed, long-eared, burrowing African mammal, which lives off termites caught by sticking out its tongue as an anteater does for ants.

I was so fascinated that I went on—I copied the dictionary's next page. And the same experience came when I studied that. With every succeeding page, I also learned of people and places and events from history. Actually the dictionary is like a miniature encyclopedia. Finally the dictionary's A section had filled a whole tablet—and I went on into the B's. That was the way I started copying what eventually became the entire dictionary. It went a lot faster after so much practice helped me to pick up handwriting speed. Between what I wrote in my tablet, and writing letters, during the rest of my time in prison I would guess I wrote a million words.

I suppose it was inevitable that as my word-base broadened, I could for the first time pick a book and read and now begin to understand what the book was saying. Let me tell you something: from then until I left that prison, in every free moment I had, if I was not reading in the library, I was reading on my bunk. You couldn't have gotten me out of books with a wedge. Between Mr. Muhammad's teachings, my correspondence, my visitors—usually Ella and Reginald—and my reading of books, months passed without my even thinking about being imprisoned. In fact, up to then, I never had been so truly free in my life.

The Norfolk Prison Colony's library was in the school building. A variety of classes was taught there by instructors who came from such places as Harvard and Boston universities. The weekly debates between inmate teams were also held in the school building. You would be astonished to know how worked up convict debaters and audiences would get over subjects like "Should Babies Be Fed Milk?"

Available on the prison library's shelves were books on just about every general subject. Much of the big private collection that Parkhurst had willed to the prison was still in crates and boxes in the back of the library—thousands of old books. Some of them looked ancient: covers faded, old-time parchment-looking binding. Parkhurst, I've mentioned, seemed to have been principally interested in history and religion. He had the money and the special interest to have a lot of books that you wouldn't have in general circulation. Any college library would have been lucky to get that collection.

As you can imagine, especially in a prison where there was heavy emphasis on rehabilitation, an inmate was smiled upon if he demonstrated an unusually intense interest in books. There was a sizable number of well-read inmates, especially the popular debaters. Some were said by many to be practically walking encyclopedias. They were almost celebrities. No university would ask any student to devour literature as I did when this new world opened to me, of being able to read and *understand.*

I read more in my room than the library itself. An inmate who was known to read a lot could check out more than the permitted maximum number of books. I preferred reading in the total isolation of my own room.

When I had progressed to really serious reading, every night at about ten P.M. I would be outraged with the "lights out." It always seemed to catch me right in the middle of something engrossing.

Fortunately, right outside my door was a corridor light that cast a glow into my room. The glow was enough to read by, once my eyes adjusted to it. So when "lights out" came, I would sit on the floor where I could continue reading in that glow.

At one-hour intervals the night guards paced past every room. Each time I heard the approaching footsteps, I jumped into bed and feigned sleep. And as soon as the guard passed, I got back out of bed onto the floor area of that light-glow, where I would read for another fifty-eight minutes—until the guard approached again. That went on until three or four every morning. Three or four hours of sleep a night was enough for me. Often in the years in the streets I had slept less than that.

1965

CRITICAL THINKING POINTS: *After you've read*

1. What kind of a teacher do you think Malcolm X would have been in the classroom? What in this piece leads you to believe the way you do?

2. Malcolm X refers to skipping words he didn't know while he was reading as one of his "book-reading motions." What are some others and are they as easily remedied?

3. What might have Malcolm X learned in the streets that served him well in this experience?

SOME POSSIBILITIES FOR WRITING

1. Malcolm X says, "I didn't know *which* words I needed to learn." Pick a page at random from a dictionary and write about any words you "need" to learn.

2. Compare and contrast this piece with the selection from *Up from Slavery* presented in this book. What do you think accounts for the similarities and differences in these pieces?

3. Compare and contrast this piece with the selection from *Lummox: Evolution of a Man* later in this book. How does Magnuson's "conversion" in jail compare to that of Malcolm X? How important are some of the differences? Why?

Miss Rinehart's Paddle

Jeri McCormick

Jeri McCormick (b. 1934) teaches creative writing at senior centers and elderhostels. Her poems have appeared most recently in *Poetry Ireland Review, Cumberland Poetry Review,* and *Rosebud.* Her book of poems, *When It Came Time,* was published in 1998 by Salmon Publishing Ltd. in Ireland.

the other side of power

CRITICAL THINKING POINTS: *As you read*

1. Were you the kind of student who got into trouble or the kind who did everything right?
2. The poem is saturated with violent images. What are some of them?
3. Name some of the kinds of power that teachers have over students.

The long hard rumor
had hit us years before
but there was nothing we could do
to fend sixth grade off.
One September morning
we filed into Miss Rinehart's room
to face the thick glasses,
heavy oxfords, spit curls.

The weapon occupied
her middle drawer
and was rarely used on girls,
though Betty Jo got five whacks
for her haphazard map of Brazil —
the Amazon all smeared and off-course,
Rio de Janeiro inland by inches.

I sat through six months
of imagined failures,
ended up a jittery stooge
with all *A*'s, the best parts in plays
and only now wonder
about the other side of power.

1991

CRITICAL THINKING POINTS: *After you've read*

1. What might the author mean when she calls herself "a jittery stooge / with all A's, the best parts in plays"?

2. What did you feel as you read this poem? Was it painful, funny, or sad to read? What made it so?

3. Recall elementary or middle school teachers who were especially "mean." What made them mean? What did you fear about them?

SOME POSSIBILITIES FOR WRITING

1. Many of us can recall memorable episodes from elementary, middle, or high school classrooms that changed the way we feel about teaching and/or learning. Think of such an episode. What makes it a memorable moment? What changes did the event lead to?

2. Talk to your parents and grandparents about their experiences in school. Write an essay comparing your experiences in school to those of your parents or grandparents.

3. Physical discipline is rarely practiced much anymore in this country. What other kinds of discipline do teachers and/or school systems employ? Which methods do you think are the most effective?

50% Chance of Lightning

Cristina Salat

Cristina Salat is founder of Kulana, a racially diverse artist's sanctuary in the rainforests of Hawaii. An author and filmmaker, her work has been published by Bantam Books, Children's Television Workshop, and *Popular Photography.*

Well, what's the point of being gay if I'm never going to be with anybody?

CRITICAL THINKING POINTS: *As you read*

1. Watch for the different responses Robin and Malia have toward college. What are they? Were you eager to apply to college and leave home, like Malia, or not quite ready, like Robin? Why?
2. Speculate about how Robin's mother died. What details in the story led you to that theory?
3. Are the people you know more like Malia (concrete goals, even down to the type of car she hopes to drive) or more like Robin (abstract wishes, such as simply "be happy")? Are you more like Malia or Robin? In what ways?

I wonder if I'll ever have a girlfriend." Robin stamps her sneakers against the wet pavement, tired of waiting.

Malia laughs. "Is that all you think about?"

"Well, what's the point of being gay if I'm never going to be with anybody?" Robin shifts the big umbrella they are sharing to her other hand. Fat silver drops of rain splatter above the plastic dome. She wishes the bus would run on time for once.

"Independent women. We vowed, remember? No guy chasing," Malia says.

Robin shoots Malia a look.

"Or girl chasing," Malia adds quickly.

"You can't talk," Robin says, trying not to feel each strand of her hair as it frizzes. "You have someone."

"That's true." Malia smiles.

Robin looks at the gray, wet world through her clear umbrella. It's hat weather. Black baseball hat and hair gel. She uses both, but nothing really helps on damp days like this. "It's silly to worry how you look. Rain can make you alive if you let it!" Robin's mother used to say. She loved stormy weather almost as much as Robin didn't.

"It's Friday! How come you're so quiet?" Malia asks. "You're not obsessing about your hair, are you? It looks fine. I'd trade you in a second . . . so don't start in about my perfect Filipino hair!" She grins, reading Robin's mind.

Robin can't help smiling. They've known each other a long time.

"Guess what!" Malia changes the subject. "Tomorrow is me and Andrew's six-month anniversary. That's the longest I've ever gone out with anybody."

Robin sighs. "You guys will probably get old together." And I'll be the oldest single person on the face of the planet, she thinks gloomily.

Malia's forehead wrinkles into a slight frown. "No. I'm leaving. I can't wait to get out of here." A large electric bus lumbers to the curb and stops with a hiss. "I sent my applications out yesterday. NYU, Bryn Mawr, Hampshire, and RIT, in that order," Malia says as she boards.

They squeeze onto the heated bus between packed bodies in steaming overcoats. The bus lurches forward.

"Where did you decide?" Malia asks, grabbing onto a pole near the back.

Robin shrugs.

Malia raises one eyebrow. "It's almost Thanksgiving. You are still going to try for NYU and Hampshire with me, aren't you?"

"I guess," Robin says. "I haven't had time to decide anything yet." It's not like she hasn't been thinking about it.

College catalogs are spread across the floor of her bedroom. All she has to do is figure out where she wants to spend the next four years of her life. New York? Massachusetts? Zimbabwe? There's an endless stream of choices.

"You better make time," Malia says. "You shouldn't wait until the deadlines."

"Give me a break, okay?" Robin stares past the seated heads in front of her.

"Cranky, cranky." Malia elbows Robin's arm.

A woman wipes one hand across a steamed window for an outside view and pulls the bus cord. She vacates her seat and Malia and Robin squeeze past someone's knees to claim it. With Malia balanced on her lap, Robin turns her head toward the window and watches the city swish by. She tries to picture herself next fall, suitcases packed, excited to be going. She's almost eighteen; she should want to leave home. A new room. New city. New friends.

I can't leave, not yet! The air in the bus is thick and warm; it's hard to breathe enough in. Outside the window, sharp edged buildings and signs fly past. Robin's head feels light and disconnected. She presses her face against the cold glass. She doesn't have to leave. She can apply to San Francisco State or USF right here in the city. Or she won't go at all. Malia's mom didn't go to college. Robin's dad didn't go either, but he wants her to. "You're smart, like your mother," he's always saying. But what if she doesn't want to go?

It's okay, Robin repeats to herself. No one can make me.

Outside the window she watches a small, mixed terrier approach the curb, sniffing the ground. Its fur is wet and matted, standing up in points. The dog steps into the stilled, waiting traffic. Robin scans the sidewalk for the dog's person. Don't they know it's dangerous to let their puppy wander into the street?

Robin stares through the window, her mind racing. Maybe it's lost. She could help. She could get off the bus and . . . A car honks loudly. Something inside her shrinks up. Malia's weight is heavy on her lap. The dog looks up and scampers back to the curb as traffic surges and the bus rumbles forward. Robin cranes her neck. She should get off, before it's too late. But she can't.

"What is it?" Malia asks, feeling Robin's shift.

Robin forces herself to lean back in the seat and breathe slowly. She's being stupid. The dog won't get run over. Its owner is probably just down the block.

They hang their jackets over the chair in Malia's small, neat room and Robin drops her baseball cap onto the desk.

"You want to see my list of goals?" Malia asks. "I read in *New Woman* if you know exactly what you want, you're more likely to get it." She hands Robin an open, spiral-bound note-book and drops next to her on the bed.

MALIA MANANSALA

Goals for Now
> Get into a good college, far away
> Major in computer science or business
> Get another part-time job for clothes, makeup, etc.
> Have fun!

Eventually
> Dressy job where I make a lot of money and get respect
> Nice apartment with classy things
> Old BMW or Jeep Cherokee (depending where I live)
> Great friends
> Marry someone loyal, sexy, and successful

"Money." Robin shakes her head. "Even if we get scholarships, we're going to be paying off college loans forever."

Malia nods. "That's why I need a big career. I'm not going to suck up to some man for money. You should make a goal list," she suggests, handing over a pen. "I need a snack."

Robin flops onto her side. Why not? At the top of a clean page, in slow, careful letters, she writes:

Goals
> Figure Out Who I Am
> Be Proud of Myself
> Fall in Love
> Do Something Good

Robin frowns at her list. How does Malia know exactly what she wants? "Hand it over." Malia comes back into the room with a tray of hot cocoa and microwaved pork buns.

"Okay, but it's not like yours."

"Do something good?" Malia makes a face. "Can you be more specific?"

"Hey, I didn't pick on your list!"

"I don't get it. When you want to do something, you just do it. This year you start telling everyone, 'I'm a lesbian, deal with it.' Why can't you be like that about college?"

"It's different," Robin says, thinking, I didn't tell everyone. My mother never got to know. Her mom drove a red Ho CRX with African pendants dangling from the rearview mirror. She took the highway a lot, to avoid city traffic. Route I South. Robin yanks her mind away.

"You are going to do more with your life than just be a lesbian, aren't you?" Malia prods.

Robin gets to her feet, shaking the damp bottoms of her baggy jeans away from her ankles. "Can I borrow something dry?"

"Come on. Seriously. What kind of job do you want?" Malia sounds like Robin's mom and dad used to—always excited about plans.

"I don't know. Something to help people," Robin says, looking through the closet.

"Peace Corps? Lawyer? Social worker?" Malia suggests.

"No," Robin says, a faded memory seeping into her mind. She used to play medicine woman when she was little, healing stuffed toy rabbits and her plastic Ujima dolls with bowls of grass-flower soup. "I always pictured myself in a fun office," she tells Malia, "where people or animals would come when they didn't feel well."

"You want to be some kind of doctor!" Malia enthuses.

Robin shakes her head. Playing medicine woman was a kid thing. "You know I can't stand blood and guts." Robin focuses her attention in the closet, taking out a black lace top and black leggings.

"How about a therapist? You could help people's minds."

"And listen to people complain all day?" Robin asks as she changes.

Malia sighs, shutting the notebook. "Well, what do you want to do tonight? I told Andrew I'd call him by four. Oh, I forgot! My mother and the jerk are going out after work. They won't be home till late. Do you want to have a party?"

"Yes!" Robin says. "Go rent some movies. I'll call for a pizza and invite everybody."

Andrew arrives first with a soggy Safeway bag tucked into his aviator jacket.

"Hey, Robbie!" he says, unpacking jumbo bottles of root beer and 7UP on the living-room table.

The doorbell rings again. Robin runs to let in Malia's friend Dan, who has brought his sister, Cybelle—a junior—and another girl. Malia has plenty of friends. Most of them are at least part Filipino.

Being a mix (African and Polish), Robin doesn't care who her friends are. She only has a few anyway, though she knows lots of people. When her mother died at the end of sophomore year, nobody knew what to say, so they acted like nothing happened. Robin still hangs out with the same people, but just because it's something to do; not because she cares.

When Malia returns from the video store, fifteen people are sprawled on the couch and floor with paper plates of mushroom and garlic pizza.

"Party woman," Andrew teases Malia, leaning down for a kiss. "You're soaked."

"It was only drizzling when I left. Sorry I took so long. I couldn't decide!" Malia takes two video cassettes out of a plastic bag. "I got a vampire movie and *The Best of Crack-Up Comedy.*"

"I love vampires!" Cybelle adjusts one of the five rhinestone studs on her left ear. "Let's get scared first."

"Go change," Andrew tells Malia. "I'll set up the movie." He nudges her toward the bedroom.

Robin watches, wondering if anyone will ever care like that about her. For some reason the wet dog she saw from the bus pops into her mind. Nobody cared enough to keep it safe.

"Hi. You're Robin Ciszek, right?" A white girl in ripped jeans and a "Save the Planet" sweatshirt sits down next to Robin on the couch. "I read your article in the school paper! I'm April, Cybelle's friend. I never thought what it feels like to be gay until I read your essay. Do you know a lot of gay people, or was the story mostly about you?" April's slate colored eyes are wide and curious.

Robin takes a big bite of pizza. It's still hard to believe she wrote an article about being gay and submitted it to the school paper. She must have been crazy.

"I hope you don't mind me asking," April says quickly. "I'm just interested."

"The story's mostly about me," she tells April. "I don't know a lot of other gay people."

"I guess you will next year," April says. "My sister goes to UC Berkeley, and she says there's like three different gay groups on campus."

Robin feels her shoulders clench up. Is college the only thing anyone can talk about? Of course, it'll be worth it to be out of high school just to get away from the stupid notes guys are taping on her locker door: ALL YOU NEED IS A REAL MAN and ROBIN C. AND MALIA M. EAT FISH.

"Personally, I'm glad I don't have to think about college for another year," April continues.

"Really? Why?" Robin asks, surprised.

April looks away, embarrassed. "It's dumb. I have this cat. I don't want to leave her."

"Guess what I brought!" Cybelle calls out as Andrew dims the living-room light. She takes a half-full bottle of brandy from her tote bag.

"I'll have a little of that," Malia says, coming back into the room in overalls and a fluffy white sweater. "To warm me up."

"Quiet—it's starting," Gary yells from the easy chair as a bold, red title flashes across the television screen.

"I want to sit on the couch," Tara giggles. "Move over, Danny."

April moves toward Robin to make room for another person. Her hip rests against Robin's. The couch armrest presses into Robin's other side.

"Oh, hold me, Andrew!" Cybelle teases Malia as eerie music fills the darkened room. Malia laughs.

April's leg relaxes against Robin's. Out of the corner of one eye, Robin looks at the girl sitting next to her. April is watching the screen. Robin's thigh sizzles.

Robin nonchalantly eases sideways until their arms and legs are touching. A faint scent of perfume tinges the air. April doesn't move away. Robin's whole left side buzzes. She sinks into the couch, holding her breath. It would be so amazing if—

If what? Just because this girl liked the article doesn't mean she's interested. Robin moves her leg away, mad at herself. On screen, a shadowy figure suddenly whirls around and grins evilly. April leans softly against Robin.

Warm drops of sweat trickle down Robin's side. The room feels dark and red. Robin could reach out, take April's hand, trace one finger over the knuckle bumps and pale, freckled skin. . . .

Halfway through the vampire movie, Robin has to go to the bathroom, bad. She is tempted, but restrains herself from squeezing April's leg as she gets up.

Away from everyone, she splashes cold water on her face, smiling. Could April really be interested? I could go back and sit away from her to see if she follows me.

Feeling hot and wild, Robin unlocks the door. It doesn't budge. She pulls harder, leaning backward, and opens it a foot.

"Hi, Robin." Cybelle grins, peeking around the corner.

"What's with you? Get away from the door," Robin says.

"Okay." Cybelle runs one hand through her porcupine patch of short, black hair. "C'mere. I want to ask you something." Cybelle pulls Robin into Malia's room. She shuts the door without flicking on the light.

"Smell my breath," she says, leaning close.

A warm rush of brandy air tickles Robin's face.

"I can't go home wasted. Do I smell like pizza or alcohol?" Cybelle asks. Her lips touch the side of Robin's mouth.

"What are you doing?" Robin asks.

Cybelle nuzzles Robin's face, tracing her lips along Robin's. "Don't you like me? Kiss me back."

Robin's heart stutters. Is this for real? Cybelle slides one hand under Robin's hair and grips the back of her neck, kissing harder.

I've wanted this for so long, Robin thinks, awkwardly moving her arms around Cybelle. It's weird not being able to see. Robin touches sharp shoulder blades through the thin cotton of Cybelle's turtleneck.

I should have helped that dog. The thought scuttles into Robin's head. Why is she thinking about that now!

Cybelle sucks on Robin's lower lip. I should have gotten off the bus and helped. I could have taken it to the pound, or home. Why didn't I do something?

Cybelle's small tongue slides into Robin's mouth. Why am I doing this? I've seen Cybelle around school and never wanted to. She's got a boyfriend. She'll probably tell everyone, "I made out with the lesbian at Malia's house," for a laugh.

Robin shifts sideways. "I have to go."

"What?"

"I'm going back to the living room." Robin feels for the wall switch and flicks on the light.

Cybelle blinks. "How come? It's okay. Nobody misses us." She smiles and tugs on Robin's arm, moving closer.

"I want to see the rest of the movie," Robin says, pulling away. It's a lame excuse, but what else can she say? "I want to kiss somebody I'm really into, and you're not it"?

Cybelle stops smiling and drops Robin's arm. "Oh sure," she laughs. "You're scared! Writing that story and you don't even know what to do! What a joke." She yanks open the door and walks out before Robin can respond.

Robin follows Cybelle to the living room and watches her take the small, open spot on the couch next to April. She glares at the back of Cybelle's spiked head. Who does she think she is? I don't have to make out if I don't want to!

Whirling around, Robin heads back to the bedroom and jams her feet into her sneakers.

"You okay?" Malia asks, coming in.

"Sure." Robin doesn't look up.

"Are you leaving? What's going on?"

"Nothing I want to talk about right now." Robin zips up her jacket. They walk to the front door. Robin flings it open. She can't wait to be outside.

"Call me tomorrow, okay? Hey." Malia grabs Robin's jacket.

Robin looks back over her shoulder. "What?"

"We're best buddies forever, right?"

If Malia moves to New York and Robin stays here . . . Nothing's forever.

"Sure," Robin says, looking away.

Malia smiles and reaches out for a hug. "I'm sorry you didn't have a good time. Let's go shopping tomorrow morning, just you and me. Okay?"

As soon as Robin steps away from Malia's house, she realizes she's forgotten her baseball cap. Angrily, she pops open her umbrella. It doesn't matter. There's a bus stop at the corner and she's just going home.

Water drops drum against the plastic shield above her head as cars zip by, their rubber tires splashing against wet asphalt. Robin glares at each car that passes. She will never own one. What if that dog got run over? She should have helped. A bolt of light illuminates the night. Robin looks helplessly down the empty street for a bus. She hates being out alone after dark, even when it's not very late.

Whenever someone worried, her dad used to say: "There's a fifty-fifty chance of something good happening." Robin's mother loved that saying. Her father hasn't said it much lately. It's hard to believe in good stuff when you're dealing with the other fifty percent. At least she ended the thing with Cybelle. That's something. Robin might want experience, but she's not desperate.

Thunder swells, filling the night. Robin cranes her neck, looking down the street. No bus. So it's fifty-fifty. Should she wait here, hoping no weirdos show up and bother her before the bus comes, or should she start walking in this lousy weather? Her parents used to take walks in the rain. They were nuts . . . but happy.

Robin starts to walk. A sharp wind whips by, threatening to turn her umbrella inside out. Okay, why not? She has nothing to lose. Robin clicks the umbrella shut. Rain falls cold against her face and settles onto her thick hair, expanding it. She walks fast, with the wooden umbrella handle held forward, staying near the street-lamps. Water trickles down her face and soaks into her clothing. She licks her lips. The rain tastes strangely good.

When she reaches the place where she saw the dog, Robin stops and studies the black road. A few torn paper bags. No blood or fur. It could be dead somewhere else. Or it could be off foraging in a garbage can or sleeping under a bush.

I'm sorry I didn't get off the bus to see if you needed help, she thinks. Next time I will. I hope you're safe. But maybe the dog didn't need help. Maybe it wasn't even scared. Maybe it was totally pleased to be out exploring and taking care of itself. Robin decides to picture the terrier that way.

From down the block a bus approaches, grumbling to a stop a few feet ahead. Robin hurries over. As the doors squeal open, she looks behind at the dark, empty street. She is afraid, but she doesn't want to be. Slowly, Robin turns away.

It is a long walk home under the wide, electric sky.

At the warm apartment on Guerrero Street, Robin finds her father asleep on their living-room couch. A paperback novel is spread open across his chest and his glasses are pushed up onto his forehead. Standing over him, dripping onto the brown shag rug, Robin feels tender and old. She removes his glasses and places the book on the glass coffee table, careful not to lose his page.

In her room, Robin drops her wet clothing to the floor and changes into an old set of flannel pajamas. Then she sits down at her drafting-table desk. Nothing's forever, and that's just the way it is. Moving college applications aside, she lifts two thick San Francisco phone books from the floor.

Robin thumbs through the thin A–L yellow pages slowly. There is something she can do. Something right.

Attorneys, Automobile . . . Bakers, Beauty . . . Carpets, Collectibles . . . Dentists, Divers . . . Environment . . . Florists . . . Health. Health clubs, health and diet, health maintenance, health service. A boxed ad catches Robin's eye.

Holistic Health Center
Dedicated to the well-being of body and mind
Licensed: nutritionists, massage therapists, acupuncturists
Courses in herbal healing, yoga, natural vision, Tai Chi

Medicine without blood and guts. Smiling to herself, Robin reaches for some loose-leaf paper and a pen. There's a new life out there, waiting for her. She just has to find it. She moves A–L aside and flips open M–Z. By ten P.M. three loose-leaf pages are filled with numbers and addresses. At the top of the first page, she writes: Call for info.

Robin stretches and climbs into bed with her new list. She rubs the soles of her bare feet against the chilled sheets. Maybe life is like rain. Alive if you let it be; lousy and depressing if you don't. She rolls onto her stomach. Under the information for the Shiatsu Institute, the College of Oriental Medicine, and the School for Therapeutic Massage, she writes: Tell Malia to get April's number from Dan. Call her?!?!?!

1994

CRITICAL THINKING POINTS: *After you've read*

1. Malia thinks that if people know exactly what they want, they're more likely to get it. Do you believe this is true? Why or why not?

2. Compare Robin's and Malia's lists of goals. Who do you think is more likely to be satisfied? Can you judge this simply from someone's goals? Why or why not?

3. Why do you think Robin doesn't get on the bus when it stops for her? What does the dog seem to represent to her? What details in the story led you to that conclusion?

SOME POSSIBILITIES FOR WRITING

1. Make two lists of your own goals: one abstract like Robin's and one concrete like Malia's. For instance, an abstract goal would be "work with people," whereas a concrete goal that is an extension of that would be "get a degree in elementary education."

2. There are advantages and disadvantages to having a life's plan like Malia does. Make a list of advantages concerning having your goals and life mapped out. Now make a list of disadvantages concerning having your goals and life mapped out.

3. Robin is harassed with notes on her locker after her article appeared in the school newspaper. Recall a time when you were teased for your ethnic background, sexual preference, or simply the way you talked or walked or something you did. Write about your experience.

Somewhere in Minnesota

Peter Klein

Peter Klein (b.1955) wrote this poem as an undergraduate student. After graduate school he stopped writing for nearly fifteen years and recently returned to writing and publishing. His work has appeared in *The Cortland Review, The North American Review, Blackbird,* and elsewhere. He lives in Nashville, Tennessee, where he works for a market research company.

your dark eyes focused / on a brilliant future.

CRITICAL THINKING POINTS: *As you read*

1. Who do you think is the "you" in this poem?
2. Because of poetry's condensed nature, every word is important. Choose some words that you feel are "important" to this poem. Why do you think so?
3. Why might the lines end where they do? How would the poem be different if the lines were longer or shorter?

somewhere in Minnesota
there is a photograph
mailed from denver
to an uncle in duluth
who left it in a diner
on a table by the salt
it marked a woman's place
in a drugstore fiction
where it lay for years
until her freshman son
found it told his friends
the subject was his steady
then threw it in a lake
this picture was of you
your mortar board smile
gleaming softly beneath
the photographer's light
your dark eyes focused
on a brilliant future.

1979

CRITICAL THINKING POINTS: *After you've read*

1. What might the author mean by such phrases as "your mortar board smile" or "your dark eyes focused / on a brilliant future"?
2. How do the places in which the photo ends up contribute to your reading of the poem? What do these places have in common?
3. Why do you think the history of the photograph is important to the narrator?

SOME POSSIBILITIES FOR WRITING

1. Page through your own high school yearbook. Write a brief impression of the memories the pictures call to mind. Be as specific as you can in communicating these impressions.
2. Look at your parents' or grandparents' high school graduation photos and write about the people as they appeared then compared to the people as you know them now.
3. Find yearbooks in your college library from ten or twenty years ago or older. What seems to be different about the people and the university then? What seems to be still the same?

LD

Jeff Richards

Jeff Richards was born and raised in Washington, D.C. He has an M.A. in creative writing from Hollins College.

His twisted brain was no disability. It was a gift.

CRITICAL THINKING POINTS: *As you read*

1. What do you associate with the term "LD"?
2. How can labels, such as "LD" or "gifted," help or hinder students in school?
3. Students with "invisible" disabilities often go unnoticed by other students. What would be the benefits and disadvantages of that kind of disability?

O ur minds are twisted but they are perfectly good minds. We are artistic, sensitive, impulsive, socially and emotionally immature. Spaced. We are angry, passive, withdrawn or overly extroverted. We tell stories in random order without references, and our academic skills are very slow in developing. At least that's the way we are when we are young, according to Neela Seldin, a specialist in LD who compiled the above list of our characteristics. When we grow older, we either adapt or don't adapt. Some of us drop out of high school and clerk at Kmart. Some of us graduate with Ph.D.s in nuclear physics and work for NASA. Some of us are well known: Harry Belafonte, Cher, Vince Vaughn; or leaders in their fields: Dr. Donald Coffey, a cancer researcher at Johns Hopkins; Dr. Florence Haseltine, a pioneer in women's health issues; Gaston Caperton, the educator and former governor of West Virginia; and Roger W. Wilkins, the civil rights activist. According to the company of Winston Churchill, Thomas Edison, Albert Einstein, Leonardo da Vinci, all of them either LD or afflicted by one of LD's numerous cousins, like dyslexia. Da Vinci often wrote from right to left. He had difficulty completing projects, leaving scores of complex plans and designs for posterity to try to assemble. Ms. Seldin describes the young disabled student as one who "can't make choices" and "can't stay with an activity." "Distractible, impulsive." The type to sketch out and set aside. . . .

Was I really that stupid? Was I unable to calculate fractions or percentages? Or understand what I read? I enjoyed comic books. *Fantastic Four. Archie. Spiderman.* Even the high-brow Classic Comics. One of my fondest memories was going to the drugstore to buy those comics with my dad, who seemed to enjoy them as much as I did even though he wasn't LD. I hated *Dick and Jane.* Who didn't? But comics aside,

I have to admit now, I could not read worth a damn. I was no whiz at fractions. And besides the baseball statistics I computed and recorded in a spiral notebook, I knew little of percentages. Though the terminology didn't exist at the time, I was LD.

My parents were upset at my failure to move to the next level but were undaunted, as concerned parents tend to be. They arranged for me to be tested at a diagnostic center. They enrolled me in summer school and endless tutoring sessions, and transported me to Longfellow School for Boys where I repeated sixth grade. I remember I was very depressed. I wanted to run away, join the circus or the merchant marine. I didn't want to leave my neighborhood buddies to go to this bizarre school in Bethesda full of boys who dressed up in blue blazers and ties everyday.

The summer before I went to school, they gave us a reading list—*Penrod* and *Tom Sawyer*, the usual collection of coming-of-age classics. I remember sitting in the bedroom of our rented beach house feeling the sticky, salt air, looking up occasionally from where I was bent over a book to see the yellow curtains blowing in the window. I'd hear the far-off waves against the shore, the wind in the pines, and I'd feel like I'd just woken up from a long sleep. I could read. I could *really* read. And later on, after I had finished another book, I would sit down at my desk and write exhaustive synopses and commentaries.

I hated my parents when they enrolled me at Longfellow but, when I went there and my new teacher read an excerpt from one of my book reports and said I had some good ideas, I accepted the possibility that they might be onto something. My teacher could understand my writing; I could understand him and follow his instructions; I did my tests and did my homework without copying from the encyclopedia. For the first time in my life, I didn't feel like a fraud.

However, I wasn't instantly cured of LD. It is a disability and not a disease. My mind is still twisted and always will be. What is different is that I learned how to deal with it. I'm easily distracted, so when I was in a college class I concentrated by taking elaborate notes. Many students borrowed my notes since I missed almost nothing of what the professor said. I think they benefited more than I did given my problems with memory. So I tested poorly. I made up for this in out-of-class assignments where I had time enough to think about what I was going to say. On these papers, teachers would act surprised and wonder if I was the same person who wrote the exams. My professors did not understand that I had a twisted mind, that I was as smart as anyone else, that I came to the same logical conclusions as everyone but it took me longer to get there because I was distracted by the interesting terrain I traveled on the way.

Today my daughter's teachers know what mine did not. This is both good and bad. It is good that they've found the terminology. The Internet has hundreds of Web sites that relate to Learning Disability, some of which define LD with as many as forty-eight different characteristics. Hannah has only a handful of these, many of them similar to mine: "academic skills very slow in developing, strong discrepancies in skills and knowledge, artistic, sensitive, excellent vocabulary but poor production, wants to tell but cannot retrieve words, mishears or doesn't hear, and problems with various motor development–related skills." I am amazed, on the one hand, by what a good job the nebulous "they" have done in codifying my disorder, but, on the other, I am frightened by what they plan to do with all this ammunition. They are, after all, tinkering with the human mind, my daughter's mind, in particular, and I don't find this reassuring.

I believe they are at the very beginning of understanding LD, but don't yet know how to treat it. Or if it is treatable. Or if it is a disability. Or a difference, which is closer to my view. When Hannah was in first grade she received a report card much like my own from Miss Probey. Only Miss Probey was a nice lady, even nicer when she turned into Mrs. Bernard in the middle of the year. Hannah's teacher was a prison guard. She looked like Miss Honey in *Matilda,* but acted more like Miss Trunchbull so let's call her Ms. Honeybull. Ms. Honeybull's range of normal was ludicrous. Only about three students could fit into it, two of whom were on Ritalin, the third naturally passive. She was always berating the students for one thing or another and keeping them in from recess for minor slipups such as talking out of turn in class or not keeping in line when the students walked from one classroom to another. Once, she even beat one of the students with a ruler for not identifying the location of the Nile River on a map. One of Ms. Honeybull's favorite victims was Hannah.

Hannah with her pretty, round Irish face like her mother's, thin lips, and long hair to her shoulders, flyaway hair like mine. She's been a vegetarian since she was five. She hates that we own a leather couch though she does grudgingly sit on it. When her skin touches the leather, sometimes she'd say, "This is disgusting," and eyeball us half in jest as if we are murderers.

When we received Ms. Honeybull's report card, we were upset that Hannah flunked absolutely everything. We knew she was having difficulty in her academic subjects but we had received no prior warning that it was this bad, even in art which she loves. How could she flunk art or, even more inexplicable, deportment? We were aghast with the accusation that she didn't show consideration and respect for others, that she didn't play or listen to her peers, or cooperate or share, or control herself, and on and on. This was antithetical to every experience we had ever had with our daughter. Only a kid who burned down the school deserved grades like this, said my wife. We arranged a conference with Ms. Honeybull. She defended her views. We defended ours. Nothing much was accomplished. As we left the conference room, Ms. Honeybull blurted out, "Your daughter is unteachable."

"Now I understand," I might have said but didn't. It wasn't that Hannah was unteachable. It was that Ms. Honeybull was incapable of reaching Hannah. Connie, my wife, thought it went beyond that. "They're trying to push her out of school." Which seems obvious to me now as I look back on it. We did what my parents did when we were growing up. We tested Hannah. We hired a tutor. We looked for other schools.

By the fall of the next year Hannah was enrolled in the Lab School of Washington, one of the premier schools in the world for children and adults with learning disabilities. Unlike Ms. Honeybull, the teachers are trained to deal with a wide range of students, using art, theater, dance, woodworking, you must know math.

Sally Smith, the founder and director of LSW, is the recognized leader in the field of learning disabilities. In addition, she is the head of the graduate program in LD at American University, author of five books on the subject and countless articles. As tough a character as you're likely to find, she could squeeze blood out of a turnip. So the school is well endowed. But not exclusive. Most of the students are funded and come from the public schools. The waiting list to get in is endless, as is the waiting list for teachers who want to teach there. But the real judge of LSW's success is that 90 percent of the students go on to college.

Hannah is thriving in this environment. She is much further along in her reading, writing, and arithmetic than I was at her age. She is happy. The teachers never punish her. They never single her out, except for praise. They have given her the award for good behavior practically every week she has been there. If she accumulates enough of these awards over a certain period of time, she is allowed to have lunch with the handsome gym instructor that all the girls swoon over.

In the fall the Lab School gives a gala at which they honor successful people with LD. I think it was the year they invited the Fonz that a paleontologist from Johns Hopkins, Dr. Steven M. Stanley, said in his speech to the overflow audience at the Omni–Shoreham Hotel that he thought he wasn't disabled. I don't remember his words exactly but they confirmed my belief. His brain, like my own, was twisted. It took him through that same illogical Alice in Wonderland world that I go through daily, and when he came out on the other side, usually he came out with a scatter-brained idea. But sometimes when he came out, his ideas were great, the very same ideas, he thought, that made it possible for him to rise to the top of his field. His twisted brain was no disability. It was a gift. What Hannah has, what I have, what my mom had, and what our ancestors had were gifts. And yet, I'm still apprehensive for Hannah. Will she be at the Lab School forever? Or will they recommend a transfer to a more traditional school once she catches up developmentally with her peers? Either way, I wonder how well she will do in college and beyond. Will she be able to compete in the real world? My concerns are no doubt little different from other parents'. Yet other parents do not have to go to the expense, the extra time, and the heartache that Connie and I do. Somehow I feel cheated that we are forced to send Hannah to a special school with kids who are basically the same as she. I wonder why this is so, why she must be isolated from the average student population, the $1 + 1 = 2$ Crowd.

2000

CRITICAL THINKING POINTS: *After you've read*

1. Richards writes, "My professors did not understand that I had a twisted mind, that I was as smart as anyone else, that I came to the same logical conclusions as everyone but it took me longer to get there because I was distracted by the interesting terrain I traveled on the way." How does he "prove" himself in college?

2. Richards makes the point that being LD might be a disability or simply a difference. What might be the impact of each alternative point of view? What
   is associated with each word?

3. How is Richards better able to parent Hannah because he has a similar
   disability?

SOME POSSIBILITIES FOR WRITING

1. Research the effects on a generation of people—most often boys and young
   men—heavily medicated by drugs such as Ritalin.

2. How might public schools incorporate some of the ideologies of the Lab
   School?

3. Research what kinds of services are available for students with disabilities
   on your campus.

School's Out: One Young Man Puzzles Over His Future Without College

Laura Sessions Stepp

Laura Sessions Stepp is a *Washington Post* staff writer.

"You see these clothes I'm wearing?" he asks. "I bought them. These shoes I'm wearing? I bought them. That car out there? I'm paying for it."

CRITICAL THINKING POINTS: *As you read*

1. What are some stereotypes about high school students who choose not to go to college? Where do those stereotypes come from?
2. What kind of town does Ben Farmer live in? How does that influence him and his choices?
3. Keep a list of reasons you feel Ben did not go to college.

Ben Farmer at 19, steering his silver Camaro Z28 down Main Street on a Friday night, glances at the Dairy Freeze and thinks about the buddies he graduated from high school with last year. They're off at college, probably partying tonight, the beer, the girls, at Virginia Tech, Radford, wherever.

He passes a karate studio, beauty supply store and boarded-up movie theater with a marquee begging passersby to "Shop Altavista First."

He could be at college. He had the grades, he's got the brains, but here he is, listening to the cough in his 330-horsepower engine and worrying about his spark plugs.

"There was a lot of unknowns about college," he says after he thinks about it. "It was going to be this big, tough, hard, hard time in which all you'd do is write papers, which I don't like to do." So for now he assembles air conditioning ducts in a factory, for $7 an hour, which is as much as his mother makes in her new job at the bank, her first sit-down job in all the years she's been raising him.

Nobody in his family ever went to any kind of college. His mom wanted him to go. She helped him with the application and the financial aid forms. But he didn't go, he took a $7 job in a town with a lot of $7 jobs, a little river town in central Virginia, where the Southern railroad met the Norfolk and Western, spawning a furniture factory, textile mill and other small manufacturers.

Ten to 12 hours a day, he hammers sheet metal, then goes home to shower off the dirt and fibers. Some nights he heads out to the driving range to hit golf balls. Weekends, he drives over to South Boston to watch guys do what he would like most to do, race stock cars. He has thought about signing on with a NASCAR pit crew, a great job except you're never home.

Altavista is home. He knows everybody, he's already got a job, and now he's met a girl, named Apryl East. He's having visions of a little house one day with a two-car garage, "going to work and going on vacation, not worrying where your next meal is coming from."

So now he's thinking of asking his boss at Moore's, an electrical and mechanical construction firm, if the company will pay him to take night classes at the local community college and then move him indoors to a better-paying job, a sit-down job. Apryl, who goes to Virginia Tech, encourages this line of thinking.

The fall after Ben and 70 others graduated from the local high school, 2.5 million American seniors enrolled in either a two-year or a four-year college.

Almost a million did not. They were overwhelmingly poor, male and white. Much to the surprise of social scientists who traditionally have looked for educational problems among minorities, low-income black and Hispanic men are more likely to go to college right out of high school than white guys like Ben. So are young women of any background. If Ben had a twin sister, she'd likely be enrolled.

There are Ben Farmers all over: in the coal towns of Pennsylvania, the suburban sprawl west of Sacramento and especially in the rural South. They've always been there, hidden in the pockets of America where they pump gas, assemble machine parts and put their pay on the family's kitchen table. They do work that needs to be done—building houses, running backhoes, riveting airplanes, surveying land and fixing the BMWs of upscale college types who occasionally might call them rednecks. America might well lose all its advanced-degree business school graduates with less pain than it would lose these young men.

They're proud of the work they do. At the same time, they've found it harder and harder to acquire full-time jobs with decent pay increases and good health insurance. Their earnings, adjusted for inflation, have fallen or stalled. Altavista, population 3,400, has several thousand people commuting there to work, so there are jobs. But fewer and fewer: Altavista has lost 1,300 jobs in a little over a year.

Other young Altavista men in Ben's position fear they're headed nowhere in a society that prefers paper-pushers to pipe fitters. They don't want to manage accounts payable for a living, or scan X-rays for cancerous tumors. They're proud of doing hard, physical work. But people around them say that white-collar jobs, available only with a college diploma, are the only way to win at life. This attitude, says Patricia Gandara, a professor of education at the University of California, Davis, can make these young white men feel invisible.

"Latinos and African Americans have horrendous problems, too, but at least they have a group identity," says Gandara, who studies low-income, primarily minority youths. "These poor white males don't know where in the culture they fit. Some are really alienated and angry."

Ken Gray, a professor of workforce education at Pennsylvania State University, worries about them, too. "No one's interested in the Bubbas," he says.

Ben is no Bubba, more an easygoing, smart kid with a goatee and a vague future. Off work, he wears American Eagle polo shirts, khakis and Nike sandals.

"You see these clothes I'm wearing?" he asks. "I bought them. These shoes I'm wearing? I bought them. That car out there? I'm paying for it." It's a matter of pride and obligation that richer people can't understand.

He has friends whose parents pay their school expenses, their apartment rent. One of his pals lives off campus in a nice two-bedroom apartment with a big leather couch and an air hockey table.

"On some days I wish I were him," Ben says. On other days? All he'll say about his buddy is this: "If you asked him how much his cell phone bill is, he wouldn't know."

Ben's a guy whose mother taught him to "always keep good credit and pay your bills on time." You get his drift.

His father, Walter, a truck driver who left Ben and Ben's mom when Ben was 3, hasn't played much of a role in his life. But Walter's parents, Marvin and Frances, sure have. Until his early teens, he'd spend the school months in Altavista with his mom, Patsy Moore, and all summer with Marvin and Frances, big NASCAR fans who followed the circuit.

"I think I disappointed Granny the most not going to college, and Mom second," he says.

His mom, eating dinner with Ben in his favorite restaurant, El Cazador, says she's still wondering why he didn't go to college. Hasn't he learned from her example?

Researchers would say that some kids never want to venture much farther along life's path than did the people they know and love best. Moore, a sweet woman of 42, doesn't understand this, as she explains to Ben over a taco salad that he helped her choose.

"You've seen me struggle from week to week," she says. "You can't want that."

No, he doesn't want that. But what does he want? More pressing still, what can he realistically expect to attain?

Ben has loved hot rods since he was a baby. He ran Matchbox cars over his grandmother's rug for hours at a time before he could walk, and as he got older he took up dirt bikes with a bunch of boys his age who lived in the country near his granny.

"We stayed outside all the time," he recalls.

As they got older, their little group carved a dirt track in woods of scrub pine and began racing cars and trucks. Ben's two best friends eventually acquired race cars and the gang started spending time at Big Daddy's South Boston Speedway, a NASCAR-sanctioned short track. Ben began to dream of becoming another Tony Stewart or a pit crew chief.

His teachers couldn't understand this fascination. He's such a good student, they'd sigh, as if you couldn't be interested in both math and Chevys, which happen to have a serious relationship through mechanical engineering. He pulled down A's and B's in high school, taking calculus and Latin. But his teachers didn't foresee a career in engineering, they just seemed to see a car-crazy kid.

One problem they didn't count on: His friends' families all had more money than his, and to dress the way they did and do the things they did, Ben had to get a job.

So at age fifteen he found one at the Amoco Food Shop south of town. He stopped playing high school basketball and started stocking shelves. Making money became something of an obsession. Not big money, though. That would have required college.

When Ben's friends started talking about four-year colleges, Ben would go silent. When they took the SAT in their junior year, Ben didn't. "I thought to myself, where would I find the money?"

His mom encouraged him to try a two-year school, and so he got an application to Danville Community College. But his heart wasn't in it. The message of his guidance counselor and some of his teachers, he says, was that four-year colleges or universities were the only goal worth aiming for.

Those who hold bachelor's degrees have a hard time understanding why anyone wouldn't want one. At Ben's high school, administrators took pride in the fact that they send proportionately more graduates to four-year colleges than other schools in the area. They talked about former students who chose Columbia, Duke or the University of Virginia. For Ben, even $8,000 to $10,000 a year for in-state tuition, room and board didn't seem in the cards.

Other young men in Ben's position report similar experiences.

"They were good at giving out papers to kids going to college, but didn't pay no attention to students going to community college," says Jason Spence, who makes bulletproof vests on the night shift at BGF Industries. Jason and Ben both remember sitting through school assemblies where the same students won award after award, scholarship after scholarship—to four-year schools.

Ben's mother recognized she needed someone to help jump-start her son, but when she sought out school authorities, she says, she received only an offhand kind of attention. "I'd never done this before. They told me I could take Ben to Danville and Lynchburg. It wasn't very helpful."

Ben says he asked at school if, on career day, organizers could bring in someone who worked in the racing industry. With several local drivers around, it would have been easy to find someone, but nothing happened.

"You feel like kind of an outsider," he says.

He might not have felt that way a decade ago, because young men and young women here could still come right out of high school and go to work for family-run industries offering decent starting wages and chances for promotion. They didn't need higher education to enjoy job security at places like Lane Furniture, famous for its cedar chests. But once the Lane family lost direct control of the company in the late 1980s, things started to change. Gradually the manufacturing of cedar chests and dining sets moved to the cheap labor market of China, and fewer and fewer workers filled the million-square-foot brick and wood complex that had dominated, indeed was, Altavista's skyline.

Last year, on Aug. 31, the last hope chest rolled off the assembly line. Other industries in the area started folding or cutting back, and by this past spring, the unemployment rate in central Virginia had hit a 10-year high. When a health supplements lab in town advertised for 40 new jobs, the cars lined up for interviews the first morning snaked for blocks through town.

Ben worried about his mother—she'd get a job, then be laid off under a last-hired, first-fired policy. "She's had a string of bad luck," he says.

Rather then head for college in the hope of improving their chances for a good job, Ben and other young men like him sought out jobs right away that offered health insurance, pension plans and savings programs.

Max Everhart, who lives around the corner from Ben, was one of them. Also a bright young man, he went to work at a machine bearings plant for $10 an hour plus benefits. "It's a good job," Max says. "I'm lucky to have it."

Ben felt the same way when he got hired four months ago at Moore's. With 300 employees, it's one of the few companies in town that is growing. In its vast, open garage he bends, shapes and glues ducts with men like Smoky Hudson and Melvin Mann, who have been doing this kind of work for 30 years. He has learned to respect them.

These guys "really work for their money," he says. "They get their hands dirty."

T.O. Rowland, a 33-year-old welder at Moore's, tells Ben he earns as much money as his wife, a schoolteacher with a master's degree. This makes Ben wonder again: Why do people make such a big deal over college?

This is a question that resonates only in some quarters of the educational establishment. Ken Gray, the Penn State professor, says: "The real opportunities for youth are grossly distorted by colleges. Seventy-one percent of jobs don't require anything beyond a high school education."

But that doesn't mean people can't or shouldn't keep learning, acquiring new skills. In Altavista, Central Virginia Community College runs a satellite center in the former Lane executive building here. The idea is to reach people in high-layoff areas. Center director Linda Rodriguez says the response from older workers, especially older female workers, has been terrific.

But young men like Ben aren't coming in.

When she approached high school authorities about coming to visit classes, she was met with some of the same lack of enthusiasm for community college that Ben's mom did. School authorities said there was no time in the calendar for her visits—the students were too busy taking tests—and offered a one-time assembly instead.

One evening last winter, as Ben arrived at the Amoco store to start his shift, the store manager pushed a paper napkin over to him across the counter. "Someone left this for you," he said.

On the napkin next to the beef jerky, the name Apryl East was scribbled along with a phone number. Ben smiled, remembering the blonde with the cornflower-blue eyes and infectious laugh who had stopped by a couple of weeks earlier. She was after him. Sweet.

Eight months later, the blonde is riding with him in his Camaro as they return from a football game between his old high school and hers in nearby Gretna, where she led cheers and played piccolo in the marching band. Now she's a senior at Virginia Tech, planning on teaching elementary school.

Apryl swears that her best friend left the napkin without her knowledge. Ben doesn't know whether to believe her but he also doesn't care.

He eventually did call her, they went out to a movie. Now a wallet photo of the two of them is propped next to the odometer in his beloved car.

Increasingly, their conversation involves the years to come, and tonight is no exception. Ben ran into a guy at the game whose girlfriend is taking courses in motorcar management at a community college.

"That kinda makes me want to try it," he tells Apryl.

He could choose to stay on at Moore's and go to school at the same time, "maybe get a job on computers" at Moore's. He also has had a couple of conversations with NASCAR driver Stacy Compton. Perhaps, while he's still young, he should just chuck everything—except Apryl—and enlist Compton's help signing on with a racing crew. The sponsors and money for his own car might follow.

"I am so not sure," he says.

Apryl has accepted his confusion, for now.

"I'd like you to go to college," she tells Ben, "but it's okay with me if you don't." Her three best friends are all at different universities. But neither her dad, a supervisor at Moore's, nor her mom, a secretary in a printing shop, attended college, and they've been happy together. From what she has observed at home, college isn't crucial to the married life she dreams of.

What is important, she has told Ben gently, is that he get his behind in gear. He can always try one avenue and move to another if he doesn't like it. He's not yet 20, she reminds him.

Where will he find the motivation?

"From me," she says. She laughs but she's serious. "I'm going to get out of college, come back home and tell him to do it. I can be his little mentor."

A few hours before Ben picks her up for the game, over lunch at a downtown diner, she admits that when she learned that Ben wasn't in college, "I was shocked. I told my mom he didn't get the right kind of guidance."

So why does she stick with him? "He's got a great personality. He's funny." Unlike her previous boyfriend, "he treats me well. Oh, and another thing I like about him? My dad and he have bonded. He says when we have kids, he wants to be the kind of dad he never had."

She takes a breath, then adds, "Ben's everything I ever wanted." She laughs again, then cups her hand over her mouth as if she has revealed just a little too much.

2002

CRITICAL THINKING POINTS: *After you've read*

1. Do you have any friends who are not in college? Is it difficult to explain to them what it is like? Why or why not?
2. If you could predict a future for Apryl and Ben, what might it be? Why?
3. If you were going to give Ben some advice, what would it be?

SOME POSSIBILITIES FOR WRITING

1. Compare and contrast your life now to the life you might have had if you had not gone to college.
2. In so many ways, Ben is a product of the environment and people around him. Imitating the "feature reporter" tone of this essay, write a similar one with you as the subject.
3. "No one's interested in the Bubbas," this essay asserts. Is that true? Why do you think the way you do?

8th Grade Final Exam
Salina Kansas, 1895

Various tests from the days of yore occasionally make the rounds of Internet information loops. This exam was taken from the original document on file at the Smoky Valley Genealogical Society and Library in Salina, Kansas.

What is the cost of a square farm at $15 per acre, the distance around which is 640 rods?

CRITICAL THINKING POINTS: *As you read*

1. How well do you think you would do on this test? Why?
2. Do you think your teachers could pass it? Why or why not?
3. Are there any questions where your answer might be correct for today but not for 1895? Why?

Grammar

(Time, one hour)

1. Give nine rules for the use of Capital Letters.
2. Name the Parts of Speech and define those that have no modifications.
3. Define Verse, Stanza and Paragraph.
4. What are the Principal Parts of a verb? Give Principal Parts of do, lie, lay and run.
5. Define Case, Illustrate each Case.
6. What is Punctuation? Give rules for principal marks of Punctuation.
7–10. Write a composition of about 150 words and show therein that you understand the practical use of the rules of grammar.

Arithmetic

(Time, 1.25 hours)

1. Name and define the Fundamental Rules of Arithmetic.
2. A wagon box is 2 ft. deep, 10 feet long, and 3 ft. wide. How many bushels of wheat will it hold?

3. If a load of wheat weighs 3942 lbs., what is it worth at 50 cts.per bu, deducting 1050 lbs. for tare?
4. District No.33 has a valuation of $35,000. What is the necessary levy to carry on a school seven months at $50 per month, and have $104 for incidentals?
5. Find cost of 6720 lbs. coal at $6.00 per ton.
6. Find the interest of $512.60 for 8 months and 18 days at 7 percent.
7. What is the cost of 40 boards 12 inches wide and 16 ft. long at $20 per inch?
8. Find bank discount on $300 for 90 days (no grace) at 10 percent.
9. What is the cost of a square farm at $15 per acre, the distance around which is 640 rods?
10. Write a Bank Check, a Promissory Note, and a Receipt.

U.S. History

(Time, 45 minutes)

1. Give the epochs into which U.S. History is divided.
2. Give an account of the discovery of America by Columbus.
3. Relate the causes and results of the Revolutionary War.
4. Show the territorial growth of the United States.
5. Tell what you can of the history of Kansas.
6. Describe three of the most prominent battles of the Rebellion.
7. Who were the following: Morse, Whitney, Fulton, Bell, Lincoln, Penn, and Howe?
8. Name events connected with the following dates: 1607, 1620, 1800, 1849, and 1865.

Orthography

(Time, one hour)

1. What is meant by the following: Alphabet, phonetic orthography, etymology, syllabication?
2. What are elementary sounds? How classified?
3. What are the following, and give examples of each: Trigraph, sub-vocals, diphthong, cognate letters, linguals?
4. Give four substitutes for caret 'u'.
5. Give two rules for spelling words with final 'e'. Name two exceptions under each rule.

6. Give two uses of silent letters in spelling. Illustrate each.

7. Define the following prefixes and use in connection with a word: Bi, dis, mis, pre, semi, post, non, inter, mono, super.

8. Mark diacritically and divide into syllables the following, and name the sign that indicates the sound: Card, ball, mercy, sir, odd, cell, rise, blood, fare, last.

9. Use the following correctly in sentences, Cite, site, sight, fane, fain, feign, vane, vain, vein, raze, raise, rays.

10. Write 10 words frequently mispronounced and indicate pronunciation by use of diacritical marks and by syllabication.

Geography

(Time, one hour)

1. What is climate? Upon what does climate depend?

2. How do you account for the extremes of climate in Kansas?

3. Of what use are rivers? Of what use is the ocean?

4. Describe the mountains of N.A.

5. Name and describe the following: Monrovia, Odessa, Denver, Manitoba, Hecla, Yukon, St. Helena, Juan Fernandez, Aspinwall and Orinoco.

6. Name and locate the principal trade centers of the U.S.

7. Name all the republics of Europe and give capital of each.

8. Why is the Atlantic Coast colder than the Pacific in the same latitude?

9. Describe the process by which the water of the ocean returns to the sources of rivers.

10. Describe the movements of the earth. Give inclination of the earth.

1895

CRITICAL THINKING POINTS: *After you've read*

1. Perhaps too easy an answer as to why much of this material is so foreign to you is that you were never "taught it." What are some of the reasons that is so?

2. Which sections of the test do you think you would do the best at? The worst? Why?

3. Which individual questions would be the hardest and the easiest for your class to answer? Why?

SOME POSSIBILITIES FOR WRITING

1. Design your own test (or section of a test) to give to students in 1895. Try not to "trick" anyone or to concentrate on objects or areas that would be unfamiliar to them simply because those subjects didn't exist at the time.

2. What are some of the most difficult tests you have taken in school? What made them difficult? Were they fair or unfair tests? What made them fair or unfair?

3. If you were to design a fair but difficult test for a course you are taking this semester, what kinds of questions might you ask? Why?

Further Suggestions for Writing— "Where We're Coming From"

1. What do you expect to miss the most and least about high school and/or home? Why?

2. What kind of high school student were you? What traits would you like to keep as a college student? What would you like to change and why? What could you do to facilitate this?

3. Recall a time when you were thrust into a situation where you did not quite fit in. Describe your experience. How does it compare to starting college?

4. Recall some recent experience that was new, different, foreign, and perhaps even frightening. Reflect on what you learned or how your preconceptions changed. What idea(s) gradually dawned on you?

5. Think of some significant accomplishment in your life. Write about how curiosity, discipline, risk taking, initiative, and/or enthusiasm contributed to that accomplishment. Did other qualities contribute as well?

6. Think of a time when you lacked the verbal skills you needed to communicate effectively. It may have been conducting a college interview, writing a letter to a friend, or expressing your ideas in class. Write about how it made you feel and how you coped with the problem.

7. If you participated in any organized programs in high school, describe what that activity did or did not teach you.

8. Identify a talent you have or information you possess that is unique, such as tap dancing, scuba diving, or how to make maple syrup. Write at least a page about why this is important to you and why others should know about it.

9. Aesop says, "Never trust the advice of a man in difficulties." No doubt you've received advice before coming to college. What makes for good advice? For bad? What kind of advice were you given? Which will be the easiest or the hardest for you to follow? Why?

10. Choose one of the pieces of advice in this chapter and try to convince someone that it is particularly good or bad advice.

11. Think of a problem with your high school, perhaps within a team, student organization, or group of friends. Propose some specific solutions for this problem.

12. Working in a group, examine how our society guides students to college. Did you feel that you received "the right kind of guidance"? Why or why not?

13. Some students seem eager to answer questions in class, to join the discussion, while others do not. How do you usually react in these situations? Why?

14. Interview two or three experienced students about their first year. What kinds of pressure and problems did they have? How did they handle them? Seek their advice on things you are concerned about.

15. Most people want to succeed at what they do, and college is no exception. Why and how much do you want to succeed at college? What does success at college mean for and to you?

16. What cocurricular activities do you plan to pursue in college? How do these activities relate to your academic or career plans?

17. Choose a campus organization you are thinking about joining and investigate it. Prepare a report on this organization to deliver to the class.

18. If you are new to the town where your school is located, or even if you are not, find something interesting, odd, or unique about it and present your findings to the class.

19. Go to an on-campus event of any kind that you have never experienced before, such as a symphony, a ballet, a poetry reading, or a debate. The possibilities are endless. With an open mind, summarize, describe, and/or evaluate it. Do you think you would ever attend another event of this kind? Why or why not?

20. Prepare for a crucial situation that is likely to happen to you as a college student this semester. Imagine exactly what might happen and write a description of it. Explain why this situation is likely to be so crucial. Include all the possible outcomes from the best to the worst, and figure out what you might do to prepare for the situation before it occurs.

21. Contrast "Saved" with "One Writer's Beginnings." What are some of the reasons these pieces display the differences they do? What support do you have for your position?

22. Find and watch Spike Lee's 1992 film *Malcolm X*. How does seeing this film affect your reading of the selection "Saved"?

23. Research and write a brief report about the Dawes Act (or General Allotment Act) of 1887. How do the philosophical and political implications of this act further your understanding of Zitkala-Sa's "Incurring My Mother's Displeasure"?

24. Read *Be True to Your School* by Bob Greene (1988) and/or *Please Don't Kill the Freshman: A Memoir* by Zoe Trope (2003) or similar high school memoirs. How does either of these high school experiences compare to yours or to each other? Why do you think that is so?

25. Read *Bullseye: Stories and Poems by Outstanding High School Writers* edited by Pawlak, Lourie, and Padgett (1995) and/or *Coming of Age in America: A Multicultural Anthology* edited by Frosch and Sotto (1995) and/or *Early Harvest: Student Writing from the Rural Readers Project* edited by Rachele Syme (2000) or similar collections. Which pieces seem to be the most honest to you? Why?

26. Read *Aquamarine Blue 5: Personal Stories of College Students with Autism* by Dawn Prince-Hughes (2002) and/or *Learning Outside the Lines: Two Ivy League Students with Learning Disabilities and ADHD Give You the Tools*

to Succeed edited by Mooney and Cole (2002) and/or Learning Disabilities and Life Stories edited by Rodis, Garrod, and Boscardin (2002), or some similar collection. After reading these experiences from these points of view, what insights and/or new awareness do you have?

27. Read Don't Tell Me What to Do, Just Send Money: The Essential Parenting Guide to the College Years by Johnson and Schelhas-Miller (2000) and/or Empty Nest . . . Full Heart: The Journey from Home to College by Andrea Van Steenhouse (2002) and/or Letting Go: A Parents' Guide to Understanding the College Years by Coburn and Treeger (2003), or a similar guide for parents of college students. After reading these experiences from these points of view, what insights and/or new awareness do you have?

28. Choose at least three films from the list at the end of this chapter. What do they seem to say about high school? What support do you have for your position?

29. Choose one of your responses to "Some Possibilities for Writing" in this chapter and do further research on some aspect of the topic. Write about how and why this new information would have improved your previous effort.

30. Find the original text from which one of the selections in this chapter was taken. What led you to choose the text you did? How does reading more from the text affect your original reading? Is there more you would like to know about the text, its subject, or its author? Where might you find this further information?

Selected Films—"Where We're Coming From"

Almost Famous (2000, USA). Cameron Crowe's semi-autobiographical tale of a high-school boy who is given the chance to write a story about an up-and-coming rock band as he accompanies it on their concert tour. Comedy/Drama. 122 min. R.

American Graffiti (1973, USA). The action takes place over one typical night for a group of high school graduates. Cowritten and directed by George Lucas (the auteur behind the Star Wars trilogy). Comedy. 110 min. PG.

The Boy Who Could Fly (1986, USA). After the death of her father, teenage Milly moves into a new neighborhood with her mother and brother. Amid the struggles to fit in at a new school in a new town, Milly befriends an autistic neighbor boy who believes he can fly and who changes the lives of everyone around him. Family/Fantasy. 114 min. PG.

Boyz N the Hood (1991, USA). The film follows the stories of childhood friends who grow up in a Los Angeles ghetto. Drama. 107 min. R.

The Breakfast Club (1985, USA). Forced to spend a Saturday detention in school, five disparate high school kids find that they have more in common than they ever realized. John Hughes directed. Comedy/Drama. 97 min. R.

Breaking Away (1979, USA). Oscar winner (for best original screenplay) about a teen just out of high school searching for his identity through bicycle racing. Filmed on location at Indiana University. Comedy/Drama. 100 min. PG.

Can't Hardly Wait (1998, USA). It's graduation night for a group of high school seniors, and each of them must face the future while learning to let go of the past. Comedy. 100 min. PG-13.

Class (1983, USA). Two prep school roommates come up against class differences and a salacious secret neither one is fully aware of. Comedy/Drama. 98 min. R.

Crooklyn (1994, USA). The life of a 1970s Brooklyn family told through the viewpoint of a nine-year old girl. Spike Lee's semi-autobiographical tale of his childhood, coauthored with his sister, Joie. Comedy/Drama. 115 min. PG-13.

Do the Right Thing (1989, USA). Spike Lee's film of racial tensions that finally boil over in the Bed-Stuy district of Brooklyn during the hottest day of the summer. Comedy/Drama/Crime. 120 min. R.

Election (1999, USA). An obnoxious overachiever running for student body president is opposed by an unlikely candidate egged on by a vindictive teacher. Comedy. 103 min. R.

Elephant (2003, USA). A violent incident rocks the students and faculty at a high school in Portland, Oregon. Drama. 81 min. R.

Fame (1980, USA). Follows four students through their years in the New York City High School for the Performing Arts. The kids fall into four clearly defined stereotypes: brazen, gay and hypersensitive, prickly, and shy. Drama. 134 min. R.

Fast Times at Ridgemont High (1982, USA). Based on the factual book by Cameron Crowe, who returned to high school as an adult masquerading as a student for a year. Featured the film debuts of Forest Whitaker, Eric Stoltz, Anthony Edwards, and Nicolas Cage. Comedy. 90 min. R.

Ferris Bueller's Day Off (1986, USA). Days away from graduation, Ferris and his best friends, Cameron and Sloane, explore Chicago on a day of hooky. John Hughes directed. Comedy. 102 min. PG-13.

Finding Forrester. (2000, USA). Jamal is a basketball player and gifted student whose writing talent is nurtured by a famously reclusive author, William Forrester (Sean Connery). 136 min. Drama. PG-13.

Grease (1978, USA). John Travolta stars in this musical where Greasers and Goody-Goodies sing and dance their way through broken hearts, drag races, and phantom pregnancies at 1950s Rydell High School. Comedy/Musical. 110 min. PG.

Heathers (1989, USA). In a half-hearted attempt at popularity, Veronica mixes with popular girls Heather I, II, and III until she meets the darkly rebellious Jason Dean, who shows her that the flip side to popularity can be murder. Dark Comedy. 102 min. R.

Hoop Dreams (1994, USA). Recruited to attend an elite high school by professional basketball player Isaiah Thomas, Arthur Agee and William Gates are filmed for nearly five years as they struggle through successes and failures on their way to college. Documentary. 170 min. PG-13.

Hoosiers (1986, USA). A coach with a dark past and the town drunk pair up to train a small-town high-school basketball team in Indiana for the state championships. Drama. 115 min. PG.

Kids (1995, USA). A young skater sets out to deflower as many virgins as possible, but things go badly when one gets tested for HIV. Drama. 91 min. R.

Malcolm X (1992, USA). A biopic of the controversial and influential Black Nationalist leader. Directed by Spike Lee. Drama. 209 min. R.

Mystic Pizza (1988, USA). Three young women of blue-collar Portuguese descent work in a pizzeria in the coastal town of Mystic, Connecticut, and one dreams of going to Yale. Romantic comedy. 104 min. R.

Not Another Teen Movie (2001, USA). A send-up of teen movies from the past two decades. The film plays with stereotypes of stereotypes and mixes stock plots into one incomprehensible storyline—and it all takes place at John Hughes High School. Comedy. 89 min. R.

O (2001, USA). An update of *Othello* with a teen cast, taking place in a white prep boarding school in the South. The only black student, Odin, is the star basketball player. Drama. 95 min. R.

October Sky (1999, USA). Based on the memoir *Rocket Boys* by Homer H. Hickam Jr., this true story begins in 1957 with the Soviet Union's historic launch of the Sputnik satellite. Homer sees Sputnik as his cue to pursue a fascination with rocketry, but winning the science fair is his only ticket to college and out of life in a West Virginia coal-mining town. Drama. 108 min. PG.

Orange County (2002, USA). An Orange County teen and aspiring writer yearns for admission to Stanford. Comedy. 82 min. PG-13.

The Outsiders (1983, USA). Based upon S.E. Hinton's popular novel, *The Outsiders* follows the lives of a group of high-school-aged boys who sit on the margins of society. Drama. 91 min. PG.

Perfect Score (2004, USA). Six high school seniors decide to break into the Princeton Testing Center so they can steal the answers to their upcoming SAT tests and all get perfect scores. 92 min. PG-13.

A Raisin in the Sun (1961, USA). On the brink of the Civil Rights movement, an impoverished African-American family unexpectedly receives a small windfall, enough money to make someone's dreams come true. Beneatha dreams of going to medical school, while her father dreams of opening his own business, and her grandmother dreams of owning her own home in an integrated neighborhood. Based on the groundbreaking play by Lorraine Hansberry. Drama. 128 min. N/R.

Rebel Without a Cause (1955, USA). A James Dean classic. Dean stars as a troubled teen who comes to a new town hoping to start over and finds both friends and enemies. Drama. 111 min. N/R.

Risky Business (1983, USA). With his parents out of town, entrepreneurial Tom Cruise decides to spend the time waiting to hear from colleges dancing in his underwear and organizing a prostitution ring. By the time he gets to college, he's a wiser man. Comedy. 99 min. R.

Rushmore (1999, USA). The king of Rushmore prep school is put on academic probation. Comedy. 133 min. R.

Say Anything . . . (1989, USA). A young kickboxer falls for the smart girl. She's college bound; he's maybe not. Comedy/Drama. 89 min. PG-13.

Sixteen Candles (1984, USA). Samantha Baker's angst-ridden love-life, as well as her sixteenth birthday, is lost in the uproar caused by her older sister's wedding. Comedy/Drama. 93 min. PG.

Thirteen (2003, USA). A thirteen-year-old girl's relationship with her mother is put to the test as she discovers drugs, sex, and petty crime in the company of her cool but troubled best friend. Drama. 100 min. R.

Valley Girl (1983, USA). A Valley Girl falls for a Hollywood punk (played by Nicholas Cage) and struggles to do the right thing despite what her trendy, snobby friends think. Comedy. 95 min. R.

Weird Science (1985, USA). Two high-school science nerds "create" the perfect woman, who proceeds to turn their lives upside down. Sci-Fi/Fantasy/Comedy. 94 min. PG-13.

For critical thinking points on these films, see Appendix (p.281).

Two

School Daze

LIFE IN THE FIRST YEAR

Many first-year students often walk around in a daze—sleep deprived, homesick, scared, overwhelmed, or feeling like a castaway in a strange land. The selections in this chapter focus on the sometimes humorous and sometimes very serious transitions, new interactions, balancing acts, and experiences that make up the first year of college.

READING SELECTIONS

A Day in the Life Of . . .

My First Week at Mizzou

from *Diary of a Freshman*

Take This Fish and Look at It

Hunters and Gatherers

Theme for English B

from *Lummox: Evolution of a Man*

The English Lesson

Outside In: The Life of a Commuter Student

from *I Walk in Beauty*

from *The Freshman Year Thrill Ride*

A Day in the Life Of . . .

Greg Adams

Greg Adams (b. 1970), a songwriter and poet, is currently working as a newspaper editor.

. . . REWIND.

CRITICAL THINKING POINTS: *As you read*

1. From its title, what do you expect the poem to be about?
2. Why is this a poem and not a short story or a diary entry? What things specifically make this a poem?
3. What are some of the narrator's personality traits? How do you know that?

> 8:04 a.m., Kleenex, lamp
> light, Irish Spring, Pert
> Plus, boxers, pants, shirt,
> Malt-O-Meal, milk, vitamin.
> parking lot, bridge, college
> algebra, Burger King, hot chocolate,
> short story, bridge, parking
> lot, keys, stereo, guitar.
> local news, frozen chicken, instant
> potatoes, salt, butter,
> milk, aspirin, Rolaids, rented
> video, beer, popcorn, Kleenex.
> beer, more beer, salt, burnt
> kernels, credits, STOP, Close
> Up, mint floss, sleep sofa, allergy
> pill, lights, REWIND.

1994

CRITICAL THINKING POINTS: *After you've read*

1. Which of these details seem to particularly reflect college life? How might that contribute to your reading of the poem?
2. Imagine you could ask the narrator, "So, how was your day?" What do you think he would say? Why?
3. Why do you think there are no verbs in the poem? What effect does that have?

SOME POSSIBILITIES FOR WRITING

1. Rewrite the poem so it is pertinent to your day. Include specific details in the way the author does. Try it again, but this time make it about a day in your life when you were in high school.

2. Write about some part of your daily routine—getting up, going to bed, walking the dog, driving to work (the more mundane the better)—as seen by a disinterested, objective third person. Try as hard as you can not to tell readers what you want them to know, but instead show them with concrete details.

3. Again, write about some part of your daily routine, but as observed by a person who wants readers to like or to dislike you. Or, as observed by a person who wants readers not to trust you. Or, from your own point of view, which reflects a particular state of mind such as happiness, depression, joy, or boredom. Try as hard as you can not to tell readers what you want them to know, but instead show them with concrete details.

My First Week at Mizzou

FROM *ANOTHER YEAR IN THE LIFE OF A NERD*   Andrew Hicks

Andrew Hicks (b. 1978) graduated with a degree in journalism from the University of Missouri–Columbia. He traces his ostracism from popular society to the age of 5, when he was moved up to first grade after a month of kindergarten. "Apparently, I was finger painting and taking naps on a higher level than the other kids." Hicks's four "Years in the Life" comedy diaries have garnered critical praise from *Netsurfer Digest* and *The Web*.

I have only one class on Fridays, the omnipresent Spanish class, so that leaves plenty of time for leisure, studying and keeping up on letter correspondence. . . . Okay, you got me, I slept all afternoon.

CRITICAL THINKING POINTS: *As you read*

1. Among the first things writers should consider is their purpose and audience. What do you think are the purpose and audience of this piece? What elements lead you to think the way you do?

2. Recall your experience of first coming to campus. How was your experience different from Hicks's experience? How was it similar?

3. What are some stereotypes you associate with nerds? Why? Does the narrator conform to or violate any of these? Is he really a nerd?

August 22, 1995

The first day of the end of my life. Yes, the college experience has begun for your favorite nerd and so far it hasn't been that much different from the high school experience, except that I am now completely independent, miles from home and—oh yeah—stone cold drunk. No, of course I'm not. That statement was incorrect. I'm actually *fall-down* drunk. That last statement was also incorrect, as I've obviously never been drunk in my life. I've been exempt from peer pressure thus far in my life, except for the time those guys got me hooked on phonics, a habit I haven't been able to break since. Still, who knows what will happen to me now that I'm stuck on the grounds of a large state university, open and susceptible to all forms of temptation. I may even convert from the original "Star Trek" to "Star Trek: The Next Generation."

Dorm life, obviously, is my first experience of living in close quarters with another person, if you don't count the year and a half I was shacked up with "Golden Girl" Estelle Getty. I'd be remiss if I didn't take up valuable space in the book berating my roommate, but he's actually a pretty nice guy. A quiet guy, too. Keeps to himself. At least that's what the neighbors will tell the police after he kills me in my sleep. Think I'm being paranoid? Then you haven't seen the stack of *Soldier of Fortune* magazines, the poster of the Army guy carrying an automatic gun, the American flag hanging over the bed. Now are you starting to see the scenario? I own several Japanese electronic products, including the laptop computer I'm typing this on. What if this militant patriot decides to make sure I never buy foreign again? Still, he's probably just a normal American teenager, hence the Kathy Ireland poster on the wall. Of course, she's fully-clothed, so maybe he's not so normal after all.

At least my roommate passed one TV compatibility test, the one that asks "Do you like 'America's Funniest Home Videos'?" I could never voluntarily share a room with someone who found Bob Saget amusing. I still have to see about a second TV compatibility test, this one concerning late-night talk show hosts. As far as I'm concerned, there are two kinds of people in the world, the Letterman people and the Leno people. I've only met one Conan person in my life, but this was a McCluer student named Sumar who had continuing flashbacks to Woodstock '94, so that tells you something. My family and I are all staunch Letterman men, but of course my two best friends are Leno people, so what good does that test do? See, I've been here one day and already my theories on life are falling apart.

August 24, 1995

Today was the first day of classes. My first class on Mondays, Wednesdays and Fridays doesn't start until 10:40, but since I made no attempt to conceal that fact from my employers, I had to get up bright and early this morning to serve people their heart attacks.

The one good thing about getting up at 6:30 is that there aren't any other people using the showers. As you may imagine, with an ample body like mine, I'll never be president of the Public Showers Fan Club. I am grateful that there are stalls to separate the showers, but I still sometimes accidentally reveal too much, as evidenced a few days ago, when somebody said, "Hey, that pasty white shower curtain has a crack in it." Of course it wasn't a shower curtain, but I didn't tell the guy that.

The stalls are only shoulder high, so even though certain parts are strategically concealed, you still have to make small talk with the other people in the shower room. I've already found out saying "nice penis" doesn't cut it as far as small talk goes. And I've also found out, darn the luck, that coed dorms don't mean coed showers. *Animal House,* you lied to me!

At 10:40 I was off to Spanish class, which I had thought would be my first challenging Spanish class. After all, it had taken both ounces of my brain power to test into Spanish 2 during the Summer Welcome. Once I got to class, though, and heard the jocks and frat boys saying "*Como* . . . uh . . . my llama . . . uh . . . " I canceled any previous thoughts regarding the degree of difficulty.

My other class today was an Honors class regarding the study of the book of Revelation and other apocalyptic literature, a subject I've always found fascinating, to the point where I've actually watched the 1973 Christian movie *A Thief in the Night* more than once. Enduring a movie that bad more than once should automatically save anyone's soul from hell.

Even though the University policy states that instructors can't do anything but discuss the semester syllabus (syllabi, in the plural) on the first day, both classes did assign homework. For the Revelation class I have to walk up to complete strangers on the street and record their opinions on how the world would end, which isn't exactly a casual icebreaker for conversation. I might as well be asking them to imagine their sweet grannies burning in hellfire for all eternity.

August 25, 1995

I went to my remaining three classes today and, let me tell you, it ain't gonna be that hard for me this semester. Part of that stems from the fact that my English class centers strictly on autobiographical writing. See what I mean? All I ever do is write about myself. If only the class had been even more specific and focused on humorous autobiographical writing, I would have been set for life. But I'm sure the instructor has a sense of humor. You should have seen the suspenders he was wearing.

Three of my "instructors" are full-fledged professors, not bad for freshman courses at a large state school. The other two instructors are ambitious grad students, including my Spanish teacher, who insists on the annoying habit of speaking in Spanish all the time. She said yesterday that if you want to be good at playing football, you play football. And if you want to be good at speaking Spanish, you speak Spanish. Or something like that. I'm not sure about the exact explanation because she said it in Spanish. See, it's a no-win situation. Excuse me, *es un no-gana situacion*.

Psychology class should prove to be interesting for the mere fact that it consists of over 500 students. I have a sneaking suspicion I'm the only person in the class and the other 499 were just extras brought in for an experiment to see how I would react to the crowd. I was clever enough to anticipate that scenario and decided to throw off the results by jumping up and down, yelling "Mickey Mouse is in my pocket! You can't have him! None of you! Stand back, I have a light saber!" What I didn't anticipate was the appearance of the Mizzou police five minutes later to haul me away.

Last night we had a meeting of all the guys in my dorm. Seeing all the people I live with all at once made one thing perfectly clear to me—I have to keep my door locked at all times. As far as roommate relations go, there have been no significant developments. The guy just doesn't talk. And he keeps putting up more of the gun/military posters, the latest featuring a skull with criss-crossed guns, reading "Mess with the best, die like the rest." Oh yeah, one more thing—I haven't been sleeping too well either.

August 26, 1995

I have only one class on Fridays, the omnipresent Spanish class, so that leaves plenty of time for leisure, studying and keeping up on letter correspondence. . . . Okay, you got me, I slept all afternoon. I think I was entitled, though, after getting up at 6:30 this morning to work in the dining hall. I am gradually getting the hang of proper food-handling procedures, as today I only contaminated the food with two deadly bacteria instead of the usual three.

My first dining hall shift was a barbecue picnic at the football field, where—it has been constantly mentioned—the Astroturf has been replaced by real grass. What they didn't mention was that we were serving the Astroturf on buns with barbecue sauce for dinner. Apparently, all the rules about hygiene outlined at the orientation meeting don't apply to outdoor meals. The swarm of flies swimming in the cole slaw clued me in to that fact. Towards the end of the evening, the flies had actually constructed a miniature waterslide leading into the cole slaw and were taking turns sliding down the damn thing.

This is the first Friday night here on campus and I imagine there's plenty of drinking going on. I myself have had two pitchers of Brita filtered water, so watch out! You can tell I've loosened up out here. I used to drink only tap water, but the water here has so much lead in it there's a pencil sharpener attached to the sink.

It's been an exciting Friday night for me. A trip to the laundry room and the computer lab in the same evening. I thought the computer lab would be fairly empty due to it being Friday night and all but the first time I went in the computers were all in use. "Why aren't you people out getting drunk?" I demanded. "Leave the computer room to dorks like me who have nothing better to do." But no one budged. Oh well, I can always come back later to coerce preteen girls over the Internet.

August 29, 1995

Although there's not much spiritual conviction to be found in most Mizzou students (their philosophy in life centers more around "two boobs and a brewski" than the Bible), there are still quite a few Christian organizations on campus, many of which go to great lengths to attract students' attention. Today, for example, there was a street preacher yelling at the top of his lungs at one intersection about "fornication" and "hay-ell," with the traditional evangelist flair, the kind of college student who would be more at home at Oral Roberts University than a large state school.

As I was walking past this spectacle, I overheard a girl commenting. She was a Jim Morrison–worshiping vampire clone with purple hair and a nose ring. She said three words concerning the street preacher: "That guy's weird." I considered stopping and pointing out the full irony of the girl's comment but decided against it.

My week at Mizzou has proven to me that there are quite a few people out there who stretch the bounds of "normal," whatever that may be defined as. Today in my Revelation course a group of students reported back on their interviews with people about their opinions on the world's end. Although most respondents did have the traditional Rapture / Tribulation / Antichrist / Armageddon beliefs or the naturalistic science-geek perspective of the earth ending due to "cyclical forces," there were some that just couldn't be classified.

One person thought the earth would literally shrink to one-eighth its original size and people would have to push each other off into space to retain their position, until the only people left were murderers whom God would cast into hell. Of course, this guy's brain has probably shrunk to one-eighth its original size. . . . Another person, a Black power advocate, said that, due to negligence by white supremacists, the ozone hole would widen, giving all white people skin tumors. Only people of African origin would survive. I think this guy must have graduated from McCluer.

The professor then told us of a book manuscript with conclusive proof that the world would end on November 14, 1999, to which one person responded, "Do we get off class for it?" A humorous exchange I had nothing to do with but nevertheless felt compelled to transcribe so maybe I can sell it to *Reader's Digest* one day.

1995

CRITICAL THINKING POINTS: *After you've read*

1. Why would/does anyone keep a journal? What do you think would be some of the advantages of doing so?

2. What might be some of the differences between keeping a journal for yourself and going online with one? Pay attention not only to what you would say but also how you would say it.

3. Hicks wrote his *Another Year in the Life of a Nerd* series years before "blogs" became so popular. Why do you think writing blogs is a current craze?

4. Imagine the author reading his journal some ten or twenty years in the future. What do you think he will think and/or feel about it then?

SOME POSSIBILITIES FOR WRITING

1. Create or re-create your own journal of your first few days of classes.

2. Imagine you are one of the characters who appears in this journal and rewrite one or more scenes from that character's point of view.

3. Write about the funniest incident that has happened to you since arriving on campus. Then write about the saddest or most disappointing incident.

Diary of a Freshman

AN EXCERPT   Charles Macomb Flandreau

Charles Macomb Flandreau (1871–1938), born in Minnesota, was a newspaperman, a writer, and a Harvard graduate who wrote memoirs of his college days "embodied" in a series of satiric stories found in *Harvard Episodes* (1897) and *Diary of a Freshman* (1901).

I was careful not to say that I had failed or flunked, or hadn't passed, as that was not the impression I wished to convey.

CRITICAL THINKING POINTS: *As you read*

1. What is a "double entendre"? How is this technique used in this piece?
2. Pay attention to the attitude and tone of the advisor and the student. What do you think each was trying to accomplish?
3. This scene took place on a college campus more than one hundred years ago. What things are still true of college students? What things are still true of advisors and administrators?

My advisor is a young man and seems like an appreciative, well-disposed sort of person (he offered me a cigar after I had sat down in his study), so I didn't have any difficulty in telling him right off what I had come for.

"I've heard from my hour examinations," I said, "and I find that I have been given E in all of them." (I was careful not to say that I had failed or flunked, or hadn't passed, as that was not the impression I wished to convey.)

"We have met the enemy and we are theirs," he answered pleasantly. "Yes, I heard about that," he went on, "and I hoped you would come in to see me." Then he waited awhile—until the clock began to get noisy—and at last he glanced up and said— "What was it doing when you came in? It looked like snow this afternoon." But I hadn't gone there to discuss meteorology, so I ignored his remark.

"I can scarcely think I could have failed in everything," I suggested.

"It is somewhat incredible, isn't it?" the young man murmured.

"I never stopped writing from the time an examination began until it stopped," I said.

"What did you think it was—a strength test?" he asked brutally.

"I told all I knew."

"Yes," he acknowledged; "your instructors were convinced of that."

"And I don't think I got enough credit for it. If I had the books here, I feel sure I could make this plain."

"Well, let's look them over," he answered readily; and much to my astonishment he went to his desk and brought back all my blue-books.

I confess I hadn't expected anything quite so definite as this, but I tried to appear as if I had hoped that it was just what might happen. We sat down side by side and read aloud—first an examination question (he had provided himself with a full set of the papers) and then my answer to it.

"Explain polarized light," he read.

"The subject of polarized light, as I understand it, is not very well understood." I began; at which my adviser put his hands to his head and rocked to and fro.

"If you don't mind," I said, "I think I'd rather begin on one of the others; this physics course is merely to make up a condition, and perhaps I've not devoted very much time to it; it isn't a fair test." So we took up the history paper and read the first question, which was: "What was the Lombard League?" My answer I considered rather neat, for I had written: "The Lombard League was a coalition formed by the Lombards." I paused after reading it and glanced at my adviser.

"It was a simple question, and I gave it a simple answer," I murmured.

"I'm afraid you depreciate yourself, Mr. Wood," he replied. "Your use of the word 'coalition' is masterly."

"But what more could I have said?" I protested.

"I don't think you could have said *anything* more," he answered inscrutably.

I read on and on, and he interrupted me only twice—once in the philosophy course to point out politely that what I constantly referred to as "Hobbe's Octopus" ought to be "Hobbe's Leviathan," and once in the questions in English Literature, to explain that somebody or other's *Apologia Pro Vita Sua* was not—as I had translated it—"an apology for living in a sewer." (I could have killed Berrisford for that—and it sounded so plausible, too; for any one who lived in a sewer would naturally apologize.) He let me proceed, and after a time I couldn't even bring myself to stop and contest the decisions as I had done at first; for I dreaded the way he had of making my most serious remarks sound rather childish. So I rattled on, faster and faster, until I found myself mumbling in a low tone, without pronouncing half the words; and then I suddenly stopped and put the blue-book on the table and stared across the room at the wall. He didn't express any surprise, which, on the whole, was very decent of him, and after a minute or two of silence, during which he gathered up the evidence and put it back in his desk, we began to talk football and our chances of winning the big game. He said some nice things about Duggie, and hoped the rumor that he was overtrained wasn't true. I told him that I lived in the same house with Duggie and knew him very well, and feared it was true. He seemed glad that I knew Duggie. I stayed for about fifteen minutes so as not to seem abrupt or angry at the way my visit had turned out, and then left. We didn't refer to the exams again, so I don't see exactly how I can ever right the wrong they have done me. If my adviser were a different kind of man, I could have managed it, I think.

1901

CRITICAL THINKING POINTS: *After you've read*

1. Can you discover from this dialogue any of the reasons the student may have failed his exams? What are some of them?

2. The narrator says, "I told all I knew." "Yes," his advisor says, "your instructors were convinced of that." Why do you think the advisor treated the student in the way he did? What kinds of things does the advisor wish to accomplish?

3. Do you believe the student actually learned anything from this encounter? Why or why not? What might the student have learned?

SOME POSSIBILITIES FOR WRITING

1. Have you ever found yourself in a situation similar to this one? Write the scene.

2. Imagine you are going to film this scene. Write it as if it were a movie script. Now update the scene to the present day. What might change about the characters and their dialogue? Why do you think so?

3. Failing is one thing, but coming to terms with your failure is even more difficult. Write about a time when it was hard for you to face your failure.

Take This Fish and Look at It

Samuel H. Scudder

Samuel H. Scudder (1837–1911) was a famous entomologist who attended Harvard University.

I was piqued; I was mortified. Still more of that wretched fish! But now I set myself to my task with a will, and discovered one new thing after another, until I saw how just the Professor's criticism had been. The afternoon passed quickly; and when, towards its close, the Professor inquired: "Do you see it yet?"

CRITICAL THINKING POINTS: *As you read*

1. Consider why observation skills are necessary for students to grow and learn. In what academic situations are these skills most critical? How do you rate yourself as an observer?
2. Consider the type of student Scudder was before his episode with the fish. How might he have changed as a student? As a scientist? As a person?
3. What are some clues to the era in which the essay is set?

I t was more than fifteen years ago that I entered the laboratory of Professor Agassiz, and told him I had enrolled my name in the Scientific School as a student of natural history. He asked me a few questions about my object in coming, my antecedents generally, the mode in which I afterwards proposed to use the knowledge I might acquire, and, finally, whether I wished to study any special branch. To the latter I replied that, while I wished to be well grounded in all departments of zoology, I proposed to devote myself specially to insects.

"When do you wish to begin?" he asked. "Now," I replied.

This seemed to please him, and with an energetic "Very well," he reached from a shelf a huge jar of specimens in yellow alcohol. "Take this fish," he said, "and look at it; we call it a haemulon; by and by I will ask what you have seen."

With that he left me, but in a moment returned with explicit instructions as to the care of the object entrusted to me.

"No man is fit to be a naturalist," said he, "who does not know how to take care of specimens."

I was to keep the fish before me in a tin tray, and occasionally moisten the surface with alcohol from the jar, always taking care to replace the stopper tightly. Those were not the days of ground-glass stoppers and elegantly shaped exhibition jars; all the old students will recall the huge neck-less glass bottles with their leaky, wax-besmeared corks, half eaten by insects, and begrimed with cellar dust. Entomology was a cleaner science than ichthyology, but the example of the Professor, who had unhesitatingly plunged to the bottom of the jar to produce the fish, was infectious; and though this alcohol had a "very ancient and fishlike smell," I really dared not show any aversion within these sacred precincts, and treated the alcohol as though it were pure water. Still I was conscious of a passing feeling of disappointment, for gazing at a fish did not commend itself to an ardent entomologist. My friends at home, too, were annoyed when they discovered that no amount of eau-de-Cologne would drown the perfume which haunted me like a shadow.

In ten minutes I had seen all that could be seen in that fish, and started in search of the Professor—who had, however, left the Museum; and when I returned, after lingering over some of the odd animals stored in the upper apartment, my specimen was dry all over. I dashed the fluid over the fish as if to resuscitate the beast from a fainting fit, and looked with anxiety for a return of the normal sloppy appearance. This little excitement over, nothing was to be done but to return to a steadfast gaze at my mute companion. Half an hour passed—an hour—another hour; the fish began to look loathsome. I turned it over and around; looked it in the face ghastly; from behind, beneath, above, sideways, at a three-quarters' view—just as ghastly. I was in despair; at an early hour I concluded that lunch was necessary; so, with infinite relief, the fish was carefully replaced in the jar, and for an hour I was free.

On my return, I learned that Professor Agassiz had been at the Museum, but had gone, and would not return for several hours. My fellow students were too busy to be disturbed by continued conversation. Slowly I drew forth that hideous fish, and with a feeling of desperation again looked at it. I might not use a magnifying-glass; instruments of all kinds were interdicted. My two hands, my two eyes, and the fish: it seemed a most limited field. I pushed my finger down its throat to feel how sharp the teeth were. I began to count the scales in the different rows, until I was convinced that was nonsense. At last a happy thought struck me—I would draw the fish; and now with surprise I began to discover new features in the creature. Just then the Professor returned.

"That is right," said he; "a pencil is one of the best of eyes. I am glad to notice, too, that you keep your specimen wet, and your bottle corked."

With these encouraging words, he added: "Well, what is it like?"

He listened attentively to my brief rehearsal of the structure of parts whose names were still unknown to me: the fringed gill-arches and movable operculum, the pores of the head, fleshy lips and lidless eyes; the lateral line, the spinous fins and forked tail; the compressed and arched body. When I finished, he waited as if expecting more, and then, with an air of disappointment: "You have not looked very carefully; why," he continued more earnestly, "you haven't even seen one of the most conspicuous features of the animal, which is plainly before your eyes as the fish itself—look again, look again!" and he left me to my misery.

I was piqued; I was mortified. Still more of that wretched fish! But now I set myself to my task with a will, and discovered one new thing after another, until I saw how just the Professor's criticism had been. The afternoon passed quickly; and when, towards its close, the Professor inquired: "Do you see it yet?"

"No," I replied, "I am certain I do not, but I see how little I saw before."

"That is next best," said he, earnestly, "but I won't hear you now; put away your fish and go home; perhaps you will be ready with a better answer in the morning. I will examine you before you look at the fish."

This was disconcerting. Not only must I think of my fish all night, studying, without the object before me, what this unknown but most visible feature might be; but also, without reviewing my discoveries, I must give an exact account of them the next day. I had a bad memory; so I walked home by Charles River in a distracted state, with my two perplexities.

The cordial greeting from the Professor the next morning was reassuring; here was a man who seemed to be quite as anxious as I that I should see for myself what he saw.

"Do you perhaps mean," I asked, "that the fish has symmetrical sides with paired organs?"

His thoroughly pleased "Of course! Of course!" repaid the wakeful hours of the previous night. After he had discoursed most happily and enthusiastically—as he always did—upon the importance of this point, I ventured to ask what I should do next.

"Oh, look at your fish!" he said, and left me again to my own devices. In a little more than an hour he returned, and heard my new catalogue.

"That is good, that is good!" he repeated; "but that is not all; go on"; and so for three long days he placed that fish before my eyes, forbidding me to look at anything else, or to use any artificial aid. "Look, look, look," was his repeated injunction.

This was the best entomological lesson I ever had—a lesson whose influence has extended to the details of every subsequent study; a legacy the Professor had left to me, as he has left it to so many others, of inestimable value, which we could not buy, with which we cannot part.

A year afterward, some of us were amusing ourselves with chalking outlandish beasts on the Museum blackboard. We drew prancing starfishes; frogs in mortal combat; hydra-headed worms; stately crawfishes, standing on their tails, bearing aloft umbrellas; and grotesque fishes with gaping mouths and staring eyes. The Professor came in shortly after, and was as amused as any at our experiments. He looked at the fishes.

"Haemulons, every one of them," he said; "Mr. _____ drew them."

True; and to this day, if I attempt a fish, I can draw nothing but haemulons.

The fourth day, a second fish of the same group was placed beside the first, and I was bidden to point out the resemblances and differences between the two; another and another followed, until the entire family lay before me, and a whole legion of jars covered the table and surrounding shelves; the odor had become a pleasant perfume; and even now, the sight of an old, six-inch, worm-eaten cork brings fragrant memories.

The whole group of haemulons was thus brought in review; and, whether engaged upon the dissection of the internal organs, the preparation and examination of the bony framework, or the description of the various parts, Agassiz's training in the method of observing facts and their orderly arrangement was ever accompanied by the urgent exhortation not to be content with them.

"Facts are stupid things," he would say, "until brought into connection with some general law."

At the end of eight months, it was almost with reluctance that I left these friends and turned to insects; but what I had gained by this outside experience has been of greater value than years of later investigation in my favorite groups.

1874

CRITICAL THINKING POINTS: *After you've read*

1. Professor Agassiz says, "A pencil is one of the best of eyes." What does he mean? How and why might this be true?

2. Scudder says, "I see how little I saw before." Professor Agassiz answers, "That is next best." What does the professor mean? In what ways is this realization a step toward the lesson Scudder learns?

3. What makes this a humorous story? Would it be as effective without the humor? Why or why not?

SOME POSSIBILITIES FOR WRITING

1. Recall a teacher who taught you a lesson you didn't expect to learn. What led to your acquiring that lesson? Write an essay describing your experience.

2. Observation is a skill that is used constantly in social and academic situations. What are some experiences you've had in which your observation skills were absolutely integral to your success? Choose one experience and describe it.

3. Recall a personal experience that turned out poorly because your observation skills failed you. Write about the situation and speculate how it could have turned out differently if you had been more observant.

Hunters and Gatherers

Jennifer Hale

"Hunters and Gatherers" is an excerpt from a journal that Jennifer Hale (b. 1977) kept for an Introduction to College Learning Strategies course.

Not knowing what to expect for college, I was poorly prepared. I have not brought with me the special tools required for a successful transition to college life.

CRITICAL THINKING POINTS: *As you read*

1. What kind of student does the author seem to be? What specifically from the journal do you base your opinion on?
2. Each student brings his or her unique perspective to college. What is the author's perspective? What is yours?
3. Consider how the author "learned" her course work as she wrote in her journal. Have you ever used this technique of applying course work to your personal life?

Due to the fact that I am currently a history major I have the extreme pleasure of learning the same thing in three classes. In Anthropology, US History and World History all my professors are talking about pre-historical societies and hunting/gathering groups as a foundation for the classes. This is highly beneficial for a person who selectively attends class such as I. I can take notes for one class and still do well in the others. However lackadaisical this approach may seem I have still learned a great deal. In studying hunting and gathering societies I have found parallels to my own life.

In a hunting and gathering society the food-getting strategies involve the collection of "naturally" occurring plants and animals. In this type of community there are little economic practices. Except for the occasional bartering there is no currency exchange. Primitive societies like this one are also extremely superstitious, having natural gods that provide for people and are also feared by the clan.

Maybe the connection is not clear to you, so I will give examples.

In hunting/gathering societies the food getting strategies involve the collection of naturally occurring plants and animals.

Not knowing what to expect for college, I was poorly prepared. I have not brought with me the special tools required for a successful transition to college life. These "tools" would be things like tape, nail-polish remover, highlighter, and, of course, sleeping pills. Fortunately I live in a very fertile and lush place where these things are easily attainable. However, like primitive societies, I must make offerings to the God that provides these needed "tools," namely my roommate Karen. I try to use naturally occurring products when Karen is out of the room so not to anger her but sometimes a complimentary can of Coke helps to keep the peace. Another item that I find I can't live without is cereal. Luckily for me Karen thinks all food goes bad a week after it is bought (an idea I introduced into her puny skull) so she often throws out perfectly good food. At this point I do "creative hunting/gathering" by removing the good trash (cereal) and throw the bad trash down the trash shoot. This way I am not stealing the food only recycling it. I also get points for taking out the garbage.

In this type of community there are little economic practices. Except for the occasional bartering there is no currency exchange.

Besides prison, maybe college life is the most cash free environment alive today. However true this may be, there is still a free exchange of goods. Since money is used for tobacco, alcohol, and weed, other ways of obtaining goods must be developed. After all, necessity is the mother of invention. The use of CDs from a neighbor might involve the use of one of your good sweaters. Term papers can be bought for carpeting, and let's not underplay the value of sexual favors.

Primitive societies also are extremely superstitious, having natural gods that both provide for the clan and are feared by it.

I can't stress the importance of abusing your roommate enough. Hey, the way I see it, this college thing is an egalitarian society, and we all should share. Or at least that's what I tell myself as I am eating out of the trash. However wonderful this might seem there are prices to pay. Like tuition.

1996

CRITICAL THINKING POINTS: *After you've read*

1. In what other ways might first-year students become "hunters and gatherers"? How else might they be described?

2. In addition to the concrete tools the author mentions, what kinds of personal skills are needed to make the transition to college life? Does this student possess any of those?

3. Read or reread Andrew Hicks's "My First Week at Mizzou." How is Hale similar to Hicks? How is she different?

SOME POSSIBILITIES FOR WRITING

1. Build on Hale's list of the tools necessary for college life. Make it your own personal list, however far fetched.

2. Hale says, "Not knowing what to expect for college, I was poorly prepared." Write briefly about one way you have already realized you were poorly prepared for college. What steps should you take to rectify this situation?

3. Use specific course work from one of your classes and find parallels to your personal or social life, in the same way the author of "Hunters and Gatherers" does. Some possibilities might include concepts you've learned in your courses in psychology, sociology, economics, or any other social science field.

Theme for English B

Langston Hughes

Langston Hughes (1902–1967) is known for the use of jazz and black folk rhythms in his poetry. He was born in Joplin, Missouri, and educated at Lincoln University in Pennsylvania. He was a prominent figure during the Harlem Renaissance in the 1920s and was referred to as the Poet Laureate of Harlem.

It's not easy to know what is true for you or me

CRITICAL THINKING POINTS: *As you read*

1. What do you imagine were the teacher's goals in making such an assignment? How successfully did the student fulfill them?
2. The narrator's specific audience is his instructor. What other audience might Hughes have had in mind?
3. What kinds of students might enroll in "English B"?

The instructor said,
> Go home and write
> a page tonight.
> And let that page come out of you—
> Then, it will be true.

I wonder if it's that simple?
I am twenty-two, colored, born in Winston-Salem.
I went to school there, then Durham, then here
to this college on the hill above Harlem.
I am the only colored student in my class.
The steps from the hill lead down into Harlem,
through a park, then I cross St. Nicholas,
Eighth Avenue, Seventh, and I come to the Y,
the Harlem Branch Y, where I take the elevator
up to my room, sit down, and write this page:

It's not easy to know what is true for you or me
at twenty-two, my age. But I guess I'm what
I feel and see and hear, Harlem, I hear you:
hear you, hear me—we two—you, me, talk on this page.
(I hear New York, too.) Me, who?

Well, I like to eat, sleep, drink, and be in love.
I like to work, read, learn and understand life.
I like a pipe for a Christmas present,
or records—Bessie, bop, or Bach.
I guess being colored doesn't make me not like
the same things other folks like who are other races.
So will my page be colored that I write?
Being me, it will not be white.
But it will be
a part of you, instructor.
You are white—
yet a part of me, as I am a part of you.
That's American.
Sometimes perhaps you don't want to be a part of me.
Nor do I often want to be a part of you.
But we are, that's true!
As I learn from you,
I guess you learn from me—
although you're older—and white—
and somewhat more free.

This is my page for English B.

1924

CRITICAL THINKING POINTS: *After you've read*

1. Why isn't it easy, as Hughes says, to write "a page that comes out of you," especially one that is "true"?

2. Hughes says, "I like to eat, sleep, drink, and be in love." Why does he begin with general items? Why might Hughes include detailed directions to his home?

3. Hughes says, "So will my page be colored that I write? / Being me, it will not be white. / But it will be / a part of you, instructor." What do you think he means? How is his page a "part" of the instructor?

SOME POSSIBILITIES FOR WRITING

1. Hughes wrote his theme as a poem. Rewrite his poem as prose and add longer scenes built on the details in the poem.

2. Write one page that describes your identity. Keep in mind you have limited space, so be specific and selective about what you include. How, like Hughes, are you made up of what you "feel and see and hear"?

3. Write about a time when a teacher did, should have, or could have learned from you.

Lummox: Evolution of a Man

AN EXCERPT   **Mike Magnuson**

Mike Magnuson (b. 1963) earned a one-year suspension for poor academic performance after his first year of college. This excerpt details the Labor Day weekend before he returned to classes. *Lummox* is Magnuson's third book. He teaches creative writing at Southern Illinois University at Carbondale.

He's going to fill his mind with ideas and beauty, and even if nobody thinks Mike's capable of knowing this shit, knowing about beauty and truth and art and all that, by God Mike can know about it anyway.

CRITICAL THINKING POINTS: *As you read*

1. What is a "lummox"? Do you think Mike Magnuson is a lummox? Why or why not?
2. What are grounds for suspension at your school?
3. How does Magnuson teach himself to be a better reader while he's in jail?

A thin jailer is standing in the cell's doorway, requesting that Mike get on his feet. Mike complies, gets right up, and isn't wobbly one bit. He feels pretty good, all things considered. Says happily to the jailer, "I'm glad *that's* over."

"What's that?" the jailer says.

"Being in jail."

The jailer grins, but not with amusement. Says, "You're not going home, buck. You're here till Tuesday morning."

Mike figures the jailer's giving him shit. "Give me a break, man." He says. "That's three days from now."

The jailer says, "You gotta wait till your arraignment."

Mike doesn't move. "Till Tuesday?"

"Monday, that's Labor Day. No court."

Block C in Eau Claire County Jail has twelve lock-down cells—one prisoner to a cell—that open to a barred-in holding area with three picnic-type tables in it. One of the tables is covered with books and magazines and board games, and the other two are set up for smoking and watching the TV, which is situated high up, just outside the bars.

75

Around 8:30 A.M. Mike arrives on Block C. The jailer assigns him to Cell 6. Tells Mike here's the shitter and here's the shower and lunch is at eleven, supper at five and lockdown at nine. And that's that. Mike's cooling out in the hoosegow. He's looking at three days of hard county time.

The place doesn't seem too intimidating, though. A few inmates are playing Risk at one of the tables, smoking cigarettes, and a guy there with long black hair and aviator glasses waits till the jailer leaves, gets up from his spot on the bench, comes right over to Mike and introduces himself.

Says he's Tom. He hopes Mike will enjoy his stay. "I'm the welcoming committee around here," he says.

He invites Mike to take a seat, which Mike does, then he offers Mike a cigarette, which he takes, then he gives Mike the straight skinny on Block C.

Tom's nine months into a yearlong stretch here for stealing a few car stereos and doing some other stupid shit, and he would get out during the week to work on Huber Law, but he can't seem to find himself a job, and, well, it's pretty goddam quiet here during the weekdays. Pretty relaxing. But on the weekends the block fills up with drunks, and that's cool with Tom because the food's a lot better on the weekends than it is during the week. Check out the feast for Sunday lunch, hey. We're talking turkey dinner with all the trimmings. And there's of course the Risk game here, which on occasion is very competitive, very quality. And there's this fine stack of magazines and books.

"I myself," Tom says, "have read every book in the stack."

"Cool," Mike says.

The other inmates on Block C aren't as talkative as Tom, but they're completely not dangerous-seeming in a way. A couple of them say they're in for bouncing checks. One guy's in for his second DUI. One guy's in for his third. Another guy, a really skinny fellow with sunken eyes, he won't say what he's in for, but Mike doesn't figure it's for anything but a fuckup.

After a while, Mike tells everybody his story. The getting-drunk-at-the-Brat-Kabin part, the stealing-the-hand, the giving-fake-names-to-the-cops, and everybody busts complete gut about it. They all say they wish they were in for what Mike's in for.

And there you have it: Mike's buddies with everybody.

Lunch is sliced roast beef with mashed potatoes, gravy, peas, and a tin cup full of milk. Awesome chow, that's for sure. He'd never be eating this good at home. And after lunch, everybody yawns and wanders off to their cells, and in no time the only sound in Block C is peaceful petty-criminal snoring, but Mike's still awake. He's in jail, man. This ain't something a person should sleep through! He's got to be remembering this so he can tell his grandchildren about it. Or something.

Okay, so there's a stack of books. Maybe he'll find something to read till his fellow inmates wake up. He's never actually enjoyed reading, and in fact he hasn't read a book cover to cover since he was ten. Some Hardy Boys book, he thinks it was. Or maybe a book about airplanes. But here in Block C: Hell, it's so quiet, basically a boredom situation while everybody's napping, he figures reading is the perfectly natural thing to do.

So there's piles of *Sports Afield* and *Outdoor Life*, all raggedy and with pages torn or missing. And there's some books with sociological type titles: *Rehabilitation of the Thief. The Social Animal. A Case Against Recidivism.* And so forth.

Finally, he finds a thin black paperback, a movie tie-in book for the film *Rollerball.* Mike didn't see *Rollerball* when it came out, must have been ten years ago, but he remembers that it was about a sort of futuristic roller derby to the death or whatever. The more he thinks about it, he remembers *Rollerball* because there were ads on TV for it and somebody was playing the beginning of Bach's Toccata and Fugue in D Minor on the organ. Toccata and Fugue in D Minor. One of Mike's all-time favorites. If *Rollerball* is about *that*, it's going to be kickass.

He takes the book to his cell, stretches out, opens it up. He's expecting music, sure, or at least a novel about roller derby, but this book isn't either of those things, not really. *Rollerball* is a book of short stories by some guy named William Harrison, a guy who's seen fit to write a preface to his book, a few pages in which he talks about all sorts of things Mike doesn't remotely understand.

William Harrison writes this:

> Nowadays a well-documented Cultural Decline has befallen us and the students in the universities are too depraved to listen to talk of standards and so, I insist, am I.

He also writes this:

> The author of the story knows this and derives considerable pleasure from this fact; he is a miniaturist—with all the minor and subversive enjoyments of that role—and he sets a small hieroglyph against the armor of the body politic.

Mike reads this whatever-it-is five or six times, grows bewildered, and promptly falls asleep.

When he wakes, the book's still balanced on his chest. Outside his cell a few inmates are gathered around one of the picnic tables, playing Risk with Tom, who seems to be winning. Tom's saying, "Strategy, I'm telling you. The game is about strategy." The inmates are playing Risk for cigarettes, betting one smoke for one country occupied, two smokes for a continent.

Mike reopens *Rollerball*, rereads that sentence about body politic. Like, what in the hell is *that*? And he decides to move forward in the book and maybe find something he can understand there. He sees a story listed on the contents page called "Rollerball Murder." The movie story. He finds it, begins to read. The story's fifteen pages long, mostly explaining the rules of roller derby to the death, and also talking about some other junk like corporations replacing governments and people being all miserable and ignorant and bloodthirsty as a result.

As far as Mike can tell, ain't no Toccata and Fugue in D Minor *anywhere* in this story. He reads the entire story three times, slowly and carefully, and the only thing he reads about music is a one-line reference to corporate hymns and brass bands on the last page. But the thing is, by the time he's read the story three times, he doesn't care if there's a Toccata in there. There's people fucking each other and getting fucked over and fucking other people over. There's action: motorcycles, dudes getting killed. And somewhere near the end of the story the main character, a fellow name of Jonathan E., realizes that playing roller derby to the death is a pretty horseshit thing to do. And Mike finds himself saying, aloud, "No kidding, it's horseshit."

Suppertime comes. Another nice meal: fried chicken and green beans and potato salad and apple cobbler. Exceptional.

And during the evening Mike joins his fellow offenders in a television film festival. The movie is your made-for-TV type about a grizzly bear loose somewhere in the Northwest, terrorizing folks renting cabins on their summer vacations. Great flick, everybody's thinking. They're cheering for the bear, hoping he rips every one of them vacationers to shreds. And the bear rips up a few, too. And everybody applauds and whistles. But near the end of the movie, when an enterprising young forest ranger manages finally to kill the bear and everything in the movie is happily-ever-after, the skinny inmate with the sunken eyes falls to pieces, breaks down and weeps. The skinny guy can't endure a happy ending on Block C.

In the morning, after pancakes and sausage, Mike resolves to spend his whole day reading. He's slept well. Sure, he stinks bad because he worked landscaping all yesterday and then got drunk and still hasn't changed his clothes or showered or brushed his teeth. But he's feeling fresh in the physical and spiritual way. This incarceration thing, he's thinking, and the solitude thing in Cell 6, it's exactly the kind of mental preparation he needs before commencing the fall term. He can pull his shit together in here.

Now, you've probably heard that people's lives can sometimes change in one moment, that somebody is one person for a long time, then they experience something incredible, and they are thereafter altered. Folks who go for Christ, they'll for sure tell you that. For He comes to touch you once. And you must be ready to accept Him. And for sure, hey: Damn near every rock 'n' roll musician you've ever heard about says something like: "After I saw the Beatles on *Ed Sullivan,* I knew I wanted to play." Or "When I heard Hendrix in London." All people do this shit; it's easier for them to say *Right here, at this very instant, that's when I knew,* than to say, *Well, I kinda poked along in life and eventually I knew what I wanted to do with myself.*

But on this Sunday morning in the Eau Claire County Jail, on Cell Block C, in cell number 6, Mike's moment comes to him, the instant where everything in his life has been pointing in this direction and everything in his life will be different afterwards.

He reads a story in *Rollerball* called "A Cook's Tale."

It's about a middle-aged man with a job. He's the head cook at the University of Minnesota Hospital. He's large and gruff and is known as the Swede. And unbeknownst to any of his coworkers in the hospital kitchen, he's read the entire Modern Library, four hundred books, in alphabetical order, over a period of eight years. The Swede's name is John Olaf, and the story is about him finally letting his secret slip.

A woman named Emma works in the hospital kitchen, and on the day the story begins, she's weepy as fuck-all because her husband who's a graduate student, has just failed a major examination. She can't work worth a hoot as a result, is defensive about her husband, saying that he's not dumb and that he's been studying very hard to pass that test, and it's the Swede's job, it's what he gets paid for, to convince her to pull herself together. He's got a kitchen to run here. And he treats Emma hard, jokes about her husband, but when he sees her weeping there before her industrial dishwasher, his heart gets meat-tenderized for her. He feels sorry for her. So he tries comforting her, and the only words that come to him are a few words from Proust. "Pain she was capable of causing me; joy, never; pain alone kept the tedious attachment alive."

This perks her up all right. She wants to know where the quote comes from, and the Swede, he tells Emma he's just heard it somewhere; he can't remember where.

They have an affair, of course, because in stories, Mike supposes, that's one of the things people do. That Swede's married to a woman who can't understand why he's spent all that money and all that time reading four hundred books of the Modern Library. Emma is married to a man who's more interested in his studies than in her. Therefore, it's natural that they should come together. But the Swede never lets on to Emma that he's read all those books. He's large, coarse, and oafish, hardly the educated-looking type, and he figures that even if he tells Emma he's read all those books, she won't believe him. To Emma, the Swede is a fresh breath of uneducated air. To the Swede, Emma is everything his wife is not. They picnic. They hang around together. They talk and all that stuff.

Near the end of the story, Emma invites the Swede to a party at her apartment, a party where her husband's friends and professors are chatting about intellectual things. The Swede gets horrifically drunk at the party. At one point, an intellectual accuses the Swede of being a Classicist, and the Swede punches him. The Swede—and Mike knows this is the point of the story—is just as smart as these intellectuals, but he doesn't know how to behave like them. He's a large, coarse, oafish dude, and nothing's going to change that.

At the very end of the story, the Swede makes love to Emma, quietly, in Emma's bedroom, while the party rages outside the door, and then he goes home to his wife, carrying a loaf of fresh-baked bread under his arm.

Lovely.

Here's the math of it, folks. Mike reads this story and can't help thinking that the Swede equals Mike Magnuson. "A Cook's Tale" is exactly the story of Mike's life—well, except for the lovemaking part and the book-reading part. But there's the Swede: large, ungainly, loud. And there's Mike: same. Which is, in Mike's view, cause for joy. In the story, see, the Swede triumphs in a small way over the world. He can't socialize properly with intellectuals? So what? The Swede *is* an intellectual, and that's all that matters about being an intellectual: being one. So Mike resolves right then and there that he's going to do something grand like the Swede's done. He's going to read four hundred books or something like that. He's going to fill his mind with ideas and beauty, and even if nobody thinks Mike's capable of knowing this shit, knowing about beauty and truth and art and all that, by God Mike can know about it anyway.

And Mike goes ahead and does school the right way. He gets his shit together. He goes to court on Tuesday morning, gets some laughs in the courtroom when the judge reads selected excerpts from the arresting officer's report aloud: "The suspect identified himself as Bart Starr. This court hasn't heard *that* one before." But the judge releases Mike to his own recognizance. And Mike walks home. On the way, he stops by the lilac where he pitched his wallet, and sure enough, the wallet's there. Nobody's touched it. This is a nice town. This is a place where nobody will steal your wallet.

And Mike cleans himself up and gets to his first class on time, and to his next class and to his next class and so on. And he does his homework. He gets some good grades on tests and papers and presentations. He speaks up in class, tries to say intelligent things and sometimes even does, and when he's not in class he's sitting at a study carrel in the library or hanging out in the Student Union, smoking cigarettes or drinking coffee with folks from his classes and discussing with them the meaning of the universe and so forth, and by God he starts making the best friends a person could have at college: the smart ones, the crazy ones, the ones with goofy haircuts and who wear goofy clothes, the ones with alternative worldviews and alternative ways of living, the ones who know they're brilliant and have every intention of overthrowing the world when they get the chance.

You add it all up: Looks like Mike's turning out okay after all.

2002

CRITICAL THINKING POINTS: *After you've read*

1. Magnuson recognizes the difference between being as smart as "intellectuals" and acting like them. Why is this important in his story?

2. What contributes to Magnuson's plan for an evolution? Is it realistic that he experiences the kind of transformation he does over just a few days? Why or why not?

3. Most memoirs or nonfiction books about the experiences of an author are written in the first person. Why do you think Magnuson wrote about his experiences in the third person? What might this accomplish? How might this piece be different if told from the first-person point of view?

SOME POSSIBILITIES FOR WRITING

1. Magnuson writes, "you've probably heard that peoples' lives can sometimes change in one moment, that somebody is one person for a long time, then they experience something incredible, and they are thereafter altered." Have you ever experienced or witnessed this?

2. How does being in jail during the weekend before school begins affect Magnuson? Do you think Magnuson considers the repercussions of being in jail? Why or why not?

3. What characteristics of the Swede, John Olaf, in "A Cook's Tale" does Magnuson identify with? Are there any characters in books, films, or TV programs with whom you've felt some connection? How? Why?

The English Lesson

Nicholasa Mohr

Nicholasa Mohr is a writer from New York City. Her fiction for both young readers and adults often features Puerto Rican characters in urban settings, such as the El Barrio (East Harlem) section of New York where Mohr was born. She won a 1981 American Book Award from the Before Columbus Foundation for *Felita* (1979); her other books include *El Bronx Remembered: A Novella and Stories* (2nd edition, 1986), *Rituals of Survival: A Woman's Portfolio* (1985), and *Nilda: A Novel* (2nd edition, 1986).

Adult Education offered Basic English, Tuesday evenings from 6:30 to 8:00, at a local public school. Night customers did not usually come into Rudi's Luncheonette until after eight. William and Lali promised that they would leave everything prepared and make up for any inconvenience by working harder and longer than usual, if necessary.

CRITICAL THINKING POINTS: *As you read*

1. Have you ever struggled to learn a second language? What was most difficult about it for you?
2. In what ways is Mrs. Hamma condescending toward her students? How might she feel if she realized this?
3. Why are some English-speaking people often intimidated by groups of people speaking another language? Is that the case for Mrs. Hamma?

R emember our assignment for today everybody! I'm so confident that you will all do exceptionally well!" Mrs. Susan Hamma smiled enthusiastically at her students. "Everyone is to get up and make a brief statement as to why he or she is taking this course in Basic English. You must state your name, where you originally came from, how long you have been here, and . . . uh . . . a little something about yourself, if you wish. Keep it brief, not too long; remember, there are twenty-eight of us. We have a full class, and everyone must have a chance." Mrs. Hamma waved a forefinger at her students. "This is, after all, a democracy, and we have a democratic class; fairness for all!"

Lali grinned and looked at William, who sat directly next to her. He winked and rolled his eyes toward Mrs. Hamma. This was the third class they had attended together. It had not been easy to persuade Rudi that Lali should learn better English.

"Why is it necessary, eh?" Rudi had protested. "She works here in the store with me. She don't have to talk to nobody. Besides, everybody that comes in speaks Spanish—practically everybody, anyway." But once William had put the idea to Lali and explained how much easier things would be for her, she kept insisting until Rudi finally agreed. "Go on, you're both driving me nuts. But it can't interfere with business or work—I'm warning you!"

Adult Education offered Basic English, Tuesday evenings from 6:30 to 8:00, at a local public school. Night customers did not usually come into Rudi's Luncheonette until after eight. William and Lali promised that they would leave everything prepared and make up for any inconvenience by working harder and longer than usual, if necessary.

The class admitted twenty-eight students, and because there were only twenty-seven registered, Lali was allowed to take the course even after missing the first two classes. William had assured Mrs. Hamma that he would help Lali catch up; she was glad to have another student to make up the full registration.

Most of the students were Spanish-speaking. The majority were American citizens—Puerto Ricans who had migrated to New York and spoke very little English. The rest were immigrants admitted to the United States as legal aliens. There were several Chinese, two Dominicans, one Sicilian, and one Pole.

Every Tuesday Mrs. Hamma traveled to the Lower East Side from Bayside, Queens, where she lived and was employed as a history teacher in the local junior high school. She was convinced that this small group of people desperately needed her services. Mrs. Hamma reiterated her feelings frequently to just about anyone who would listen. "Why, if these people can make it to class after working all day at those miserable, dreary, uninteresting, and often revolting jobs, well, the least I can do is be there to serve them, making every lesson count toward improving their conditions! My grandparents came here from Germany as poor immigrants, working their way up. I'm not one to forget a thing like that!"

By the time class started most of the students were quite tired. And after the lesson was over, many had to go on to part-time jobs, some even without time for supper. As a result there was always sluggishness and yawning among the students. This never discouraged Mrs. Hamma, whose drive and enthusiasm not only amused the class but often kept everyone awake.

"Now this is the moment we have all been waiting for." Mrs. Hamma stood up, nodded, and blinked knowingly at her students. "You may read from prepared notes, as I said before, but please try not to read every word. We want to hear you speak; conversation is what we're after. When someone asks you about yourself, you cannot take a piece of paper and start reading the answers, now can you? That would be foolish. So . . . "

Standing in front of her desk, she put her hands on her hips and spread her feet, giving the impression that she was going to demonstrate calisthenics.

"Shall we begin?"

Mrs. Hamma was a very tall, angular woman with large extremities. She was the tallest person in the room. Her eyes roamed from student to student until they met William's.

"Mr. Colón, will you please begin?" Nervously William looked around him, hesitating. "Come on now, we must get the ball rolling. All right now . . . did you hear what I said? Listen, 'getting the ball rolling' means getting started. Getting things going, such as—" Mrs. Hamma swiftly lifted her right hand over her head, making a fist, then swung her arm around like a pitcher and, with an underhand curve, forcefully threw an imaginary ball out at her students. Trying to maintain her balance, Mrs. Hamma hopped from one leg to the other. Startled, the students looked at one another. In spite of their efforts to restrain themselves, several people in back began to giggle. Lali and William looked away, avoiding each other's eyes and trying not to laugh out loud. With assured countenance, Mrs. Hamma continued.

"An idiom!" she exclaimed, pleased. "You have just seen me demonstrate the meaning of an idiom. Now I want everyone to jot down this information in his notebook." Going to the blackboard, Mrs. Hamma explained, "It's something which literally says one thing, but actually means another. Idiom . . . idiomatic." Quickly and obediently, everyone began to copy what she wrote. "Has everyone got it? OK, let's GET THE BALL ROLLING, Mr. Colón!"

Uneasily William stood up; he was almost the same height standing as sitting. When speaking to others, especially in a new situation, he always preferred to sit alongside those listening; it gave him a sense of equality with other people. He looked around and cleared his throat; at least everyone else was sitting. Taking a deep breath, William felt better.

"My name is William Horacio Colón," he read from a prepared statement. "I have been here in New York City for five months. I coming from Puerto Rico. My town is located in the mountains in the central part of the island. The name of my town is Aibonito, which means in Spanish 'oh how pretty.' It is name like this because when the Spaniards first seen that place they was very impressed with the beauty of the section and—"

"Make it brief, Mr. Colón," Mrs. Hamma interrupted, "there are others, you know."

William looked at her, unable to continue.

"Go on, go on, Mr. Colón, please!"

"I am working here now, living with my mother and family in Lower East Side of New York City," William spoke rapidly. "I study Basic English por que . . . because my ambition is to learn to speak and read English very good. To get a better job. Y—y también, to help my mother y familia." He shrugged. "Y do better, that's all."

"That's all? Why that's wonderful! Wonderful! Didn't he do well, class?" Mrs. Hamma bowed slightly toward William and applauded him. The students watched her and slowly each one began to imitate her. Pleased, Mrs. Hamma looked around her; all together they gave William a healthy round of applause.

Next, Mrs. Hamma turned to a Chinese man seated at the other side of the room.

"Mr. Fong, you may go next."

Mr. Fong stood up; he was a man in his late thirties, of medium height and slight build. Cautiously he looked at Mrs. Hamma, and waited.

"Go on, Mr. Fong. Get the ball rolling, remember?"

"All right. Get a ball rolling . . . is idiot!" Mr. Fong smiled.

"No, Mr. Fong, idio*mmmmmm!*" Mrs. Hamma hummed her m's, shaking her head. "Not an—It's idiomatic!"

"What I said!" Mr. Fong responded with self-assurance, looking directly at Mrs. Hamma. "Get a ball rolling, idiomit."

"Never mind." She cleared her throat. "Just go on."

"I said OK?" Mr. Fong waited for an answer.

"Go on, please."

Mr. Fong sighed, "My name is Joseph Fong. I been here in this country United States New York City for most one year." He too read from a prepared statement. "I come from Hong Kong but original born in city of Canton, China. I working delivery food business and live with my brother and his family in Chinatown. I taking the course in Basic English to speak good and improve my position better in this country. Also to be eligible to become American citizen."

Mrs. Hamma selected each student who was to speak from a different part of the room, rather than in the more conventional orderly fashion of row by row, or front to back, or even alphabetical order. This way, she reasoned, no one will know who's next; it will be more spontaneous. Mrs. Hamma enjoyed catching the uncertain looks on the faces of her students. A feeling of control over the situation gave her a pleasing thrill, and she made the most of these moments by looking at several people more than once before making her final choice.

There were more men than women, and Mrs. Hamma called two or three men for each woman. It was her way of maintaining balance. To her distress, most read from prepared notes, despite her efforts to discourage this. She would interrupt them when she felt they went on too long, then praise them when they finished. Each statement was followed by applause from everyone.

All had similar statements. They had migrated here in search of a better future, were living with relatives, and worked as unskilled laborers. With the exception of Lali, who was childless, every woman gave the ages and sex of her children; most men referred only to their "family." And, among the legal aliens, there was only one who did not want to become an American citizen, Diego Torres, a young man from the Dominican Republic, and he gave his reasons. " . . . and to improve my economic situation." Diego Torres hesitated, looking around the room. "But is one thing I no want, and is to become American citizen"—he pointed to an older man with a dark complexion, seated a few seats away—"like my fellow countryman over there!" The man shook his head disapprovingly at Diego Torres, trying to hide his annoyance. "I no give up my country, Santo Domingo, for nothing," he went on, "nothing in the whole world. OK, man? I come here, pero I cannot help. I got no work at home. There, is political. The United States control most the industry which is sugar and tourismo. Y—you have to know somebody. I tell you, is political to get a job, man! You don't know nobody and you no work, eh? So I come here from necessity, pero this no my country—"

"Mr. Torres," Mrs. Hamma interrupted, "we must be brief, please, there are—"

"I no finish lady!" he snapped. "You wait a minute when I finish!" There was a complete silence as Diego Torres glared at Susan Hamma. No one had ever spoken to her like that, and her confusion was greater than her embarrassment. Without speaking, she lowered her eyes and nodded.

"OK, I prefer live feeling happy in my country, man. Even I don't got too much. I live simple but in my own country I be contento. Pero this is no possible in the situation of Santo Domingo now. Someday we gonna run our own country and be jobs for everybody. My reasons to be here is to make money, man, and go back home buy my house and property. I no be American citizen, no way. I'm Dominican and proud! That's it. That's all I got to say." Abruptly, Diego Torres sat down.

"All right." Mrs. Hamma had composed herself. "Very good; you can come here and state your views. That is what America is all about! We may not agree with you, but we defend your right to an opinion. And as long as you are in this classroom, Mr. Torres, you are in America. Now, everyone, let us give Mr. Torres the same courtesy as everyone else in this class." Mrs. Hamma applauded with a polite light clap, then turned to find the next speaker.

"Bullshit," whispered Diego Torres.

Practically everyone had spoken. Lali and the two European immigrants were the only ones left. Mrs. Hamma called upon Lali.

"My name is Rogelia Dolores Padillo. I come from Canovanas in Puerto Rico. Is a small village in the mountains near El Yunque Rain Forest. My family is still living there. I marry and live here with my husband working in his business of restaurant. Call Rudi's Luncheonette. I been here New York City Lower East Side since I marry, which is now about one year. I study Basic English to improve my vocabulario and learn more about here. This way I help my husband and his business and I do more also for myself, including to be able to read better in English. Thank you."

Aldo Fabrizi, the Sicilian, spoke next. He was a very short man, barely five feet tall. Usually he was self-conscious about his height, but William's presence relieved him of these feelings. Looking at William, he thought being short was no big thing; he was, after all, normal. He told the class that he was originally from Palermo, the capital of Sicily, and had gone to Milano, in the north of Italy, looking for work. After three years in Milano, he immigrated here six months ago and now lived with his sister. He had a good steady job, he said, working in a copper wire factory with his brother-in-law in Brooklyn. Aldo Fabrizi wanted to become an American citizen and spoke passionately about it, without reading from his notes.

"I proud to be American citizen. I no come here find work live good and no have responsibility or no be grateful." He turned and looked threateningly at Diego Torres. "Hey? I tell you all one thing, I got my nephew right now fighting in Vietnam for this country!" Diego Torres stretched his hands over his head, yawning, folded his hands, and lowered his eyelids. "I wish I could be citizen to fight for this country. My whole family is citizens—we all Americans and we love America!" His voice was quite loud. "That's how I feel."

"Very good," Mrs. Hamma called, distracting Aldo Fabrizi. "That was well stated. I'm sure you will not only become a citizen, but you will also be a credit to this country."

The last person to be called on was the Pole. He was always neatly dressed in a business suit, with a shirt and tie, and carried a briefcase. His manner was reserved but friendly.

"Good evening fellow students and Madame Teacher." He nodded politely to Mrs. Hamma. "My name is Stephan Paczkowski. I am originally from Poland about four months ago. My background is I was born in capital city of Poland, Warsaw. Being educated in capital and also graduating from the University with degree of professor of music with specialty in the history of music."

Stephan Paczkowski read his notes carefully, articulating every word. "I was given appointment of professor of history of music at University of Krakow. I work there for ten years until about year and half ago. At this time the political situation in Poland was so that all Jewish people were requested by government to leave Poland. My wife who also is being a professor of economics at University of Krakow is of Jewish parents. My wife was told she could not remain in position at University or remain over there. We made arrangements for my wife and daughter who is seven years of age and myself to come here with my wife's cousin who is to be helping us.

"Since four months I am working in large hospital as position of porter in maintenance department. The thing of it is, I wish to take Basic English to improve my knowledge of English language, and be able to return to my position of professor of history of music. Finally, I wish to become a citizen of United States. That is my reasons. I thank you all."

After Stephan Paczkowski sat down, there was a long awkward silence and everyone turned to look at Mrs. Hamma. Even after the confrontation with Diego Torres, she had applauded without hesitation. Now she seemed unable to move. "Well," she said, almost breathless, "that's admirable! I'm sure, sir, that you will do very well . . . a person of your . . . like yourself, I mean . . . a professor, after all, it's really just admirable." Everyone was listening intently to what she said. "That was well done, class. Now, we have to get to next week's assignment." Mrs. Hamma realized that no one had applauded Stephan Paczkowski. With a slightly pained expression, she began to applaud. "Mustn't forget Mr. Paczkowski; everyone here must be treated equally. This is America!" The class joined her in a round of applause.

As Mrs. Hamma began to write the next week's assignment on the board, some students looked anxiously at their watches and others asked about the time. Then they all quickly copied the information into their notebooks. It was almost eight o'clock. Those who had to get to second jobs did not want to be late; some even hoped to have time for a bite to eat first. Others were just tired and wanted to get home.

Lali looked at William, sighing impatiently. They both hoped Mrs. Hamma would finish quickly. There would be hell to pay with Rudi if the night customers were already at the luncheonette.

"There, that's next week's work, which is very important, by the way. We will be looking at the history of New York City and the different ethnic groups that lived here as far back as the Dutch. I can't tell you how proud I am of the way you all spoke. All of you—I have no favorites, you know."

Mrs. Hamma was interrupted by the long, loud buzzing sound, bringing the lesson to an end. Quickly everyone began to exit.

"Good night, see you all next Tuesday!" Mrs. Hamma called out. "By the way, if any of you here wants extra help, I have a few minutes this evening." Several people bolted past her, excusing themselves. In less than thirty seconds, Mrs. Hamma was standing in an empty classroom.

William and Lali hurried along, struggling against the cold, sharp March wind that whipped across Houston Street, stinging their faces and making their eyes tear.

In a few minutes they would be at Rudi's. So far, they had not been late once.

"You read very well—better than anybody in class. I told you there was nothing to worry about. You caught up in no time."

"Go on. I was so nervous, honestly! But, I'm glad she left me for one of the last. If I had to go first, like you, I don't think I could open my mouth. You were so calm. You started the thing off very well."

"You go on now, I was nervous myself!" He laughed, pleased.

"Mira, Chiquitín," Lali giggled, "I didn't know your name was Horacio. William Horacio. William Horacio. Ave María, so imposing!"

"That's right, because you see, my mother was expecting valiant warrior! Instead, well"—he threw up his hands—"no one warned me either. And what a name for a Chiquitín like me."

Lali smiled, saying nothing. At first she had been very aware of William's dwarfishness. Now it no longer mattered. It was only when she saw others reacting to him for the first time that she was once more momentarily struck with William's physical difference.

"We should really try to speak in English, Lali. It would be good practice for us."

"Dios mío . . . I feel so foolish, and my accent is terrible!"

"But look, we all have to start some place. Besides, what about the Americanos? When they speak Spanish, they sound pretty awful, but we accept it. You know I'm right. And that's how people get ahead, by not being afraid to try."

They walked in silence for a few moments. Since William had begun to work at Rudi's, Lali's life had become less lonely. Lali was shy by nature; making friends was difficult for her. She had grown up in the sheltered environment of a large family living in a tiny mountain village. She was considered quite plain. Until Rudi had asked her parents for permission to court her, she had only gone out with two local boys. She had accepted his marriage proposal expecting great changes in her life. But the age difference between her and Rudi, being in a strange country without friends or relatives, and the long hours of work at the luncheonette confined Lali to a way of life she could not have imagined. Every evening she found herself waiting for William to come in to work, looking forward to his presence.

Lali glanced over at him as they started across the wide busy street. His grip on her elbow was firm but gentle as he led her to the sidewalk.

"There you are, Miss Lali, please watch your step!" he spoke in English.

His thick golden-blond hair was slightly mussed and fell softly, partially covering his forehead. His wide smile, white teeth, and large shoulders made him appear quite handsome. Lali found herself staring at William. At that moment she wished he could be just like everybody else.

"Lali?" William asked, confused by her silent stare. "Is something wrong?"

"No." Quickly Lali turned her face. She felt herself blushing. "I . . . I was just thinking how to answer in English, that's all."

"But that's it . . . don't think! What I mean is, don't go worrying about what to say. Just talk natural. Get used to simple phrases and the rest will come, you'll see."

"All right," Lali said, glad the strange feeling of involvement had passed, and William had taken no notice of it. "It's an interesting class, don't you think so? I mean—like that man, the professor. Bendito! Imagine, they had to leave because they were Jewish. What a terrible thing!"

"I don't believe he's Jewish; it's his wife who is Jewish. She was a professor too. But I guess they don't wanna be separated . . . and they have a child."

"Tsk, tsk, los pobres! But, can you imagine, then? A professor from a university doing the job of a porter? My goodness!" Lali sighed. "I never heard of such a thing!"

"But you gotta remember, it's like Mrs. Hamma said, this is America, right? So . . . everybody got a chance to clean toilets! Equality, didn't she say that?"

They both laughed loudly, stepping up their pace until they reached Rudi's Luncheonette.

The small luncheonette was almost empty. One customer sat at the counter.

"Just in time," Rudi called out. "Let's get going. People gonna be coming in hungry any minute. I was beginning to worry about you two!"

William ran to the back to change into his workshirt.

Lali slipped into her uniform and soon was busy at the grill.

"Well, did you learn anything tonight?" Rudi asked her.

"Yes."

"What?"

"I don't know," she answered, without interrupting her work. "We just talked a little bit in English."

"A little bit in English—about what?"

Lali busied herself, ignoring him. Rudi waited, then tried once more.

"You remember what you talked about?" He watched her as she moved, working quickly, not looking in his direction.

"No." Her response was barely audible.

Lately Rudi had begun to reflect on his decision to marry such a young woman. Especially a country girl like Lali, who was shy and timid. He had never had children with his first wife and wondered if he lacked the patience needed for the young. They had little in common and certainly seldom spoke about anything but the business. Certainly he could not fault her for being lazy; she was always working without being asked. People would accuse him in jest of overworking his young wife. He assured them there was no need, because she had the endurance of a country mule. After almost one year of marriage, he felt he hardly knew Lali or what he might do to please her.

William began to stack clean glasses behind the counter.

"Chiquitín! How about you and Lali having something to eat? We gotta few minutes yet. There's some fresh rice pudding."

"Later . . . I'll have mine a little later, thanks."

"Ask her if she wants some," Rudi whispered, gesturing toward Lali.

William moved close to Lali and spoke softly to her.

"She said no." William continued his work.

"Listen, Chiquitín, I already spoke to Raquel Martinez who lives next door. You know, she's got all them kids? In case you people are late, she can cover for you and Lali. She said it was OK."

"Thanks, Rudi, I appreciate it. But we'll be back on time."

"She's good, you know. She helps me out during the day whenever I need extra help. Off the books, I give her a few bucks. But, mira, I cannot pay you and Raquel both. So if she comes in, you don't get paid. You know that then, OK?"

"Of course. Thanks, Rudi."

"Sure, well, it's a good thing after all. You and Lali improving yourselves. Not that she really needs it, you know. I provide for her. As I said, she's my wife, so she don't gotta worry. If she wants something, I'll buy it for her. I made it clear she didn't have to bother with none of that, but"—Rudi shrugged—"if that's what she wants, I'm not one to interfere."

The door opened. Several men walked in.

"Here they come, kids!"

Orders were taken and quickly filled. Customers came and went steadily until about eleven o'clock, when Rudi announced that it was closing time.

The weeks passed, then the months, and this evening, William and Lali sat with the other students listening to Mrs. Hamma as she taught the last lesson of the Basic English course.

"It's been fifteen long hard weeks for all of you. And I want you to know how proud I am of each and every one here."

William glanced at Lali; he knew she was upset. He felt it too, wishing that this was not the end of the course. It was the only time he and Lali had free to themselves together. Tuesday had become their last evening.

Lali had been especially irritable that week, dreading this last session. For her, Tuesday meant leaving the world of Rudi, the luncheonette, that street, everything that she felt imprisoned her. She was accomplishing something all by herself, and without the help of the man she was dependent upon.

Mrs. Hamma finally felt that she had spent enough time assuring her students of her sincere appreciation.

"I hope some of you will stay and have a cup of coffee or tea, and cookies. There's plenty over there." She pointed to a side table where a large electric coffeepot filled with hot water was steaming. The table was set for instant coffee and tea, complete with several boxes of assorted cookies. "I do this every semester for my classes. I think it's nice to have a little informal chat with one another; perhaps discuss our plans for the future and so on. But it must be in English! Especially those of you who are Spanish-speaking. Just because you outnumber the rest of us, don't you think you can get away with it!" Mrs. Hamma lifted her forefinger threateningly but smiled. "Now, it's still early, so there's plenty of time left. Please turn in your books."

Some of the people said good-bye quickly and left, but the majority waited, helping themselves to coffee or tea and cookies. Small clusters formed as people began to chat with one another.

Diego Torres and Aldo Fabrizi were engaged in a friendly but heated debate on the merits of citizenship.

"Hey, you come here a minute, please," Aldo Fabrizi called out to William, who was standing with a few people by the table, helping himself to coffee. William walked over to the two men.

"What's the matter?"

"What do you think of your paisano. He don't wanna be citizen. I say—my opinion—he don't appreciate what he got in this country. This a great country! You the same like him, what do you think?"

"Mira, please tell him we are no the same," Diego Torres said with exasperation. "You a citizen, pero not me. Este tipo no comprende, man!"

"Listen, you comprendo . . . yo capito! I know what you say. He be born in Puerto Rico. But you see, we got the same thing. I be born in Sicily—that is another part of the country, separate. But I still Italiano, capito?"

"Dios mío!" Diego Torres smacked his forehead with an open palm. "Mira"— he turned to William—"explain to him, por favor."

William swallowed a mouthful of cookies. "He's right. Puerto Rico is part of the United States. And Sicily is part of Italy. But not the Dominican Republic where he been born. There it is not United States. I was born a citizen, do you see?"

"Sure!" Aldo Fabrizi nodded. "Capito. Hey, but you still no can vote, right?"

"Sure I can vote; I got all the rights. I am a citizen, just like anybody else," William assured him.

"You some lucky guy then. You got it made! You don't gotta worry like the rest of—"

"Bullshit," Diego Torres interrupted. "Why he got it made, man . . . "

As the two men continued to argue, William waited for the right moment to slip away and join Lali.

She was with some of the women, who were discussing how sincere and devoted Mrs. Hamma was.

"She's hardworking . . . "

"And she's good people . . . " an older woman agreed.

Mr. Fong joined them, and they spoke about the weather and how nice and warm the days were.

Slowly people began to leave, shaking hands with their fellow students and Mrs. Hamma, wishing each other luck.

Mrs. Hamma had been hoping to speak to Stephan Paczkowski privately this evening, but he was always with a group. Now he offered his hand.

"I thank you very much for your good teaching. It was a fine semester."

"Oh, do you think so? Oh, I'm so glad to hear you say that. You don't know how much it means. Especially coming from a person of your caliber. I am confident, yes, indeed, that you will soon be back to your profession, which, after all, is your true calling. If there is anything I can do, please . . . "

"Thank you, miss. This time I am registering in Hunter College, which is in Manhattan on Sixty-eighth Street in Lexington Avenue, with a course of English Literature for beginners." After a slight bow, he left.

"Good-bye." Mrs. Hamma sighed after him.

Lali, William, and several of the women picked up the paper cups and napkins and tossed them into the trash basket.

"Thank you so much, that's just fine. Luis the porter will do the rest. He takes care of these things. He's a lovely person and very helpful. Thank you."

William shook hands with Mrs. Hamma, then waited for Lali to say good-bye. They were the last ones to leave.

"Both of you have been such good students. What are your plans? I hope you will continue with your English."

"Next term we're taking another course," Lali said, looking at William.

"Yes," William responded, "it's more advanced. Over at the Washington Irving High School around Fourteenth Street."

"Wonderful." Mrs. Hamma hesitated. "May I ask you a question before you leave? It's only that I'm a little curious about something."

"Sure, of course." They both nodded.

"Are you two related? I mean, you are always together and yet have different last names, so I was just . . . wondering."

"Oh, we are just friends," Lali answered, blushing.

"I work over in the luncheonette at night, part-time."

"Of course." Mrs. Hamma looked at Lali. "Mrs. Padillo, your husband's place of business. My, that's wonderful, just wonderful! You are all just so ambitious. Very good . . . "

They exchanged farewells.

Outside, the warm June night was sprinkled with the sweetness of the new buds sprouting on the scrawny trees and hedges planted along the sidewalks and in the housing project grounds. A brisk breeze swept over the East River on to Houston Street, providing a freshness in the air.

This time they were early, and Lali and William strolled at a relaxed pace.

"Well," Lali shrugged, "that's that. It's over!"

"Only for a couple of months. In September we'll be taking a more advanced course at the high school."

"I'll probably forget everything I learned by then."

"Come on, Lali, the summer will be over before you know it. Just you wait and see. Besides, we can practice so we don't forget what Mrs. Hamma taught us."

"Sure, what do you like to speak about?" Lali said in English.

William smiled, and clasping his hands, said, "I would like to say to you how wonderful you are, and how you gonna have the most fabulous future . . . after all, you so ambitious!"

When she realized he sounded just like Mrs. Hamma, Lali began to laugh.

"Are you"—Lali tried to keep from giggling, tried to pretend to speak in earnest—"sure there is some hope for me?"

"Oh, heavens, yes! You have shown such ability this"—William was beginning to lose control, laughing loudly—"semester!"

"But I want"—Lali was holding her sides with laughter—"some guarantee of this. I got to know."

"Please, Miss Lali." William was laughing so hard tears were coming to his eyes. "After . . . after all, you now a member in good standing . . . of the promised future!"

William and Lali broke into uncontrollable laughter, swaying and limping, oblivious to the scene they created for the people who stared and pointed at them as they continued on their way to Rudi's.

1977

CRITICAL THINKING POINTS: *After you've read*

1. Why do William and Lali wait until the last night of class to mimic Mrs. Hamma? Is this scene funny to anyone but them? Why or why not?

2. Does William and Lali's desire to improve their English skills remind you of the drive for knowledge experienced by other characters in this collection? Who are they? How are the experiences alike? How are they different?

3. Explore the relationships between William and Lali and between Rudi and Lali. How are the relationships different? What does Lali share with William that she doesn't share with her husband? Why?

SOME POSSIBILITIES FOR WRITING

1. Research the support services offered to returning adult students on your campus. Write a report to be delivered to your class.

2. How do the lives of Mrs. Hamma's students compare to your life as a college student? What obstacles do her students face that you do not? What strengths and/or resources do you have that they might not have, or vice versa?

3. Diego Torres holds an opposing view from the rest of the members of the class concerning citizenship. What parts of each of these views seem to make the most sense to you? Why?

Outside In

　　　　　　　　Patti See

Patti See (b. 1968) is a Senior Student Services Coordinator at the University of Wisconsin–Eau Claire, where she also teaches in the Women's Studies Program. Her poetry, fiction, and essays have been published in *Salon Magazine, HipMama, The Southeast Review, Women's Studies Quarterly,* and other magazines and anthologies.

I didn't know as a freshman that there are many ways to experience college and mine was just one of them. I didn't know that there were other students in my classes who weren't having the "traditional" college experience.

CRITICAL THINKING POINTS: *As you read*

1. What is a first-generation college student?
2. What is the significance of the title? In what ways is See "outside in"?
3. What are some general characteristics of "commuters"? What do you think of when you hear the word "commuter"?

I t was long ago and far away, the way many of us think of our undergraduate years. I started college in the mid-'80s, a time when women my age defined themselves with big hair and a closet-full of stone-washed denim. There were few causes for college students then, just *Just Say No,* and abortion if you were into that sort of thing. I pined for a cause, for a purpose, for a normal life as a college student. I was a commuter, living a community away from the university with room-mates who spent winters in Florida.

I didn't know as a freshman that there are many ways to experience college and mine was just one of them. I didn't know that there were other students in my classes who weren't having the "traditional" college experience. I only focused on the fact that I wasn't living in a dorm with a stranger, trying out different men like shoes, joining a sorority or student organization, experimenting with lifestyles.

I was embarrassed that my parents didn't pay for me to go to college away from home. They gave me a place to live, a car with insurance, every meal, everything that allowed me to commute the twenty minutes to school. At eighteen I didn't realize that putting myself through college, managing work and books, might be an experience in self-reliance. As the youngest of eight children, most of whom had gone to the university closest to home, I accepted that commuting was just what my family did. Like other teenagers, I thought my family was abnormal.

Though I was the last of their children to go to college, my parents still had no idea what it was about. They saw college as extended high school, what people did these days, go to classes for another four years, get another diploma, get a job that pays more than factory work.

My father was a railroad man who worked his way up from switchman to yard master over forty years. My mother's career was built around children and rosary beads. She was never without either of them for almost forty years and had no way nor need to retire from either. I didn't consider the humble beginnings of my peers, didn't know then that half of the university population was made up of first-generation college students like me. I only focused on my own history. I didn't see myself as progress.

At new student orientation, the summer before my first semester, I watched the other first-years wander around campus with their parents, touring buildings, reading the course catalogue over lunch. I didn't even consider telling my parents about orientation. I recognized even then I was in it alone. One morning when I was suffering from something as banal as menstrual cramps or a hangover, my mother said into my pale face at breakfast, "If you feel sick at school, just go to the office and tell them you need to come home. You can do that, can't you?"

I didn't bother to explain there was no office, no one to tell, that the campus spans for miles. I nodded an "okay."

When I walked into my first class of 250 students, more bodies than my entire high school and its faculty combined, I had no point of reference. It was straight out of *The Paper Chase*, I thought then, without the sophistication. That was the first time in my life I was truly anonymous, a number, and I liked being in a flood of strangers. I graduated from a Catholic high school where everyone knew everyone else, and I was tired of it.

I learned early on that college freshmen don't talk to one another in class, and I had no way outside of class to get to know any of them. My first semester, the closest I came to forming any sort of relationship with another person on campus was with janitors and professors. We swapped a familiar nod and hello in the hallways and nothing more. My first year of college evolved around my courses and working as a supermarket cashier and a nightclub waitress. I didn't give much thought to changing my situation, or even, in retrospect, outwardly disliking it. It was just what I did. I often felt so involved in the lecture and class discussions (though I didn't actually open my mouth in class till my sophomore year) that I felt as if I was going one on one with the professor.

Around midterm, my Psych. professor wrote in the margin of a paper he returned, "Interesting insights. I'd like to talk about this sometime." My first reaction was, "Well—hadn't we?" Sure, 249 other students were in the class, but I knew he was talking to me. I just took his comments a step further. Leaving class, walking to my car, all the time I drove down Highway 53, he was there in the passenger seat, conversing with me as I wrote my paper in my mind. Students who live in the dorms or even in off-campus housing in clusters of men and women don't have the opportunity to bring their professors home with them. Why would they? They've got clubs to join, games to attend, dorms to decorate, parties to go to. Poor things. That mentality sustained me throughout my undergraduate years. I relied solely on what went on in the classroom. I thought that was all there was to college: rigid professors who lectured to blank faces. I didn't have a blank face, and after taking my professors home with me, I no longer saw them as rigid.

Intellectually, I thrived. Socially, I didn't. I hung onto the three friends from high school who were still in the area. One was a commuter like me, engaged to a mechanic and simply looking for a piece of paper that allowed her to teach. She didn't seem to care that she had no connections, since she had already begun her real life by picking out china and flatware. Sometimes we had lunch together and talked about old friends who'd gone away to school. Once we went together to the bookstore to rent our textbooks, but it felt all wrong. Too high school for me. I had already adapted to the life of a loner on campus.

Another high school friend bounced from menial job to menial job and had enough money to celebrate with me at the end of the week. We spent weekends in honky-tonk bars, under-aged but dressed much older, and talked about the people we worked with, men and women twice our age, putting in their time at jobs they hated. We promised that wouldn't happen to us.

Another friend was a mother at nineteen, a woman who once wrote poetry like me. I loaned her my American Literature text books and visited her when her boyfriend was gone. We smoked cigarettes and watched movies when the baby was asleep, and sometimes I coaxed her into talking about what she read.

My life as a student was a balancing act between my old life as a "townie" and my new life as a "college girl," perfected by the twelve-mile difference between my childhood home and the university. I didn't get the do-over I always imagined students were given when they went away to school. I didn't get to reinvent myself, no longer a jock, a class clown, a stoner. I was just invisible. Looking back, I know that becoming nobody was the seed of my reinvention of myself. Time and distance help me recognize that without my experience I wouldn't be writing this now. But then, I was merely an outsider in both worlds. Friends and family teased me for staying home on a Saturday night reading and becoming a Beatnik. I was anonymous to other first-year students in my courses because, I thought then, I didn't live in a dorm. The saddest part of my college career, I see now, was that there were no late night talks about Neitzche or Anne Sexton or hot men in my gym class. Anything. Nothing. I had no one to tell what I was learning, no shared knowledge, so I made a game of sharing with myself on the way to and from school. I learned a lot in my twenty-minute commute.

I wouldn't have continued in school, would have quit to work in the plastics factory, the allure of a 401(K), if not for my passion for knowledge and desire to be somebody. I didn't know at eighteen who that somebody might be, but I had an inclination I'd find it in books, not a time card.

I started out as a journalism major because it was easy to explain to my parents. They understood what journalists do. My siblings chose "working" professions: nursing, dietetics, accounting. I was the only freak hooked on knowledge for learning's sake, not a job. Early in my sophomore year I declared English, though even months before I graduated my mother told relatives, "She's going to be a journalist." I never tried to explain what a liberal-arts degree meant. Even the phrase in my mother's mouth made me self-conscious. "English major," she said, like some people say in-surance with the emphasis on the "in." It's like the way she still says someone "knows computer," something foreign and odd, too much for her mouth in one breath. I couldn't explain that I was a writer in training, taking in the world and its details until I was ready to write it. It's something I just knew, like having blue eyes. Even in high school after I bought a pair of sea-green Incredible Hulk–eyed contacts, I was still blue underneath, still a writer. It's something inside, like serendipity that works only if you know what you're looking for or where you've been.

That meant as a freshman I discovered Walt Whitman and e.e. cummings and Kate Chopin and still talked like a townie, a walking Ole-and-Leena joke who knew proper grammar. I could diagram a sentence and write a persuasive paper to save my soul, but I was still factory-worker potential. It's what I feared as a college freshman, and even after I graduated, finding myself someday dull at the machine. That fear made me drag myself out of bed every morning at 7 A.M., eat Wheaties, and drive to school. Mornings were for classes, afternoons and evenings for work. Late nights and weekend days were for homework. It wasn't ideal, but it was productive. I was never dull but sometimes led a dull life.

Throughout my four years, I had contact with other commuters, mostly former high school classmates. Though we had similar stories, tied to the area by families and not enough money for the dorms or off-campus housing, I believed my experience was somehow different. I avoided them and their offers to car pool. These were people I'd known for thirteen years, and they were beyond interesting to me then. We knew who wet her pants in second grade and who threw up at the senior class New Year's Eve party and who made out with whom on the forty yard line after the Homecoming game. These commuters represented where I came from and wanted desperately to forget, details imbedded in my hometown DNA that I thought, at eighteen, I needed to lose in order to make room for more important details.

Though I eventually had many acquaintances, I made only one friend throughout my college career, a woman who commuted her first year when she lived with her dying grandfather. We met in a five-hour-a-week French class after she transferred from a school in her hometown. The first year I knew her, she lived in an apartment with twelve other women. I often imagined myself in her place: what all of us might talk about as we made dinner or came home from the bars. Then I met some of her roommates and discovered business majors don't have intriguing late-night discussions or even intriguing discussions in daylight. I don't recall how we got to be more than passing acquaintances or the circumstances that led me to bring her home, only twenty minutes but a lifestyle away from the college town.

"You have afghans," she said when she walked through my living room. She immediately sat in my mother's chair. What she meant was, *You live in a real home, with canned goods bursting from cupboards, no one screaming drunk upstairs at 2 A.M.*

"You have a lot of trophies," she said in my bedroom. Commuters often have no reason to pack their past lives away. I told her stories about before I was anonymous. She slept over when it was too late to drive home and we drank too much wine and ordered pizza at midnight, and I almost felt like a real college student.

Sometimes we'd get tipsy during some campus bar happy hour, and I'd tell her, "You're my only friend, man." So pathetically honest that she still teases me about it.

The first time she said, "You're so smart and nice, how can that be?" She didn't have many friends herself, and it comforted me as someone who always felt on the outside of campus life.

"Commuter," I answered, and she understood.

Later as a graduate student I continued to commute, but by then it was no longer something to be embarrassed about. It was even exotic to the other 23-year-olds too old to be slumming in student housing, while I was driving home to my rented house "in the suburbs." I was still on the outside, but I had good reason to be. I went home to see my husband and put my two-year-old to bed after class. My peers went to the bar, but some of them traveled in the front seat with me as I imagined our conversations about the literature we discussed in class.

When I was given the graduate student of the year award, my mother hinted about coming to the awards banquet. It would have been the first time either of my parents was on a college campus for something besides a commencement ceremony. Selfish or appropriate, I filled my table with professors who had influenced my life or at least my degree program.

I still commute the same route to and from school, though now I'm an instructor. When I landed my first job I considered moving nearer to campus, but—odd as it sounds—I knew I'd miss the time in the car. Even now, as I write this, the bulk of it I compose in my mind as I drive home from school, a conversation with a professor or peer or old friend, who has traveled with me a long time now.

1998

CRITICAL THINKING POINTS: *After you've read*

1. How are parental expectations or pressures addressed in this essay? How does the narrator cope with what her parents seem to expect of her? What her friends expect?

2. Why does the narrator feel isolated on campus, especially her first semester? Does she "choose" to be isolated? If so, in what ways?

3. Do you think the narrator has a positive relationship with her parents? Why or why not? What details in the essay support your answer? Can a parent–child relationship be "healthy" without being supportive? Why or why not?

SOME POSSIBILITIES FOR WRITING

1. Recall a time when you were embarrassed by your family or something in your family history.

2. See discusses the difference between her education and her parents' education. What are some differences between your education and that of your parents? What are some similarities?

3. Why do many schools require students to live in the dorms, at least for their freshman year? Does your university have any such requirement? Argue for or against mandatory student housing in an opinion piece for your school newspaper.

I Walk in Beauty

AN EXCERPT   Davina Ruth Begaye Two Bears

Davina Ruth Begaye Two Bears, a proud member of the Dinè Nation, graduated from Dartmouth University in 1990 with a degree in anthropology.

On this day I sat next to my professor, and as usual was lost. The words, ideas, arguments, and opinions whirled around me like a tornado in which I was mercilessly tossed.

CRITICAL THINKING POINTS: *As you read*

1. Human nature says that we sometimes stake our self-esteem on one failure. How and why do you think Two Bears does that?
2. What makes an Ivy League school? What might make these universities better than any others?
3. What kind of insecurities does the author have during her first year of college?

During "Freshmen Week" incoming students get a head start on *Dorm life at Dartmouth and take placement tests.*

It was during this time that our Undergraduate Advisor (UGA) group held its first meeting. I had just finished moving into Woodward, an all-female dorm. The UGA group was designed to help freshwomen/men during their first year at college. Most of the women in my dorm belonged to my group.

We decided to meet outside, and shuffled onto the front lawn, scattered with bright red and yellow leaves. As we sat in a circle, I promptly began to freeze my ass off on the damp grass. The sun was out, but it was a chilly fall day.

Our UGA, a sophomore, smiled sweetly and began to explain a name game to us. As I looked at all the unfamiliar faces, I felt afraid, intimidated, alone, and different. I was, of course, the only Navajo or Native American person in our group. A pang of home sickness stole into my heart. Our UGA finished her instructions and we began.

The rules were to put an adjective in front of our name that described us and began with the first letter of our name. The object of the game was to introduce ourselves in a way that would help us to remember everyone's name. "Musical Melody" said a proud African American woman. A friendly voice chirped, "Amiable Amy," and everyone smiled in agreement. I couldn't think of an adjective to describe me that began with D. I racked my brain for an adjective, anything! But it was useless. "Oh, why do I have to be here? I don't belong here with all these confident women. Why can't I do this simple thing?" I remember thinking. My palms were sweating, my nose was running, and my teeth began to chatter. I looked at all their faces, so fresh, so clean and confident. It was finally my turn. I still couldn't think of an adjective. In agony, I uttered "Dumb Davina." "Nooo!" they all protested. Amiable Amy interjected, "Why not Divine Davina?" I shot her a smile of gratitude, but I was horrified and embarrassed. How could I have said that and been serious? Talk about low self-esteem.

My first term at Dartmouth went well academically. I received an A, a B, and a C. But I was lonely, even though I was friends with several women in my UGA group. It was hard for me to relate to them, because I felt they did not know who I was as a Native American, and where I was coming from. They also didn't understand my insecurities. How could they, when they believed so strongly in themselves?

I look back at my first year at Dartmouth, and realize that I made it hard on myself. I took it all too seriously, but how could I have known then what I know now? It took me years to be able to think of myself in a positive light. My mother always told me, "You are no better than anybody else. Nobody is better than you." Unfortunately, at Dartmouth her gentle words were lost in my self pity.

Going home for Christmas almost convinced me to stay home. I was so happy with my family, but I didn't want to think of myself as a quitter, nor did I want anyone else to think of me that way. I came back to an even more depressing winter term. My chemistry course overwhelmed me and I flunked it.

Chemistry was torture, and I could not keep up no matter how hard I tried. A subject that I aced in high school and actually liked did me in that term, and made me feel like a loser. What went wrong? It was just too much information too fast. I was depressed, and my heart was not really in the subject. Finally, I accepted my predicament. I'm not science material, and that's that.

Why did I do so horribly? My note taking skills were my downfall. They were poor at best. The crux of my problem was trying to distinguish the important facts that I needed to write down from the useless verbiage quickly. By the time I got to writing things down, I'd already have forgotten what the professor had just said. In this way, valuable information slipped through my fingers. Not only were my note taking skills poor, but so was my ability to participate in class discussion. At Dartmouth, one was expected to follow everything that was being said, think fast, take notes, ask questions, and finally deliver eloquent opinions, answers, and arguments. It was beyond my limited experience and self-confidence to do so. "Say something!" I screamed mentally, but it was useless. Fear paralyzed me in class. Outside of class I'd talk, but not in class amid the stares of my peers. My freshman English professor and I would have conversations in her office lasting two or three hours, but in her class, when faced with all my peers, I became mute. Once Michael Dorris, my Native American studies professor, asked me outside of class why I did not speak up in his freshman seminar on American Indian policy. I was tongue-tied. Incredibly, I felt that if I spoke up in class, I would be perceived as stupid. It did not help matters that the discussions there utterly lost me most of the time during my first couple of years at Dartmouth.

On one occasion I did speak up in an education course, "Educational Issues in Contemporary Society." It was a tough course with tons of reading. Participating in the weekly seminar was a significant part of the grade. I never talked to anyone in the class. But the professor was always nice to me, saying "Hi" whenever we ran into each other. That day was just like all the other days of the past few weeks. Seated around the oblong table were about fifteen students, the professor and a teaching assistant. The professor did not lead the discussions; he was there as a participant just like us students, and we determined the content of the seminar. I came in, sat down, and my classmates began to express themselves, taking turns at center stage. I looked from one student to another and wondered how they made it look so easy, wishing that I could, too.

On this day I sat next to my professor, and as usual was lost. The words, ideas, arguments, and opinions whirled around me like a tornado in which I was mercilessly tossed. Too many unfamiliar words, analogies, and thoughts were being expressed for my brain to comprehend, edit, sort, pile, delete, save, etc. But this was nothing new—all of my classes at Dartmouth were confusing to me and extremely difficult.

Out of the blue, as I sat there lost in thought, my professor turned his kind face toward me and asked "Davina, why don't you ever say anything?" His question was totally unexpected, but not malicious. Rather, it was asked in a respectful tone that invited an answer. Everyone stared me down; they wanted to know, too. I was caught off guard, but thought to myself: this is my chance to explain why I am the way I am. I began hesitantly, frightened out of my wits, but determined to let these people know who I was and where I was coming from.

"Well, I have a hard time here at Dartmouth. I went to school in Arizona. That's where I am from. I went to school in Tuba City, Flagstaff, Bird Springs, and Winslow, Arizona. So I've gone to school both on and off the Navajo reservation. The schools on the reservation aren't that good. But in Flagstaff, I used to be a good student. Bird Springs, which is my home community, is where I learned about Navajo culture in sixth and seventh grade. I got behind though, because the school didn't have up-to-date books. I mean we were using books from the 1950s. I really liked it though, because I learned how to sing and dance in Navajo and they taught us how to read and write the Navajo language. I learned the correct way to introduce myself in Navajo, so even though I got behind and had to catch up in the eighth grade, it was the best time of my life, and I learned a lot about my language and traditions. Then when I went to eighth grade and high school in Winslow, I had to stay in the Bureau of Indian Affairs dorm away from my family, because the bus didn't come out that far. So the dorm was for all the Navajo and Hopi students who lived too far away on the reservation. Winslow was a good school, but I don't think I was prepared for an Ivy League school like Dartmouth. I mean it's so hard being here so far away from home. I used to be in the top ten percent of my class—now I'm at the bottom of the barrel! Do you know how that makes me feel?"

I couldn't help myself and I began to sob. My words were rushing out like they had been bottled up inside for too long.

"It's awful. I feel like I can't do anything here and that the students are so much smarter than me. It seems like everyone knows so much more than me. All of you, it's so easy for you to sit there and talk. It's hard for me to do that. I envy you. I feel like I'm always lost. I hardly ever understand what you guys are talking about. It's that bad. My note taking skills aren't that good either and it causes me a lot of problems in class, makes me get behind. I mean we never had to take notes like this at Winslow. And it's hard for me to participate in class discussion. I mean at Winslow we had to, but not like this. My teacher would put a check by our name after we asked one question. We didn't sit around a table and talk like we do in here. We didn't have to really get into a subject. We didn't even have to write essays. I only wrote one term paper in my junior and senior year. My English teacher would always tell us how much writing we'd have to do in college, but he never made us write! I'm barely hanging on, but here I sit and that's why I don't participate in class discussion."

I finished my tirade. It was quiet. Nobody said a word. Then my professor leaned over and jokingly admitted, "Don't feel too bad, Davina, I don't understand what they're talking about half the time either." We all smiled, and it was as if a great weight had been lifted off my shoulders. I'm so glad he prompted me to speak that day, and his comment helped me to put it all in perspective. Not everything a Dartmouth student says is profound. It was in this class that I received a citation, which distinguishes a student's work. My professor wrote, "Courage is a sadly lacking quality in the educational world we've created. Davina dared to take steps on behalf of her own growth (and ultimately for her fellows) in an area where she could reasonably expect to be tripped by an insensitive and dominating culture. It was a privilege to accompany her." For Education 20, I received a grade of D with an academic citation, simultaneously one of the worst and best grade reports a student can receive. "Only I would receive such an absurd grade," I said to myself in exasperation, but I was proud despite the D. After that day in class, my self-confidence went up a notch. In my junior and senior years at Dartmouth I began to participate in class little by little. By the time I hit graduate school, you couldn't shut me up.

1997

CRITICAL THINKING POINTS: *After you've read*

1. Two Bears says she was determined to let her classmates know "who I was and where I was coming from." Why do you think her "tirade" in class happened when it did?

2. Two Bears says, "Not everything a Dartmouth student says is profound." What might she mean? Why is realizing this important to her progression as a student?

3. How do you feel about talking in class and answering a teacher's question? Why is this easy for some people and harder for others?

SOME POSSIBILITIES FOR WRITING

1. What do you think are or should be the best predictors of success at college?
2. Two Bears's professor says, "Courage is a sadly lacking quality in the educational world we've created." What do you think he means?
3. How does self-esteem affect the way that students learn in elementary school? In high school? In college?

The Freshman Year Thrill Ride

AN EXCERPT **Missy Loney and Julie Feist**

Missy Loney and Julie Feist were first-year students when they published their list in the St. Paul *Pioneer Press*.

Just because the class is called calculus does not mean you get to use your calculator.

CRITICAL THINKING POINTS: *As you read*

1. As you read, consider how this list might be a reflection of the two authors and their personalities or how this list might apply to college students in general. What items in the list support your ideas?
2. Do you believe peers give you the most pertinent advice? Why or why not?
3. Were you offered advice from parents, teachers, siblings, and friends before you went to college? What pieces of advice were helpful? What pieces were outdated, silly, or unnecessary to you?

1. Your family become your friends, and your friends become your family.
2. If you don't wear your contacts in the shower, you don't notice the moldy walls as much.
3. If you wear a T-shirt under everything, you only have to wash once a month, or whenever you spill.
4. A bag of chips and a can of salsa can last a whole month.
5. Christmas lights are good year round.
6. When you go to bed at 4 A.M. and get up at 6 A.M., it's not worthwhile to get into PJ's or slide under the covers.
7. Some teachers really do care, others really don't.
8. The average college student has more appliances than plug-ins in her dorm room.
9. If you study at the bookstore, you don't need to buy any books.
10. Even when they're wrong, college teachers are always right.
11. The word adviser is misleading.
12. It's possible to oversleep for the 4:45 P.M. Sunday Mass.
13. To study is not the reason most people come to college.

14. You never realize the value of a couch until you don't have one.
15. You can live for an entire month on 75 cents.
16. Homesickness visits at the most peculiar times.
17. It no longer matters what the job is, as long as it pays money.
18. Life isn't fair, but you always get what you deserve.
19. In a group of 100 people, you can still be alone.
20. There are some things that Mom and Dad shouldn't know.
21. It's important to fully screen a guy before you go out with him. Blind dates are dangerous.
22. When around friends, sandbagging is a social activity.
23. Fire drills at 3 A.M. let the whole world know where everyone is sleeping.
24. If you thought you knew your roommate first semester, wait until second semester.
25. When the power is out for 12 hours, the freezer will defrost onto the carpet.
26. You never truly value your car until you don't have one.
27. Quarters are the world. They mean the difference between wearing your underwear inside out for the third time or just the first.
28. E-mail makes the world go round. It's a college student's lifeline.
29. Saying you're not going to drink and not drinking are two separate subjects.
30. Pizza, pizza, pizza. A staple diet.
31. Pizza is only delivered until 2 A.M.
32. Sleep doesn't have to always happen between 10 P.M. and 6 A.M.
33. Brushing your roommate's teeth is an exciting activity at 4 A.M.
34. Some relationships are strengthened by distance while others disappear.
35. If the sign says free food, it must be a worthwhile activity.
36. You don't get any credits for watching football.
37. All books must be removed from the shelves at least once a semester. To sell them back.
38. Getting snail mail makes the whole week wonderful.
39. Packages are even better.
40. Dorm rooms are not good places to study.
41. Just because the class is called calculus does not mean you get to use your calculator.
42. Half a bottle of perfume is a good substitute for a shower.
43. Don't talk to a "Days of Our Lives" addict between noon and 1 P.M.
44. College can change you 100 times and then mold you back into the person you were when you first came.

1997

CRITICAL THINKING POINTS: *After you've read*

1. What do you learn about the authors from their list?
2. Which items on the list strike you as particularly important to learn during your first year at college? Why? Which items on the list are ones that you need to learn on your own? Why?
3. Is it easier to accept advice from your peers than from your parents? Why or why not?

SOME POSSIBILITIES FOR WRITING

1. Create a list called "The Things I Learned in High School."
2. Create your own list of things you've learned in your first week or month or semester at college.
3. What are some "college issues" that this list does not address? Make a list of your own ideas.

Further Suggestions for Writing—"School Daze"

1. One of the most important study skills to develop as a college student is time management. How do you intend to manage studying, deadlines, test preparation, work, and social time?

2. Interview at least three first-year students about some of their fears in the classroom. Next, seek out students who have been on campus longer than you have and ask them for advice about these fears.

3. Browse through this semester's schedule of classes and make a list of courses you would love to take regardless of any requirements. Explain why you would like to take these courses.

4. One of the objectives of a university education is that it challenges your beliefs and perhaps even changes your mind. Briefly explain one thing that you are sure you will never change your mind about and why you think so. Then choose something you might be likely to reconsider, or maybe you already have begun to reconsider it. Again, be sure to include why.

5. Research the characteristics of your freshman class. After finding out as much as you can about such things as race, ethnicity, financial background, high school class rank, and ACT or SAT scores, write a profile as a report for your class. Then consult the most recent online edition of the *Chronicle of Higher Education* and write a report on how your school's profile compares to that of other, similar universities.

6. Interview your advisor about what he or she feels to be the advisor's role. How much does your advisor feel he or she can and/or should do for advisees? How much are students expected to do for themselves?

7. Schools often have programs for commuters that help them get more involved in campus social activities. Contact your Dean of Students Office or Residence Life Office to find out what kinds of programs for commuters are available on your campus. Write a report to deliver to your class.

8. Working in a group, examine the issue of having a part-time job while also being a first-year student.

9. Write about your own personal attitude toward alcohol and/or drugs and how you came to that position.

10. What connection does goal setting have to success at college? Interview two upper-class students about their opinions on setting short- and long-term goals.

11. Write a paper on one of the following: "How to Fail a Course," "How to Make and Keep Friends at College," "How to Protect Yourself at College," "How to Cope with Homesickness," "How to Succeed as a Student Athlete," or another, similar topic of your choosing.

12. Contact your Admissions Office or Dean of Students Office to find out the number of students of color on your campus. Does your university have any student groups specifically for people of certain ethnic backgrounds? What type of support do they offer?

13. Contact your Admissions Office or Dean of Students Office to discover how many nontraditional students are enrolled. What obstacles do nontraditional students face that "traditional" students do not? What support is offered to them on your campus? Write a report to be delivered to your class.

14. Argue for or against a new policy concerning alcohol on your campus.

15. Is binge drinking a problem on your campus? Begin by contacting your campus counseling services for any research they have conducted concerning binge drinking and its effects on your campus. Come up with some potential solutions to this problem.

16. Evaluate your school's program for alcohol awareness.

17. Choose a problem with your campus environment that you think would be relatively easy and inexpensive to solve, and propose a solution.

18. Do athletes on your campus have to meet the same admissions requirements as other students? What type of support services are available to student athletes? How do these services compare to those offered to the general student population?

19. In what way(s) is Patti See's search for identity or reinvention of herself in "Outside In: The Life of a Commuter Student" like Jennifer Crichton's in "'Who Shall I Be?': The Allure of a Fresh Start" in Chapter 3? How are their "re-makes" different? How do their experiences contribute to these similarities and differences?

20. Contrast the selection from Mike Magnuson's *Lummox* with Malcolm X's "Saved" in Chapter 1. Why do these pieces display the differences they do?

21. Locate some of the following poems by Langston Hughes: "Graduation," "Genius Child," "Daybreak in Alabama," "College Formal: Renaissance Casino," and "To Be Somebody" (found in either his selected or collected poems). Using these poems, write briefly on what you think Hughes's views on education might have been.

22. Find a recent college survival guide and compare it with similar guides from years ago. What insights arise from your investigation? Why do you think the way you do?

23. Read *Coming of Age* by Lorri Hewett (1996) and/or *The Cheese Monkeys: A Novel in Two Semesters* by Chip Kidd (2002) and/or *I Am Charlotte Simmons* by Tom Wolfe (2004) and/or some other novel about college life. How does the college experience portrayed in any or all of these books compare to your experience? Why do you think so?

24. Read *Out & About Campus: Personal Accounts by Lesbian, Gay, Bisexual & Transgender College Students* edited by Howard and Stevens (2000) and/or

Out on Fraternity Row: Personal Accounts of Being Gay in a College Fraternity edited by Windmeyer and Freeman (1998) or similar collections. What insights and/or new awareness have you come to from seeing these experiences from these points of view?

25. Read *Chicken Soup for the College Soul: Inspiring and Humorous Stories for College Students* edited by Jack Canfield (1999). Do any of the pieces actually inspire you? Why or why not? How do you account for the wide popularity of this book and books like it? In what ways is this collection different from this text, *Higher Learning?*

26. Choose at least three films from the list at the end of this chapter. What do they seem to say about going to college? What support do you have for your position?

27. Choose one of your responses to the "Some possibilities for writing" topics in this chapter and do further research on some aspect of the topic you addressed in your narrative. Write about how and why this new information would have improved your previous effort.

28. Find the original text from which one of the selections in this chapter was taken. What led you to choose this particular text? How does reading more from the text affect your original reading? Is there more you would like to know about the text, its subject, or its author? Where might you find this further information?

Selected Films—"School Daze"

Bonzo Goes to College (1952, USA). A smart, spunky chimpanzee stars on the varsity football team. Comedy. 80 min. N/R.

Circle of Friends (1995, Ireland–USA). Three friends from a strict Catholic small town face old inhibitions and new freedoms when they go to college in Dublin. Adapted from the Maeve Binchy novel. Romantic drama. 96 min. PG-13.

Class of '44 (1973, USA). College sequel to the sentimental coming-of-age classic *Summer of '42.* Drama. 95 min. PG.

College (1927, USA). Brilliant silent film comedian Buster Keaton tries out for every sports team on campus. Comedy. 65 min. N/R.

The Curve (1998, USA). Three college roommates create much suspense when two of them decide to kill the third in the hopes of getting good grades in compensation for the psychological stress of "losing" their roommate to suicide. Mystery/Drama/Comedy. 90 min. R.

Drive, He Said (1972, USA). Jack Nicholson directed this oddly told tale of coming-of-age angst and alienation. Scene stealer Bruce Dern plays the maniacal college basketball coach. Sports/Drama. 90 min. R.

Frosh (1993, USA). Filmmakers spent a year living in a multicultural, co-ed dormitory at Stanford University. The film documents students' difficult search for personal identity within an increasingly diverse student population. Documentary. 98 min. N/R.

Good Will Hunting (1997, USA). Will Hunting, a janitor at MIT, has a gift for mathematics; a psychiatrist tries to help him with his gift and the rest of his life. Drama. 126 min. R.

Greetings (1968, USA). In this Vietnam War farce (an early effort by director Brian De Palma) Robert De Niro helps a buddy try to fail his physical and escape the military draft. Comedy. 88 min. R.

The Heart of Dixie (1989, USA). Three white southern college women find their lives and politics shifting as they confront the civil rights movement in the late 1950s. Drama. 96 min. PG.

Higher Learning (1995, USA). Political correctness and race issues haunt several students, whose lives intersect briefly and tragically on the campus mall. Drama. 127 min. R.

Horse Feathers (1932, USA). In this classic Marx Brothers farce, Groucho heads Huxley College, whose football team is in no shape for the big game. Musical comedy. 67 min. N/R.

Kent State (1981, USA). Emmy-winning made-for-TV movie about the 1970 tragedy at Kent State University, in which National Guardsmen shot and killed four college protesters. Political drama. 120 min. N/R.

Legally Blonde (2002, USA). A sorority girl becomes the reigning brain at Harvard Law School. Comedy. 96 min. PG-13.

National Lampoon's Animal House (1978, USA). At a 1962 college, Dean Vernon Wormer is determined to expel the Delta House fraternity, but those rough-housers have other plans for him. Comedy. 109 min. R.

P.C.U. (1994, USA). A freshman falls in with dorm mates who organize offensive activities. A social satire of political correctness. Comedy. 81 min. PG-13.

Revenge of the Nerds (1984, USA). A ragtag team of nerds, geeks, losers, and freaks starts its own fraternity in rebellion against the Greek elites. Comedy. 90 min. R.

The Revolutionary (1970, USA). A college student gets caught up in the role of political revolutionary, until he's dangerously in over his head. Drama. 100 min. PG.

Rudy (1993, USA). Based on the true story of Rudy Ruettiger, a five-foot, six-inch college student who must overcome the prejudices of his blue-collar family and an elitist university system in order to fulfill his dreams of playing on the Notre Dame football team. Drama. 116 min. PG.

School Daze (1988, USA). Homecoming weekend on a southern campus highlights how some blacks deny or affirm their racial identity. Directed by Spike Lee. Musical comedy. 114 min. R.

School Ties (1992, USA). A handsome young Jewish prep school athlete hides his religion to survive anti-Semitism in the 1950s. Drama. 107 min. PG-13.

Seniors: Four Years in Retrospect (1997, USA). The filmmakers of *Frosh* returned to Stanford three years later to see how college life had changed five of the students profiled in the earlier film. Combining extensive footage shot during senior year with prophetic clips and outtakes from *Frosh*, the two directors have produced a new film focusing on the different trajectories that students from diverse backgrounds take to a fulfilling and successful college experience. Documentary. 56 min. N/R.

For critical thinking points on these films, see Appendix (p.281).

Three

Student Relations

FAMILY, FRIENDS, AND LOVERS

Much of the education at college takes place outside the classroom, as students learn to live in groups, view and treat one another as adults, and adapt to their changing family roles. This chapter explores parents adjusting to their children's growth, friendships that will last a lifetime or at least a semester, and the difficult choices involved in romantic relationships.

READING SELECTIONS

Raspberries

Ten Commandments for a College Freshman

First Love

Carmen

"Who Shall I Be?": The Allure of a Fresh Start

What It's Really Like

No More Kissing—AIDS Everywhere

The Blue-Light System

Dear Concerned Mother

The Undeclared Major

The Good Student Apologizes to His Professor and to the Girl in Room 303

Homeward Bond

Everyday Use

Raspberries

Jennifer Fandel

Jennifer Fandel (b. 1973) has a Master of Fine Arts degree from Mankato State University. She writes biographies for children.

I hang on to the bush,
ready to fall heavy
full and red.

CRITICAL THINKING POINTS: *As you read*

1. Read through the poem as quickly as you can. What are your first impressions of it?
2. Make a list of words that you think are particularly powerful, beautiful, or important to this poem.
3. Speculate about the poet's age. What makes you think that?

My love is heavy
as raspberries.
Silent as the fall
and red, turning
scarlet as an old heart
heavily thumping,
slow in beat, thinking.
My love is silent
as the waiting.
If only the sun and rain
could be enough.
I hang on to the bush,
ready to fall heavy
full and red.
Cupping his palm
he curves to me,
falling apart
at his touch.

1993

CRITICAL THINKING POINTS: *After you've read*

1. Why do you think the poet compares her love to raspberries? Do you think this is a good comparison? Why or why not?

2. How is this poem like other love poems you've read? How is it different?

3. If you didn't know the author's gender, would you guess this poem was written by a man or a woman? Why?

SOME POSSIBILITIES FOR WRITING

1. The poet writes, "My love is heavy as raspberries." What are three words other than *raspberries* that the poet could have used? The poet writes, "My love is silent as the waiting." What are three words other than *waiting* that could be used here? Choose at least two other words, and briefly record some of the insights and/or questions you come up with.

2. Love in the poem is an abstraction. Choose some other abstractions, such as growing up, injustice, or ambition, and render them in concrete, specific details and/or images of varying length.

3. Read or reread Ron Watson's "The Good Student Apologizes to His Professor and to the Girl in Room 303," later in this chapter. Both pieces might fall into the category of "love poems." How are they different? How are they the same?

Ten Commandments for a College Freshman

Joseph McCabe

Joseph McCabe (b. 1912) is an ordained minister in the United Presbyterian Church and trustee of the Princeton Theological Seminary and Herbert Hoover Presidential Library. His books include *Your First Year at College* (Westminster, 1967) and *Reason, Faith, and Love* (Parthenon, 1972).

College is a new beginning, a clean slate. . . . Burn your bad bridges. No one at college knows about that soiled baggage you've been carrying.

CRITICAL THINKING POINTS: *As you read*

1. What advice seems dated to you? What advice still seems pertinent to college students?
2. The father asks of his son, "Give me your ideas on what to scrap and what to keep." What is your response to this?
3. This piece was written in the form of a letter. What are some qualities of a letter that make this piece effective? How would this be different if it were not part of a personal letter from father to son?

Dear J.B.—

. . . As you know I am asked from time to time to talk to high school students about college and how to prepare for it. Do you think something like the following would be helpful? I'm thinking of calling it: Ten Commandments for a College Freshman. Give me your ideas on what to scrap and what to keep.

I. Thou Shalt Plan to Succeed.

Does this seem as obvious as the need for a quarterback on the football team? I don't mean *hope* to succeed. I mean that success in college will be much more likely if you really draw up a schedule of hours for study, work, and play. Lay out your day and your week. Get in the habit in high school. This will be the secret of getting things done in college and enjoying the whole experience.

II. Thou Shalt Handle Freedom Responsibly.

No one is going to tell you when to get up, go to eat, study, or go to bed. It's amazing that so many survive, and, of course, many don't. Freedom such as a student has at college is devastating for that freshman who has little sense of responsibility.

You've got to get set for freedom; it isn't doing what comes naturally.

III. Thou Shall Spread the Joy of Learning.

Learning is an exciting adventure as you have already discovered in the best of your high school courses. Beware those who are "sent" to college, for they will be taking the attitude that education is the enemy of fun. Beware the cynics. They're on every campus and their refrain runs like this, "Poor food, dorm is like a jail, dull professors, slobby team, why did you come here?" You will sometimes wish they would take their budding ulcers or sour stomach elsewhere. But if it's an education you're after, you'll get it, and you will enjoy the process.

IV. Thou Shalt Scale Down Those Reports on the Sex and Liquor Bit.

Not every co-ed takes the pill as routinely as most takes aspirin, and the extracurricular is not a perpetual beer bust. Most fellows on campus are still looking for the girl they want to marry, and it isn't going to be the b**** who was quick to bed. When you read of students getting bombed on booze, remember you're getting a minority report.

V. Thou Shalt Plan to Commit Fun—and Often.

The world of academia has two extremes. There's the playboy who can't get a book open or the body to the library and there's the grind who never lives it up at all. You should expect to go on a real study binge, but the bookworm learns less than the fellow who knows how to make learning the leitmotif and still plays with abandon. American adults don't know how to play at all. Did they unlearn it in college?

VI. Thou Shalt Know at Least One Professor or One Dean Personally.

Even at the risk of seeming to make yourself a bore! But much more likely you will be welcomed as a student mature enough to relate to a mature person, and that will set both of you up. Invite him to the Union for coffee and he'll flip inwardly—but he'll go and he will be delighted by the invitation. At the small college this kind of relationship should come about readily, but often it doesn't.

All the best universities are striving to make it happen more often. You can do this one yourself, and then say (but not to the prof or the dean), "This lowly freshman has solved the most pressing problem facing higher education in America today!" And you will be right.

VII. Thou Shalt Be Concerned.

But not simply with war on the other side of the world and the social causes of our day. Keep informed, and do what you think is right about these. But what about the cook, the maid in your dorm, the campus maintenance crew, and the night watchman? Just say, "We students appreciate you," and someone will go through the day as though it were Christmas.

VIII. Thou Shalt Be Selective.

Paper, yearbook, student government, fraternity and sorority, dances, ball games, bull sessions, dates, causes, movies, etc., etc., . . . the whole works! If you make them all, you're a bust; and if you miss them all, you're a dud. Don't spread yourself so thin that they would never miss you if you didn't show. But do choose a few, get involved, and get that good part of a college education which no classroom can ever provide.

IX. Thou Shalt Strive to Keep Healthy.

All that psychosomatic stuff has real substance. It isn't sin, it's lack of sleep that ruins so many college careers. Phys ed is required and that will get the body exercised, but there's no requirement that you eat sensibly and keep hours conducive to vigor. You will see many students just too jaded to play well or to study at all.

X. Thou Shalt Forget and Remember.

Take some time to sit down with yourself and recall those things of which you are ashamed and sorry—and then forget them. College is a new beginning, a clean slate, and all that. Burn your bad bridges. No one at college knows about that soiled baggage you've been carrying. Remember those relationships which have made life good. They were clean and decent, and to think of them is a lift. As a freshman, look back at those relationships which brought lasting joy and seek them again. Life is the fine art of forgetting—and remembering.

Well there they are, J.B. What's missing and what needs to be said better? If you forget them all, do remember the love of all of us here.

—Dad

1963

CRITICAL THINKING POINTS: *After you've read*

1. The author talks about the "soiled baggage" that someone might bring to college. What kinds of things do you think he is talking about? How might someone "burn" their "bad bridges"?

2. The author talks about "that good part of a college education which no classroom can ever provide." What kinds of things do you think he is talking about, and what might be "good" about them?

3. There are both "do's" and "do not's" in McCabe's letter. What are some other common themes throughout these ten commandments? How might the son respond to this letter? How would you respond if you received this from one of your parents?

SOME POSSIBILITIES FOR WRITING

1. The father asks, "What's missing and what needs to be said better?" What do you think? Rewrite this letter, adding your thoughts. Since 1963, what has changed in the world and at college? Incorporate those changes into your updated, contemporary version of this letter.

2. McCabe says, "You've got to get set for freedom; it isn't doing what comes naturally." Write about your first few weeks of "freedom" at college. How did you react to your freedom? Did you "get set" for it, as the author advises? In what way?

3. How does the father mask his advice to his son? Do your parents give you outright advice or do they do it more subtly? Write some "obvious" advice from someone close to you. Now write some that is not so obvious.

First Love

FROM *THE LOOM*   R. A. Sasaki

R. A. Sasaki (b. 1952) is a third-generation Japanese American, born and raised in San Francisco. In 1983, she won the American Japanese National Literary Award for her short story "The Loom." Her fiction has been published in *Short Story Review, Pushcart Prize XVII, Story,* and other journals and anthologies. "First Love" is one of nine stories in her collection *The Loom,* published in 1991.

There was an unspoken law of evolution which dictated that in the gradual march toward Americanization, one did not deliberately regress by associating with F. O. B.s. . . . George, therefore, was a shock.

CRITICAL THINKING POINTS: *As you read*

1. Watch for images of cages in the story. How might a "cage" be important to the plot?
2. Watch for references to dramas in the story. How might this be important to the plot?
3. George is considered an "F. O. B." (fresh off the boat) because he was not born in America. What are some other stereotypes or "anti"-stereotypes used in the story?

I t was William Chin who started the rumor. He had been crossing California Street on a Saturday afternoon in December when he was almost struck down by two people on a Suzuki motorcycle. As if it weren't enough to feel the brush of death on the sleeve of his blue parka, a split second before the demon passed, he had looked up and caught sight of two faces he never would have expected to see on the same motorcycle—one of which he wouldn't have expected to see on a motorcycle at all. No one would have imagined these two faces exchanging words, or thought of them in the same thought even; yet there they were, together not only in physical space, but in their expressions of fiendish abandon as they whizzed by him. He was so shaken, first by his nearness to death, then by seeing an F. O. B. hood like Hideyuki "George" Sakamoto in the company of a nice girl like Joanne Terasaki, that it was a full five minutes before he realized, still standing in amazement on the corner of California and Fourth, that Joanne had been driving.

When William Chin's story got around, there was a general sense of outrage among the senior class of Andrew Jackson High—the boys, because an upstart newcomer like George Sakamoto had done what they were too shy to do (that is, he had gotten Joanne to like him), and the girls, because George Sakamoto was definitely cool and Joanne Terasaki, as Marsha Aquino objected with utter contempt, "doesn't even like to dance." Joanne's friends remained loyal and insisted that Jo would come to her senses by graduation. George's motorcycle cronies were less generous. "Dude's fuckin' crazy," was their cryptic consensus. Opinions differed as to which of the two lovers had completely lost their minds; however, it was unanimously held that the pairing was unsuitable.

And indeed, the two were from different worlds.

Hideyuki Sakamoto ("George" was his American name) was Japanese, a conviction that eight years, or half his life, in the States had failed to shake. He had transferred into Jackson High's senior class that year from wherever it was the F. O. B.s (immigrants fresh off the boat) transferred from; and though perhaps in his case the "fresh" no longer applied, the fact that he had come off the boat at one time or another was unmistakable. It lingered—rather persisted—in his speech, which was ungrammatical and heavily accented, and punctuated by a mixture of exclamations commonly used on Kyushu Island and in the Fillmore District.

An F. O. B. at Jackson High could follow one of two routes: he could be quietly good at science or mathematics, or he could be a juvenile delinquent. Both options condemned him to invisibility. George hated math. His sympathies tended much more toward the latter option; however, he was not satisfied to be relegated to that category either. One thing was certain, and that was that George wanted no part of invisibility. As soon as his part-time job at Nakamura Hardware in Japantown afforded him the opportunity, he went out and acquired a second-hand Suzuki chopper (most hoods dreamed of owning a Harley, but George was Japanese and proud of it). He acquired threads which, when worn on his tall, wiry frame, had the effect—whether from admiration, derision, or sheer astonishment—of turning all heads, male and female alike. He had, in a short span of time, established a reputation as a "swinger." So when William Chin's story got around about George Sakamoto letting Joanne Terasaki drive his bike, the unanimous reaction among the girls who thought of themselves as swingers was voiced by Marsha Aquino: "God dog, what a waste." Joanne Terasaki, or "Jo," as she preferred to be called, was, in popular opinion, a "brain." Although her parents were living in Japantown when she was born, soon afterwards her grandparents had died and the family moved out to "the Avenues." Jo was a product of the middle-class, ethnically mixed Richmond District. She had an air of breeding that came from three generations of city living, one college-educated parent, and a simple belief in the illusion so carefully nurtured by her parents' generation, who had been through the war, that she was absolutely Mainstream. No one, however, would have thought of her in conjunction with the word "swing," unless it was the playground variety. Indeed, there was a childlike quality about her, a kind of functional stupidity that was surprising in a girl so intelligent in other respects. She moved slowly, as if her mind were always elsewhere, a habit that boys found mysterious and alluring at first, then exasperating.

Teachers found it exasperating as well, even slightly insulting, as she earned A's in their classes almost as an afterthought. Her attention was like a dim but powerful beacon, slowly sweeping out to sea for—what? Occasionally it would light briefly on the world at hand, and Jo would be quick, sharp, formidable. Then it would turn out to faraway places again. Perhaps she was unable to reconcile the world around her, the world of Jackson High, with the fictional worlds where her love of reading took her. In her mind, she was Scarlett O'Hara, Lizzy Bennet, Ari Ben Canaan. Who would not be disoriented to find oneself at one moment fleeing the Yankees through a burning Atlanta, and the next moment struggling across the finish line in girls' P. E.? Tart repartee with Mr. Darcy was far more satisfying than the tongue-tied and painful exchanges with boys that occurred in real life. Rebuffed boys thought Jo a snob, a heartless bitch. The world of Andrew Jackson High was beneath her, that was it—a passing annoyance to be endured until she went out into the wider world and entered her true element. It must be on this wider world, this future glory, that her vision was so inexorably fixed.

Or perhaps it was fixed on a point just across San Francisco Bay, on the imposing campanile of the Berkeley campus of the University of California. She had always known she would go there, ever since, as a child, she had often gone to her mother's dresser and surreptitiously opened the top drawer to take out the fuzzy little golden bear bearing the inscription in blue letters, "CAL." It was one of the few "heirlooms" that her mother had salvaged from the wartime relocation. She had taken it with her to internment camp in the Utah desert, an ineffectual but treasured symbol of a shattered life. The government could take away her rights, her father's business, her home, but they could never take away the fact that she was U. C. Berkeley, Class of '39. Jo would have that, too. People often said of Jo that she was a girl who was going places; and they didn't mean on the back (or front) of George Sakamoto's bike.

Only love or drama could bring together two people cast in such disparate roles. When auditions began for the play that was traditionally put on by the senior class before graduation, Jo, tired of being typecast as a brain, tried out for the part most alien to her image—that of the brazen hussy who flings herself at the hero in vain. For a brief moment she stood before her fellow classmates and sang her way out of the cramped cage that their imaginations had fashioned for her. The moment was indeed brief. Marsha Aquino got the part.

"You have to admit, Jo," said William Chin apologetically, "Marsha's a natural." And Jo agreed, somewhat maliciously, that Marsha was.

George, for his part, went for the lead. It was unheard of for a hood (and an F. O. B., at that) to aspire to the stage, much less the leading part. So thoroughly did George's aspect contradict conventional expectations of what a male lead would be, that the effect was quite comic. His good-natured lack of inhibition so charmed his audience that they almost overlooked the fact that his lines had been unintelligible. At the last moment, a voice of reason prevailed, and George was relegated to a nonspeaking part as one of six princes in a dream ballet, choreographed by Jo's friend Ava.

And so the two worlds converged.

"Grace," Ava was saying. "And—flair." She was putting the dream princes and princesses through their paces. "This is a ballet."

The dancers shuffled about self-consciously. After hours of work the princes and princesses, trained exclusively in soul, were managing to approximate a cross between a square dance and a track-and-field event.

"You've got to put more energy into it, or something," Jo, who was a princess, observed critically as a sheepish William Chin and Ed Bakowsky leaped halfheartedly across the floor.

"Like this, man!" George yelled suddenly, covering the stage in three athletic leaps. He landed crookedly on one knee, arms flung wide, whooping in exhilaration. There was an embarrassed silence.

"Yeah," Jo said. "Like that."

"Who is that?" she asked Ava after the rehearsal.

"I don't know," Ava said, "but what a body."

"That's George Sakamoto," said Marsha Aquino, who knew about everyone. "He's bad."

Jo, unfamiliar with the current slang, took her literally.

"Well, he seems all right to me. If it wasn't for him, our dream ballet would look more like 'The Funeral March.' Is he new?"

"He transferred from St. Francis," Marsha said. "That's where all the F. O. B.s go."

Jo had always had a vague awareness of Japanese people as being unattractively shy and rather hideously proper. Nothing could have been further from this image than George. Jo and her friends, most of whom were of Asian descent, were stunned by him, as a group of domesticated elephants born and bred in a zoo might have been upon meeting their wild African counterpart for the first time. George was a revelation to Jo, who, on the subject of ethnic identity, had always numbered among the ranks of the sublimely oblivious.

George, meanwhile, was already laying his strategy. He was not called "Sukebe Sakamoto" by his friends for nothing.

"This chick is the door-hanger type," he told his friend Doug. "You gotta move real slow."

"Yeah," Doug said. "Too slow for you."

"You watch, sucker."

He called her one weekend and invited her and Ava to go bowling with him and Doug. Jo was struck dumb on the telephone.

"Ha-ro, is Jo there?"

"This is Jo."

"Hey, man. This is George."

"Who?"

"George, man. Sakamoto."

"Oh." Then she added shyly. "Hi."

The idea of bowling was revolting, but Jo could bowl for love.

She told her mother that she had a date. Her mother mentally filed through her list of acquaintances for a Sakamoto.

"Is that the Sakamoto that owns the cleaner on Fillmore?"

"I don't think so," Jo said.

"Well, if Ava's going, I guess it's all right."

When George came to pick her up, Jo introduced him to her father, who was sitting in the living room watching television.

"Ha-ro," George said, cutting a neat bow to her startled father.

"Was that guy Japanese?" her father asked later when she returned.

"Yeah," Jo said, chuckling.

There was an unspoken law of evolution which dictated that in the gradual march toward Americanization, one did not deliberately regress by associating with F. O. B.s. Jo's mother, who was second generation, had endured much criticism from her peers for "throwing away a college education" and marrying Jo's father, who had graduated from high school in Japan. Even Jo's father, while certainly not an advocate of this law, assumed that most people felt this way. George, therefore, was a shock.

On their second date, Jo and George went to see Peter O'Toole in a musical. From then on, they decided to dispense with the formalities, a decision owing only in part to the fact that the musical had been wretched. The main reason was that they were in love.

They would drive out to the beach, or to the San Bruno hills, and sit for hours, talking. In the protective shell of George's mother's car they found a world where they were not limited by labels. They could be complex, vulnerable. He told her about his boyhood in Kyushu, about the sounds that a Japanese house makes in the night. He had been afraid of ghosts. His mother had always told him ghost stories. She would make her eyes go round and utter strange sounds: "Ka-ra . . . ko-ro . . . ka-ra . . . ko-ro . . ."—the sound made by the wooden sandals of an approaching ghost. Japanese ghosts were different from American ghosts, he said. They didn't have feet.

"If they don't have feet," Jo asked curiously, "how could they wear sandals?"

George was dumbfounded. The contradiction had never occurred to him.

They went for motorcycle rides along the roads that wound through the Presidio, at the edge of cliffs overlooking the Golden Gate. Then, chilled by the brisk winter fog, they would stop at his house in Japantown for a cup of green tea.

He lived in an old Victorian flat on the border between Japantown and the Fillmore, with his mother and grandmother and cat. His mother worked, so it was his grandmother who came from the kitchen to greet them. (But this was later. At first, George made sure that no one would be home when they went. He wanted to keep Jo a secret until he was sure of her.)

The Victorian kitchen, the green tea, all reminded Jo of her grandparents' place, which had stood just a few blocks away from George's house before it was torn down. Jo had a vague memory of her grandmother cooking fish in the kitchen. She couldn't remember her grandfather at all. The war had broken his spirit, taken his business, forced him to do day-work in white people's homes, and he had died when Jo was two. After that, Jo's family moved out of Japantown, and she had not thought about the past until George's house reminded her. It was so unexpected that the swinger, the hood, the F. O. B. George Sakamoto should awaken such memories.

But they eventually had to leave the protective spaces that sheltered their love. Then the still George of the parked car and Victorian kitchen, the "real" George, Jo wanted to believe, evolved, became the flamboyant George, in constant motion, driven to maintain an illusion that would elude the cages of other people's limited imaginations.

He took her to dances Jo had never known existed. Jo had been only to school dances, where everyone stood around too embarrassed to dance. The dances that George took her to were dark, crowded. Almost everyone was Asian. Jo knew no one. Where did all these people come from? They were the invisible ones at school, the F. O. B.s. They *dressed* (unlike Jo and her crowd, who tended toward corduroy jeans). And they danced.

George was in his element here. In his skintight striped slacks flared at the calf, black crepe shirt open to the naval, billowing sleeves and satiny white silk scarf, he shimmered like a mirage in the strobe lights that cut the darkness. Then, chameleonlike, he would appear in jeans and a white T-shirt, stocking the shelves of Nakamura Hardware. At school, George shunned the striped shirts and windbreaker jackets that his peers donned like a uniform. He wore turtleneck sweaters under corduroy blazers, starched shirts in deep colors with cuff links. When he rode his bike, he was again transformed, a wild knight in black leather.

"The dudes I ride with," George confided to Jo in the car, "see me working in the store, and they say, 'Hey, what is this, man? You square a-sup'm?' Then the guys in the store, they can't believe I hang out with those suckers on bikes. 'Hey George,' they say, 'you one crazy son-of-a-bitch.' In school, man, these straight suckers can't believe it when I do good on a test. I mean, I ain't no hot shit at English, but I ain't no dumb sucker neither. 'Hey George,' they say, 'you tryin' to get into college a-sup'm?' 'Hey, why not, man?' I say. They can't take it if you just a little bit different, you know? All them dudes is like that—'cept you."

Jo was touched, and tried to be the woman of George's dreams. It was a formidable endeavor. Nancy Sinatra was the woman of George's dreams. For Christmas Jo got a pair of knee-high black boots. She wore her corduroy jeans tighter in the crotch.

"Hey, George," Doug said. "How's it goin' with Slow Jo?"

"None of your fuckin' business, man," George snapped.

"Oh-oh. Looks bad."

On New Year's Eve Jo discovered French kissing and thought it was "weird." She got used to it, though.

"You tell that guy," her father thundered, "that if he's gonna bring that motorcycle, he doesn't have to come around here anymore!"

"Jesus Christ!" Jo wailed, stomping out of the room. "I can't wait to get out of here!"

Then they graduated, and Jo moved to Berkeley in the spring.

The scene changed from the narrow corridors of Andrew Jackson High to the wide steps and manicured lawns of the university. George was attending a junior college in the city. He came over on weekends.

"Like good ice cream," he said. "I want to put you in the freezer so you don't melt."

"What are you talking about?"

They were sitting outside Jo's dormitory in George's car. Jo's roommate was a blonde from Colusa who had screamed the first time George walked into the room with Jo. ("Hey, what's with that chick?" George had later complained.)

"I want to save you," George said.

"From what?" Jo asked.

He tried another analogy. "It's like this guy got this fancy shirt, see? He wants to wear it when he goes out, man. He don't want to wear it every day, get it dirty. He wears an old T-shirt when he works under the car—get grease on it, no problem. It don't matter. You're like a good shirt, man."

"So who's the old T-shirt?" Jo asked, suddenly catching on.

"Hey, nobody, man. Nobody special. You're special. I want to save you."

"I don't see it that way," Jo said. "When you love someone, you want to be with them and you don't mind the grease."

"Hey, outasight, man."

So he brought her to his room.

George's room was next to the kitchen. It was actually the dining room converted into a young man's bedroom. It had the tall, narrow Victorian doors and windows, and a sliding door to the living room, which was blocked by bookshelves and a stereo. The glass-doored china cabinet, which should have housed Imari bowls, held tapes of soul music, motorcycle chains, Japanese comic books, and Brut. In Jo's grandparents' house there had been a black shrine honoring dead ancestors in the corner of the dining room. The same corner in George's room was decorated by a life-sized poster of a voluptuous young woman wearing skintight leather pants and an equally skintight (but bulging) leather jacket, unzipped to the waist.

George's mother and grandmother were delighted by Jo. In their eyes she was a "nice Japanese girl," something they never thought they would see, at least in conjunction with George. George had had a string of girlfriends before Jo, which had dashed their hopes. Jo was beyond their wildest expectations. It didn't seem to matter that this "nice Japanese girl" didn't understand any Japanese; George's grandmother spoke to her anyway, and gave her the benefit of the doubt when she smiled blankly and looked to George for a translation. They were so enthusiastic that George was embarrassed, and tried to sneak Jo in and out to spare her their effusions.

They would go to his room and turn up the stereo and make love to the lush, throbbing beat of soul. At first Jo was mortified, conscious of what her parents would say, knowing that "good girls" were supposed to "wait." But in the darkness of George's room, all of that seemed very far away.

So her first experiences of love were in a darkened room filled with the ghosts of missing Japanese heirlooms; in the spaces between the soul numbers with which they tried to dispel those ghostlike shadows, sounds filtered in from the neighboring kitchen: samurai music from the Japanese program on television, the ancient voice of his grandmother calling to the cat, the eternal shuffle of slippers across the kitchen floor. When his mother was home and began to worry about what they were doing in his room, he installed a lock, and when she began pounding on the door, insisting that it was getting late and that George really should take Jo home, George would call out gruffly, "Or-righ! Or-righ!"

But there was that other world, Jo's weekday world, a world of classical buildings, bookstores, coffee shops, and tear gas (for the United States had bombed Cambodia).

Jo flitted like a ghost between the two worlds so tenuously linked by a thin span of steel suspended over San Francisco Bay. She wanted to be still, and at home, but where? On quiet weekday mornings, reading in an empty courtyard with the stillness, the early morning sun, the language of Dickens, she felt her world full of promise and dreams. Then the sun rose high, people came out, and Jo and her world disappeared in a cloak of invisibility, like a ghost.

"Her English is so good," Ava's roommate remarked to Ava. "Where did she learn it?"

"From my parents," Jo said. "In school, from friends. Pretty much the same way most San Franciscans learn it, I guess."

Ava's roommate was from the East Coast, and had never had a conversation with an "Oriental" before.

"She just doesn't know any better," Ava apologized later.

"Well where has that chick been all her life?" Jo fumed.

Then she would long for George, and he would come on the weekend to take her away. Locked together on George's bike, hurtling back and forth between two worlds, they found a place where they could be still and at peace.

George tried to be the man of her dreams. They went on hikes now instead of soul dances. He would appear in jeans and a work shirt, and he usually had an armload of books. He was learning to type, and took great pains over his essays for Remedial English.

But they began to feel the strain. It began to bother George that Jo made twenty-five cents an hour more at her part-time job in the student dining room than he did at the hardware store. He had been working longer. He needed the money. Jo, on the other hand, never seemed to buy anything. Just books. Although her parents could afford to send her to college, her high-school record had won her a scholarship for the first year. She lived in a dream world. She had it so easy.

He asked to borrow fifty dollars, he had to fix his car, and she lent it to him immediately. But he resented it, resented his need, resented her for having the money, for parting with it so easily. Everything, so easily. And he tortured her.

"Hey, is something wrong, man?" George asked suddenly, accusing, over the phone.

"Wrong?" Jo was surprised. "What do you mean?"

"You sound funny."

"What do you mean, funny?"

"You sound real cold, man," George said. His voice was flat, dull.

"There's nothing wrong!" Jo protested, putting extra emphasis in her voice to convince him, then hating herself for doing so. "I'm fine."

"You sound real far away," George went on, listlessly.

"Hey, is something bothering you?"

"No," George said. "You just sound funny to me. Real cold, like you don't care." He wanted her to be sympathetic, remorseful.

And at first she was—repentant, almost hysterical. Then she became impatient. Finally, she lapsed into indifference.

"I have the day off tomorrow," George said over the phone. "Can I come?" Jo hesitated.

"I have to go to classes," she warned.

"That's okay," he said. "I'll come with you."

There was another long pause. "Well . . . we'll see," she said.

As soon as she saw him the next day, her fears were confirmed. He had gone all out. He wore a silky purple shirt open halfway to his navel, and skintight slacks that left nothing to the imagination. There was something pathetic and vulnerable about the line of his leg so thoroughly revealed by them. As they approached the campus, George pulled out a pair of dark shades and put them on.

He was like a character walking into the wrong play. He glowed defiantly among the faded jeans and work shirts of the Berkeley campus.

Jo's first class was Renaissance Literature.

"If you want to do something else," she said, "I can meet you after class."

"That's okay, man," George said happily. "I want to see what they teaching you."

"It's gonna be real boring," she said.

"That's okay," he said. "I have my psych book."

"If you're going to study," Jo said carefully, "maybe you should go to the library."

"Hey," George said, "you tryin' to get rid of me?"

"No," Jo lied.

"Then let's go."

They entered the room. It was a seminar of about ten people, sitting in a circle. They joined the circle, but after a few minutes of discussion about Lycidas, George opened his psychology textbook and began to read.

Jo was mortified. The woman sitting on the other side of George was looking curiously, out of the corner of her eye, at the diagram of the human brain in George's book.

"Would you care to read the next stanza aloud?" the lecturer asked suddenly. "You—the gentleman with the dark glasses."

There was a horrible moment as all eyes turned to George, bent over his psychology textbook. He squirmed and sank down into his seat, as if trying to become invisible.

"I think he's just visiting," the woman next to George volunteered. "I'll read."

Afterwards, Jo was brutal. Why had he come to the class if he was going to be so rude? Why hadn't he sat off in the corner, if he was going to study? Or better yet, gone to the library as she had suggested? Didn't he know how inappropriate his behavior was? Didn't he care if they thought that Japanese people were boors? Didn't he know? Didn't he care?

No, he didn't know. He was oblivious. It was the source of his confidence, and that was what she had loved him for.

And so the curtain fell on their little drama, after a predictable denouement—agreeing that they would date others, then a tearful good-bye one dark night in his car, parked outside her apartment. Jo had always thought it somewhat disturbing when characters who had been left dead on the set in the last act, commanding considerable emotion by their demise, should suddenly spring to life not a minute later, smiling and bowing, and looking as unaffected by tragedy as it is possible to look. She therefore hoped she would not run into George, who would most certainly be smiling and bowing and oblivious to tragedy. She needn't have worried. Their paths had never been likely to cross.

Jo was making plans to study in New York when she heard through the grapevine that George was planning a trip to Europe. He went that summer, and when he returned, he brought her parents a gift. Jo's parents, who had had enough complaints about George when Jo was seeing him, were touched, and when Christmas came around Jo's mother, in true Japanese fashion, prepared a gift for George to return his kindness. Jo, of course, was expected to deliver it.

She had had no contact with him since they had broken up. His family was still living in Japantown, but the old Victorian was going to be torn down for urban renewal, and they were planning to move out to the Avenues, the Richmond District where Jo's parents lived.

As Jo's dad drove her to George's house, Jo hoped he wouldn't be home, hoped she could just leave the gift with his mother. She was thankful that she was with her father, who had a habit of gunning the engine as he sat waiting in the car for deliveries to be made, and was therefore the ideal person with whom to make a quick getaway.

George's grandmother opened the door. When she saw who it was, her face changed and she cried out with pleasure. Jo was completely unprepared for the look of happiness and hope on her face.

"Jo-chan!" George's grandmother cried; then, half-turning, she called out Jo's name twice more, as if summoning the household to her arrival.

Jo was stunned.

"This is for George," she said, thrusting the gift at George's grandmother, almost throwing it at her in her haste. "Merry Christmas."

She turned and fled down those stairs for the last time, away from the doomed Victorian and the old Japanese woman who stood in the doorway still, calling her name.

1991

CRITICAL THINKING POINTS: *After you've read*

1. Why do you think "first love" often ends tragically? Do you believe it has to? Why or why not? What are some characteristics of "first love" as it is portrayed in contemporary film or fiction? Are these characteristics apparent in this story? Why or why not?

2. When did you know that Jo and George were drifting apart and their relationship doomed? What details in the story led to this?

3. What kind of "pecking order" or hierarchy exists among Japanese Americans in the story? Why might non–Japanese Americans, especially Caucasians, misunderstand this hierarchy?

SOME POSSIBILITIES FOR WRITING

1. List some outdated terms that appear in the story. Update those terms using contemporary phrases that have approximately the same meaning. What are some of the positive and/or negative associations with these terms?

2. First-year students often leave a boyfriend or girlfriend behind when they go to college. Interview a classmate who is dealing with a long-distance relationship. How could a couple cope with the separation?

3. Recall other "first love" stories (perhaps the most famous is *Romeo and Juliet*) or films. Compare Jo and George's experience to that of another fictional couple or to a couple you know.

Carmen

Jennifer Sheridan

Jennifer Sheridan has a Master of Fine Arts degree in fiction from Columbia College in Chicago.

I thought I might throw up after all the booze, and Aaron winking at me, so I dug another vanilla wafer out of the box and drank some tap water out of my cupped palm. Carmen lay face down on her bed, trying to light a cigarette.

CRITICAL THINKING POINTS: *As you read*

1. Why do you think the story is called "Carmen"?
2. Do you know people who are as disconnected from their academic lives as Carmen and Kate? Why are they disenchanted and disengaged characters?
3. Romantic ideas surrounding young people are promoted in movies, TV, and books. How are these romantic ideas reflected or countered in the story?

My best friend Carmen leaned against the sink and arched her back. She blew smoke at the ceiling and it curled back down the face of the mirror behind her. She was telling me the story of her virginity in that slow, sultry way she had. She'd just finished the orgasm part. We were cutting all our Monday afternoon classes and sharing a cigarette in her dorm bathroom.

It had happened over Thanksgiving break the previous week, in Greece with an older cousin who spoke no English. Late, nearly dawn. Parted French doors. An ocean.

I draped my arms over the still warm hand dryer. Carmen's tan was a deep berry color that rolled out of the sleeves of her T-shirt.

"Afterwards he paced around the room," she whispered. I pictured a leopard crisscrossing by the open window. Outside the sky would glow lavender. A breeze. The sound of water. The smell of salt and sky and beach.

"What did it feel like?"

"Watching him pace?"

"Yeah." I pictured myself in her place, lying on starched white sheets as my first lover, foreign and chiseled, paced like a wild animal.

"It was awesome," she said. "It was my favorite part." Passing the cigarette, she gave me a smile no one else for miles ever saw. She knew the pacing part would be my favorite too.

"God, Carmen, leave it to you to have the perfect first time," I said.

129

"Let's get drunk," she suggested. I nodded, dropping the half-smoked cigarette into the sink. It landed in a fierce sizzle.

By five-thirty the pint of Jack Daniel's was finished and the dinner migration began. When Aaron Klinger sauntered by Carmen's doorway he winked at me. Aaron Klinger who'd phone me late at night. What was I doing? Nothing much. I'd follow the scent of stale cigarettes into his bed. But it was a secret.

I thought I might throw up after all the booze, and Aaron winking at me, so I dug another vanilla wafer out of the box and drank some tap water out of my cupped palm. Carmen lay face down on her bed, trying to light a cigarette.

At six-fifteen her date appeared, standing at the door for God knows how long before I noticed him. Byron. He had black pubic curly hair on his face and head, and bugged-out eyes. His hands fluttered over his chest, landing at his sides.

Carmen insisted I come to an ancient Warren Beatty film that I'd seen twice to make sure I really hated, but what the hell, Carmen wanted me to go.

During the movie I watched her face flicker in the light coming off the screen. Occasionally I saw Byron glaring at me from the other side. I thought about Aaron, how we smoked in silence sometimes, afterward, staring at the ceiling, not touching.

"Kate," he once said. "You know Scott, the football player?"

"Yeah?"

"Well, every day he goes to this one girl's room and they do it." He leaned on one elbow and tapped his cigarette into the ashtray lying between us. I pulled the sheet up to my chin. "She makes him a cheese omelet, and that's it." Aaron rested his chin on my sheet covered chest. His greasy hair fell onto the back of my hand as I stroked the nape of his neck.

"That's great, Aaron," I said.

In the science auditorium a ten-foot Warren Beatty leaned into an open refrigerator against a half-naked Goldie Hawn.

"Juicy bootie," Carmen growled. I laughed, but I felt a hundred years old. I just wanted to go home. Maybe the phone in my hallway would be ringing. Maybe my brother would call from Yale.

"Hey, Sis, how's that Anthro class?" He'd never called me from Yale. He didn't know what classes I had.

Outside the air smelled of frost. Carmen sang a Christmas carol. Byron jammed his hands into his pockets, his eyes on Carmen, twirling in and out of sight on perfect ballet points.

"My mother is such a bitch," she said. "I hate her guts." I thought about flannel sheets against my naked skin.

"She's just drunk," I mumbled to Byron.

"Kiss me," Carmen screamed, grabbing him. She knew how bad he wanted her. I thought it was cruel, the way she treated guys. But maybe I was wrong to feel bad. Byron didn't give a shit about her either. He wanted what he wanted; we all did. At the time I gave everyone a million times more credit than they deserved.

Byron puckered his skinny chapped lips. I could see them quiver in the moonlight. Carmen wouldn't be happy about this in the morning, if she remembered it at all.

"Carmen . . . " I started. Carmen was in my face like a guard dog.

"Mind your own fucking business," she screamed.

"Yeah," said Byron. His hand gripped her arm. Carmen turned to him with a low laugh. I tried again. This time she whipped around and slapped me hard across the face. We all heard the sound. While I stroked the stinging place on my cheek his arm wrapped around her back, sliding down over her ass. She squeaked a little as he kissed her. Carmen pulled away, almost falling over backwards. Byron licked his lips and steadied her with his spindly hands.

"Good night to you," she slurred. She'd forgotten his name. Carmen disappeared into the darkness. When I found her she was throwing up in the bushes. I half-dragged her to her room.

Carmen pulled her limp dress over her head and fell naked onto the bed. She laughed at me, standing by the sink holding an empty vanilla wafer box. I could see her shape in the dim light from the hall.

"I do love you, Katie," she mumbled, rolling toward the wall. I hung her dress on the closet doorknob and stood very still on her carpet. She whimpered slightly, a sharp stab, then nothing.

I took the two steps to the side of the bed. She rolled onto her back, cradling her long arm behind her head.

"My mom," she said.

"I know," I whispered. I pulled the damp hair out of her eyes and smoothed it down along her pillow. She smelled terrible, of vomit and whiskey. She sobbed again. Her eyelids fluttered. I ran my hand over her forehead. She leaned into my fingers, cool against her hot skin. I kissed her cheek and pressed my face against hers.

Suddenly Carmen came to life. She wrapped her sweaty, strong arms around my neck and pulled my face to hers by my hair. I clamped my jaw shut, stifling a scream. Adrenaline shot through me so fast my fingers shot out straight. The next thing I knew her mouth was on mine, her lips grinding against me, her tongue forcing my teeth apart. Carmen, my best friend. Her mouth felt swollen and hot, but her tongue was cooler. It glided finally past my stubborn teeth, into my mouth. Only after she had fallen back onto the bed, eyes shut, breathing even and deep did I feel the sensation of our tongues together, like warm snakes in a twisting, sinewy pile.

When I stood up my legs wobbled. Carmen's naked chest rose and fell, half under the sheet. I staggered through the door and up the stuffy hall. One long, fluorescent light bulb flickered purple as I passed under it.

In the morning Carmen called me on the phone.

"God, Katie," she laughed. "I feel like hell."

I was angry, not because she'd slapped me but just because of everything. She wore me out. I'd watched her dance and flirt and held her head while she barfed.

Carmen wasn't meant for quiet, Midwestern evenings. Her green-tinted skin and wild ways, her elegance made me hate myself.

She admitted sheepishly that she'd been pretty drunk the night before. No, she didn't remember the movie, or spilling her Raisinets, licking melted chocolate from her fingers.

"Do you remember kissing Byron?" I asked.

"I didn't."

"Do you remember slapping me?"

"Katie, I never did!"

"Yeah, you sure did."

I thought about Carmen putting badly typed love letters signed with Aaron's name in my mailbox, Carmen calling at two A.M. to talk about Ingmar Bergman, Carmen saying I looked like a Gypsy princess in the sweater I was sure people thought was weird.

"Katie, did I? Tell me I didn't."

"You didn't."

"I did, didn't I?"

"Yeah, you did."

"I'm sorry, Katie," she said. "Do you forgive me?"

I forgave Carmen. I met her for lunch. She looked the same. Standing at the bottom of the stairs leading up to the dining hall her hands did not shake. She reached for me, a fake worried look on her face.

"Help me up the stairs, daughter," she said in an old lady voice. "I feel like shit." She leaned against me as we climbed the stairs, mumbling how much coffee she would need, twenty-nine cups, black.

We blew off all our classes that day. We smoked and laughed and bought a bottle of gin. Coming out of the liquor store Carmen said she'd call her evil, stingy father for more money.

"If I'm lucky my mom will answer the phone. She always throws in an extra fifty," she said.

Sitting in the grass outside the library Carmen apologized again and shook her head, smiling into her lap. I watched her bring her cigarette to her lips. I watched her close her eyes. I listened to the ache behind her laugh that only I ever heard. I told her a thousand times to forget the whole thing. I promised to forget it myself. I really had no choice in the matter.

1996

CRITICAL THINKING POINTS: *After you've read*

1. Why does Kate seem to worship Carmen? What is Carmen's attitude toward Kate? What details in the story support this?

2. What do you think makes the scene in which Carmen kisses Kate a pivotal one in the plot?

3. How would the story be different if the two lead characters were male?

SOME POSSIBILITIES FOR WRITING

1. Kate and Carmen take turns being the mother and the daughter. Find examples of this role switching in the text. Why do you think they switch roles?

2. Compare and contrast Carmen's and Kate's attitudes toward sex.

3. Universities are notorious for promoting a lifestyle that accepts promiscuity and many sexual partners. What are your views of college life and its reputation for creating sexually active students? What do you think are some causes of this? What might be some of the results?

"Who Shall I Be?" The Allure of a Fresh Start

Jennifer Crichton

Jennifer Crichton is the author of *Delivery: A Nurse-Midwife's Story* (1986) and *Family Reunion* (1998). She holds an A.B. from Brown University and received a Master's degree in English from Columbia University in 2002.

Nothing seduces like the promise of a clean slate.

CRITICAL THINKING POINTS: *As you read*

1. Is a "fresh start" at college alluring to everyone? Why or why not?

2. Do you believe people, especially college freshmen, choose who they will become? Why or why not?

3. Crichton says, "We learn a lot about friends from the kinds of masks they choose to wear." In what ways do people "choose" to wear "masks"? Do you know anyone who does this? Do you sometimes wear "masks"? In what types of situations?

T he student is a soul in transit, coming from one place en route to someplace else. Moving is the American way, after all. Our guiding principle is the fresh start, our foundation the big move, and nothing seduces like the promise of a clean slate.

"Do you realize how many people saw me throw up at Bob Stonehill's party in tenth grade? A lot of people," says my friend Anne. "How many forgot about it? Maybe two or three. Do you know how much I wanted to go someplace where nobody knew I threw up all over Bob Stonehill's living room in tenth grade? Very much. This may not seem like much of a justification for going away to college, but it was for me." Going away to college gives us a chance to rinse off part of our past, to shake off our burdensome reputations.

We've already survived the crises of being known, allowing how American high schools are as notoriously well-organized as totalitarian regimes, complete with secret police, punishment without trial, and banishment. High school society loves a label, cruelly infatuated with pinning down every species of student. Hilary is a klutz, Julie is a slut, and Michele a gossiping bitch who eats like a pig.

No wonder so many of us can't wait to be free of our old identities and climb inside a new skin in college. Even flattering reputations can be as confining as a pair of too-tight shoes. But identity is tricky stuff, constructed with mirrors. How you see yourself is a composite reflection of how you appear to friends, family, and lovers. In college, the fact that familiar mirrors aren't throwing back a familiar picture is both liberating and disorienting (maybe that's why so many colleges have freshman "orientation week").

"I guess you could call it an identity crisis," Andrea, a junior now, says of her freshman year. "It was the first time nobody knew who I was. I wasn't even anybody's daughter any more. I had always been the best and brightest—what was I going to do now, walk around the dorm with a sign around my neck saying 'Former High School Valedictorian'?"

For most of my college years, I was in hot pursuit of an identity crisis, especially after a Comparative Literature major informed me that the Chinese definition of "crisis" was "dangerous opportunity," with the emphasis on opportunity. On college applications, where there were blanks for your nickname, I carefully wrote "Rusty," although none of my friends (despite the fact that I have red hair) had ever, even for a whimsical moment, considered calling me that. I was the high-strung, sensitive, acne-blemished, antiauthoritarian, would-be writer. If I went through a day without some bizarre mood swing, people asked me what was wrong. I didn't even have the leeway to be the cheerful, smiling sort of girl I thought I might have it in me to be. My reputation seemed etched in stone, and I was pretty damn sick of it. As I pictured her, Rusty was the blithe spirit who would laugh everything off, shrug at perils as various as freshman mixers, bad grades, and cafeterias jammed with aloof strangers, and in general pass through a room with all the vitality and appeal of a cool gust of wind.

But when I arrived at college, Rusty had vaporized. She was simply not in the station wagon that drove me up to campus. Much of college had to do with filling in the blanks, but changing myself would not be so easy, so predictable, so clichéd.

My parents, acting as anxious overseers on the hot, humid day I took my new self to college, seemed bound by a demonic ESP to sabotage my scarcely budding new identity. After a summer planning how I would metamorphose into the great American ideal, the normal teenage girl, I heard my mother tell my roommate, "I think you'll like Jenny—she's quite the oddball." Luckily, my roommate was saturated with all kinds of information the first day of college had flung at her, and the last thing she was paying attention to were the off-the-cuff remarks this oddball's mother was making. My unmarked reputation kept its sheen as it waited for me to cautiously build it up according to plan. My parents left without any further blunders, except to brush my bangs from my eyes ("You'll get a headache, Sweetheart") and foist on what had been a blissfully bare dormitory room an excruciatingly ugly lamp from home. As soon as the station wagon became a distant mote of dust on the highway, I pulled my bangs back over my eyes in my New Wave fashion of choice, tossed the ugly lamp in the nearest trash can, and did what I came to college to do. Anonymous, alone, without even a name, I would start over and become the kind of person I was meant to be: like myself, but better, with all failures, rejections, and sexual indiscretions relegated to a history I hoped none of my new acquaintances would ever hear of.

Why was it, I wondered, when *any* change seemed possible that year, had it been so impossible in high school? For one thing people know us well enough to see when we're attempting a change, and change can look embarrassingly like a public admission of weakness. Our secret desires, and the fact that we're not entirely pleased with ourselves, are on display. To change in public under the scrutiny of the most hypercritical witnesses in the world—other high school students—is to risk failure ("Look how cool she's trying to be, the jerk!") or succeeding but betraying friends in the process ("I don't understand her any more," they say, hurt and angry) or feeling so much like a fraud that you're forced to back down. And while we live at home, parental expectations, from the lovingly hopeful to the intolerably ambitious, apply the pressure of an invisible but very effective mold.

Jacki dressed in nothing but baggy Levi's and flannel shirts for what seemed to be the endless duration of high school, even though she came to a sort of truce with her developing woman's body in eleventh grade and wasn't averse any longer to looking pretty. Looking good in college was a fantasy she savored because in high school, "I didn't want to make the attempt in public and then fail," she explains now, looking pulled-together and chic. "I thought everyone would think I was trying to look good but I only managed to look weird. And I didn't want a certain group of girls who were very image-conscious to think they'd won some kind of victory either, that I was changing to please them.

"So I waited for college, and wore nice, new clothes right off the bat so nobody would know me any other way. I had set my expectation too high, though—I sort of thought that I'd be transformed into a kind of *femme fatale* or something. When I wasn't measuring up to what I'd imagined, I almost ditched the whole thing until I realized that at least I wasn't sabotaging myself any more. When I ran into a friend from high school, even though I had gotten used to the nice way I looked, I was scared that she could see right through my disguise. That's how I felt for a long time: a slobby girl just pretending to be pulled together."

At first, any change can feel uncomfortably like a pretense, an affectation. Dana had been a punked-out druggy in high school, so worried about being considered a grind that she didn't use a fraction of her considerable vocabulary when she was around her anti-intellectual friends. She promised herself to get serious academically in college, but the first night she spent studying in the science library, she recalls, "I half-expected the other kids to look twice at me, as if my fish-out-of-water feeling was showing. Of course, it wasn't. But it was schizophrenic at first, as if I were an impostor only playing at being smart. But when you do something long enough, that thing becomes *you*. It's not playing anymore. It's what you are."

Wanting to change yourself finds its source in two wellsprings: self-hatred and self-affirmation. Self-affirmation takes what already exists in your personality (even if slightly stunted or twisted) and encourages its growth. Where self-affirmation is expansive, self-hatred is reductive, negating one's own personality while appropriating qualities external to it and applying them like thick pancake makeup.

Joan's thing was to hang out with rich kids with what can only be described as a vengeance. She dressed in Ralph Lauren, forayed to town for $75 haircuts, and complained about the tackiness of mutual friends. But after a late night of studying, Joan allowed her self-control to slip long enough to tell me of her upbringing. Her mother was a cocktail waitress and Joan had never even found out her father's name. She and her mother had trucked about from one Western trailer park to another, and Joan always went to school dogged by her wrong-side-of-the-tracks background. That Joan had come through her hardscrabble life with such strong intellectual achievement seemed a lot more credible—not to mention interesting—than the effortless achievements of many of our more privileged classmates. Joan didn't think so, and, I suppose in fear I'd blow her cover (I never did), she cut me dead after her moment's indulgence in self-revelation. Joan was rootless and anxious, alienated not only from her background but, by extension, from herself, and paid a heavy psychic price. This wasn't change: this was lies. She scared me. But we learn a lot about friends from the kinds of masks they choose to wear.

After all, role-playing to some degree is the prerogative of youth. A woman of romance, rigorous academic, trendy New Waver, intense politico, unsentimental jock, by turn—we have the chance to experiment as we decide the kind of person we want to become. And a stereotypical role, adopted temporarily, can offer refuge from the swirl of confusing choices available to us, by confining us to the limits of a type. Returning to my old self after playing a role, I find I'm slightly different, a little bit more than what I was. To contradict one's self is to transcend it.

As occasional fugitives from our families, we all sometimes do what Joan did. Sometimes you need a radical change in order to form an identity independent of your family, even if that change is a weird but transient reaction. My friend Lisa came from a family of feminists and academics. When she returned home from school for Thanksgiving, dressed as a "ditsy dame" straight out of a beach-blanket-bingo movie, she asked me, "How do you think I look? I've been planning this since tenth grade. Isn't it great?" Well, er, yes, it was great—not because she looked like a Barbie doll incarnate but because nobody would ever automatically connect her life with that of her parents again.

Another friend, Dan, went from a Southern military academy to a Quaker college in the North to execute his scheme of becoming a serious intellectual. The transformation went awry after a few months, partly because his own self was too likably irrepressible. It wouldn't lie down and play dead. "I kept running into myself like a serpent chasing its tail," as he puts it. But his openness to change resulted in a peculiar amalgamation of cultures whose charm lies in his realizing that, while he's of his background, he's not identical to it. Most of our personalities and bodies are just as stubbornly averse to being extinguished, even if the fantasy of a symbolic suicide and a renaissance from the ashes takes its obsessive tool on our thoughts now and again. But a blank slate isn't the same as a blank self, and the point of the blank slate that college provides is not to erase the past, but to sketch out a new history with a revisionist's perspective and an optimist's acts.

And what of my changes? Well, when I was friendly and happy in college, nobody gaped as though I had sprouted a tail. I learned to laugh things off as Rusty might have done, and there was one particular counterman at the corner luncheonette who called me Red, which was the closest I came to being known as Rusty.

What became of Rusty? Senior year, I stared at an announcement stating the dates that banks would be recruiting on campus, and Rusty materialized for the first time since freshman year. Rusty was a Yuppie now, and I pictured her dressed in a navy-blue suit, looking uneasily like Mary Cunningham, setting her sights on Citibank. I was still the high-strung, oversensitive, would-be writer (I'm happy to report my skin did clear up), but a little better, who left the corporate world to be Rusty. For myself, I have the slate of the rest of my life to write on.

1984

CRITICAL THINKING POINTS: *After you've read*

1. How can even flattering reputations become "as confining as a pair of too-tight shoes"?

2. What might Crichton mean when she says, "Wanting to change yourself finds its source in two wellsprings: self-hatred and self-affirmation"?

3. Crichton says her friend Dan realized that "while he's of his background, he's not identical to it." Do you feel as though you are "identical" to your background? Why or why not?

SOME POSSIBILITIES FOR WRITING

1. Crichton creates a new persona in "Rusty." Create a new persona for yourself and write a scene that shows, not tells, what this character is like by what the character does and/or by how he or she does it.

2. In what ways is a student a "soul in transit," as Crichton says? In what ways can college offer students the chance to "re-make" themselves? To "re-make" their lives? Do you believe it will happen to you? Why or why not?

3. How have you changed since you've been at college? Have you noticed yourself acting, eating, socializing, or dressing differently than you did in high school? If you don't see any noticeable changes yet, speculate about why you might or might not change dramatically.

What It's Really Like

Frank Smoot

In addition to poems and short stories, Frank Smoot (b. 1961) has published some two hundred articles, including editorials, essays, features, interviews, and critiques of art, dance, film, literature, and music. He is currently Director of Publications and Marketing for the Chippewa Valley Museum in Eau Claire, Wisconsin.

you think it's too bad you'll never know each other

CRITICAL THINKING POINTS: *As you read*

1. What do you make of the title? Does this poem portray "what it's really like"? Why or why not?
2. What kind of people are the characters in this poem? List some adjectives that describe them.
3. Keep track of all the things that the narrator can and cannot know in this poem.

It would be comforting to know something
about her that would annoy you: she laughs
like a hyena or likes a kind of music that you hate.
But the truth is that she's nice and so are you,
and as you drive away from the small light
of the restaurant on the highway in another state
you think it's too bad you'll never know each other,
and you look at yourself in the rearview mirror,
your face lighted dimly by the dashboard,
and smile because she smiled at you.
You kick it out a little, thumbs tapping
to the sweet song on the radio, to which,
you have no way of knowing,
she's dancing as she closes up.

1995

CRITICAL THINKING POINTS: *After you've read*

1. Why is this brief moment significant enough to write about? Is it important to anyone but the characters? Why or why not?

2. Would the woman in the poem most likely be interested in the speaker? Why or why not?

3. Should the speaker of the poem have said something to the woman? Why or why not?

SOME POSSIBILITIES FOR WRITING

1. Write the next scene for one or both of the characters in the poem. Where do they go after this? Who do they talk to? What do they do?

2. Visit some gathering place for college students—a student lounge, a commons area, or a cafeteria—and write a "history" for some of the couples you see around you but know nothing about.

3. Write your own imitation of this poem, maybe "What It's Never Like," or "What It Could Have Been Like."

No More Kissing—AIDS Everywhere

Michael Blumenthal

Michael Blumenthal (b. 1949) is the author of five volumes of poems, including The Wages of Goodness (University of Missouri Press, 1992). His novel Weinstock Among the Dying (Zoland Books, 1993) won Hadassah Magazine's Harold U. Ribelow Prize for Fiction. He lives and writes in Austin, Texas.

"You must remember," / he said, "that every time you make love / you tamper with fate."

CRITICAL THINKING POINTS: *As you read*

1. What are some sexual images in the poem? List them as you read.
2. Traditionally in love poems, images of love are linked with images of death. What are some images of love that have been paired with death in this poem?
3. What might be the "etymological roots" Blumenthal writes about?

He says it to the young couple
passionately kissing on the street
and, when he does, the four of us just stand there,
laughing, on this cold wintry day in Cambridge,
nineteen hundred and eighty-eight,
as if there could be no such danger
to a kiss, as if the metaphors of love and dying
had not been literalized.

Pausing a block later, my cheeks kissed
by the cold, my lips cracking
in the January air, I think back
to what a man once told me, long before
risk had so clinical a name,
so precise a passage. *"You must remember,"*
he said, *"that every time you make love
you tamper with fate."*

Now, the early wisdoms grow clear:
the serpents slither into the year,

the elegies are writing themselves
on desires' sheets, passion and suffering
are fusing their etymological roots
into a single trunk. *Yet why should they not embrace,*
these beautiful two? They are, after all, part
of the oldest story in the world—before God,
before microbes, before the sea had licked
the earth and the air clean with its long tongue.

1989

CRITICAL THINKING POINTS: *After you've read*

1. How is this poem a reflection of the time in which it was written?
2. What might be some of the things suggested by the "oldest story in the world" that the poet refers to?
3. In what ways have the "metaphors of love and dying" been "literalized"?

SOME POSSIBILITIES FOR WRITING

1. Do you believe "that every time you make love you tamper with fate"? In what ways is this statement true? What aspects of fate are tampered with? Write a one-page response supporting or contradicting this statement.
2. Write a response from the point of view of the young couple who are kissing. What might they say to the man who yells out his warning to them? To the advice given in the second stanza? To the poet at the end of the poem?
3. In what ways has the existence of AIDS shaped your attitudes and behaviors concerning sex?

The Blue-Light System

FROM *THE MORNING AFTER: SEX, FEAR, AND FEMINISM ON CAMPUS*   Katie Roiphe

Her book *The Morning After: Sex, Fear, and Feminism on Campus* catapulted Katie Roiphe (b. 1968) into a media spotlight. Its assertions about issues of violence against women, victimization, and contemporary feminist thinking demonstrated the author's strong opinions in these areas and was critical of the direction she felt the struggle for women's rights had taken during the 1980s.

Now the idea of random encounters, of joyful, loveless SEX, raises eyebrows. The possibility of adventure is clouded by the specter of illness. It's a difficult backdrop for conducting one's youth.

CRITICAL THINKING POINTS: *As you read*

1. What kinds of precautions were you told about during the new students' orientation on your campus? Do you feel that orientation prepared you for a safe life on campus? Why or why not?

2. In this essay, what kinds of "warnings" concerning sex are aimed specifically at male college students? How do these compare to the warnings aimed at female college students?

3. Roiphe builds her essay on "oppositions," seemingly self-contradictory ideas. List some as you read.

W ith its magnolia trees, its gray Gothic buildings, Princeton's pastoral campus looks like it hasn't changed much over the last century. But when the sun goes down, it's clear that the last five years have altered the face of the campus. There are still freshmen wandering around late at night, but there are also blue lights up all over campus in case someone pulls you into the darkness. The blue lights above security phones, part of what is often called the blue-light system, were erected on many campuses in the eighties. Since the phones aren't actually used much for emergencies, their primary function seems to be to reassure the lone wanderer. Having started with fifteen lights and added some each year, Princeton now has around seventy. The blue lights mark a new and systematic sense of danger. People may have always been scared walking around campuses late at night, but now, bathed in blue light, they are officially scared.

As freshmen in the late eighties and early nineties, we arrived at college amid a flurry of warnings: "Since you cannot tell who has the potential for rape by simply looking, be on your guard with every man." "Do not put yourself in vulnerable situations." "Condoms are not perfect and they do not provide 'safe sex.'" "To eliminate risk, abstain from sex or avoid sexual intimacy beyond fantasy, massage and mutual masturbation." "Over fifty percent of all female college students experience some form of sexual victimization or sexual harassment." "No birth control is one hundred percent effective except the word 'No!'" "Are you hearing LOVE when your boyfriend is saying SEX?" "One in four college women has experienced rape or attempted rape since age fourteen." As we are settling into our new surroundings, there are fliers and counselors and videotapes telling us how not to get AIDS and how not to get raped, where not to wander and what signals not to send. By the end of freshman week, we know exactly what not to do. Once we make it through the workshops and pamphlets on date rape, safe SEX, and sexual harassment, no matter how bold and adolescent, how rebellious and reckless, we are left with an impression of imminent danger. And then there are the whistles. Female freshmen arriving at Wesleyan and other campuses are given whistles to protect them against rape and assault. For the past couple of years at Princeton, there has been someone outside the building during registration offering these whistles to female students on their way out.

Several years ago, parents and prospective students on tours of the Wesleyan campus saw more of college life than they expected. As they were touring the campus, looking at the library and the classrooms, the students playing Frisbee on the grass and the freshman dorms, the cheerful patter of the tour guide was interrupted by the impassioned words of a feminist student. She delivered a three-minute speech about the danger of rape, warning parents and prospective students to take the university's response to the rape crisis into consideration when applying to college.

She urged them to ask the administration questions about security and blue lights. The rape crisis is not just at Wesleyan but everywhere, she told them.

That spring she and another student involved in this dramatic effort at what would have once been called consciousness-raising disrupted many tours, raising the ire of the administration. Parents and prospective students were shaken. Needless to say, the admissions office was not happy to have the issue of date rape thrust at students on the brink of their decision about colleges. Parents, already worried about sending their children to a strange place, had another source of concern to add to their list. But the guerrilla feminists were effective in their purpose: they successfully planted the fear of rape in the minds of prospective students before they even reached the Wesleyan campus.

Word of mouth, then, comes from older students as well as university staff. The barrage of warnings is not just the product of a bureaucratic mechanism churning out pieces of paper. The warnings are not just official university policy filtering down to us from above. There are faces and stories behind these warnings. They have taken hold of student attention. Students run women's centers and hot lines, workshops and peer-counseling groups. They write plays and design videos and posters about rape. Campus literary magazines and political journals are filled with stories and poems about sexual danger. Most visibly, most dramatically, students organize and march against rape. I remember myself, a bewildered freshman, watching candle-lit faces weave snakelike through campus. Angry voices were chanting "Two, four, six, eight, no more date rape," and the marchers carried signs saying "Take Back the Night." I remember an older student from my high school, whom I'd always respected, always thought particularly glamorous, marching, her face flushed with emotion, and I wondered what it was about. Before the chants condensed into meaning, when they were still sounds instead of words, I wondered whom they wanted the night back from and what they wanted it back for. The confusion was not just mine.

The vague poetic symbols of the campus movement against rape speak of a more general fear. As the marchers passed, I wandered back to my dorm through the still unfamiliar campus, the darkness suddenly charged with a nameless threat.

In this era of Just Say No and No Means No, we don't have many words for embracing experience. Now instead of liberation and libido, the emphasis is on trauma and disease. Now the idea of random encounters, of joyful, loveless SEX, raises eyebrows. The possibility of adventure is clouded by the specter of illness. It's a difficult backdrop for conducting one's youth.

What further complicates sexual existence is that the sexual revolution hasn't been entirely erased by a new ethos of sexual conservatism. Free love hasn't been entirely eclipsed by safe SEX. Sexual climates do not rove across our experience like cold fronts on a weather map. Instead, they linger and accumulate. Today's culture of caution coexists with yesterday's devil-may-care. Encouraged, discouraged, condemned, condoned, youthful sexual activity is met with powerful and conflicting responses. Everywhere we look there are signs of sexual puritanism, but there are also signs of sexual abandon. Adding to the mixed messages are signs of sexual danger.

On the subway, next to a condom ad in Spanish, there is an ad for perfume showing a naked man carrying a naked woman over his shoulder. On an average day we are flooded with images of erotic promise: the topless couple in a Calvin Klein underwear ad; a poster of an ecstatic Madonna with her stomach bare, her jeans unbuttoned, her book, *SEX*, on the cover of *Newsweek*; the pornographic section of our video store; the XXX movie houses in certain neighborhoods; men with long hair, chests bare, arms around each other, in an advertisement for Banana Republic, and the list goes on. We may not always notice these images, but like buildings and trees, they are part of our landscape.

This is a culture that pulls both ways. Pat Buchanan rails about the importance of sexual morality, and Banana Republic uses SEX to sell clothes. We've been hearing Reagan and then Bush drone on about family values for as long as we can remember, but we haven't lost the myth of the casual encounter. Pressures clash. Our ears were filled simultaneously with Nancy Reagan's Just Say No and George Michael's late-'80s hit song "I Want Your SEX." An image from deep childhood perfectly captures today's conflicted sexual climate: Dr. Dolittle's two-headed creature, the pushmi-pullyu.

There's no doubt that some people are running around thinking only about pleasure and whom they're going to go home with after a party. But that is not the whole story. Many are more concerned with getting ahead and getting a nice car than getting drunk and getting laid. The pressure to do well and make money in an age of diminishing economic expectations looms larger than it did for those who went to college in the '60s and '70s.

Finding yourself pales in comparison to supporting yourself. These days desire is often tailored by a pre-professional pragmatism, and many undergraduates, although not necessarily the ones I knew, are keeping their lives, sexually and otherwise, in relative order.

Yes, they are arguing about whether to teach abstinence in New York City's public schools, and yes, there are more pressures to stay faithful and stay at home, but we still haven't lost the idea of the sexual revolution. We still hear stories from older brothers, sisters, cousins, and aunts about sleeping around and not caring, and feeling free and pretending to feel free.

I remember, when I was young, hearing my older sister tell my mother that she was the last person on earth who was faithful to her husband. I turned to look at my mother, imagining her as a dinosaur, the kind they keep at the Museum of Natural History. Everyone else, my sister told me, was into free love and all that. I remember exactly where we were sitting when we had that conversation. I remember the color of the couch. And I remember the visions of having dozens of husbands, like a bouquet of flowers, running through my mind.

The sexual revolutionaries, then, have made their impression, and we are still impressed. Warnings about sexual harassment and sexual disease compete with wanton images of sexual freedom. Even though attitudes toward sexual experimentation have changed, many people still think of it as a necessary stage. We are still intrigued and pressured and exhausted by the sexual revolution. Although we may have developed an almost blasé attitude toward the absolute ideals of libertinism, they still exert a strong presence in the way we think and the choices we make.

People tell me that SEX should be as free as it was not so long ago, that we shouldn't have to use discretion and condoms. We may have been thinking about AIDS for about as long as we've been thinking about SEX, but many of us still expect to experiment. While there is a strong cultural belief that sexual adventure is a minefield of rape and disease, there is also a lingering refrain: this is not the way it's supposed to be.

The shift from free love to safe SEX is itself part of our experience. Our sexual climate, then, incorporates the movement from one set of sexual mores to another.

The presence of the past complicates our decisions. Messages mix, and our imaginations catch hold of one, then the other, dragging our bodies this way and that. I remember the parties, dark rooms, beer, cigarettes, dancing shadows dressed in mostly black. In the corner a vodka punch, with a cherry taste. Girls were dancing with girls, some because they were interested in each other, others because they were trying to catch the attention of the boy across the room. That spring, girls had started taking their shirts off at parties. I remember the bras, black lace, white lace, pink lace. There was a drama in dancing in bras, in crushing taboos beneath our feet. For most people, boys were in the background those nights. They were not the point. Dancing without shirts was intended as a bold statement about the triumph of the female body, an eyecatching, spirit-lifting display of sexual availability. As music surged, as bodies pressed against each other, it was a show of sexuality, freedom, and power, a charade of earlier, wilder days. We definitely had something to prove, and beneath all the bacchanalian urgency, there was something calculating, something self-conscious, something designed to impress. But what was there to prove in the dark room surrounded by people who had eaten breakfast, lunch, and dinner together every day for years? The point, I think, was to exhibit a power, as well as a freedom we didn't quite have.

In the dark, without shirts, it was ourselves we were trying to impress. It was, above all, a dance of control, and the rhythm was frustration.

That same spring, most of the shirtless dancers would shout about date rape until they were hoarse at Take Back the Night. To many observers the conjunction of these two activities seemed contradictory, even hypocritical. But dancing without shirts and marching at Take Back the Night are, strange as it seems, part of the same parade. The different drums of sexual desirability, strength and vulnerability, frustration and fear, are all part of the group exhibitionism: the same show of power, and the same dance of control.

Liquor and parties still hold their allure for the freshman, but it's an allure full of complications and second thoughts. Hormones run high at this age, but they mix uneasily with worry. Maybe the freshman hasn't had much experience with boys. Maybe her parents were strict about curfews. In jeans, lipstick, and a tight black shirt, maybe she's finally at a real party with upperclassmen.

This is a generic story. Our freshman gets a beer, and a handsome boy from one of her classes, she doesn't remember which, comes up and flirts with her. She smiles at him, and in that instant she tries to calculate the risks. She tries to remember which girl she saw him with last week. She looks at his torn jeans, he looks bisexual, he looks like he might be one of those sullen-youth types who have spent a summer in the East Village injecting heroin. People are dancing to the pounding music, "However do you want me. However do you need me." The music makes it hard to hear each other, and he suggests they go up to his room to talk.

She hesitates. Flashes of the play she just saw about date rape run through her head. His invitation evokes the black-and-white print of the manual warning her about AIDS. Someone she knows has just caught herpes. All around her people are dancing. Her drink is beginning to blur the edges of her vision. Maybe she goes with him, maybe she doesn't, but either way the situation is complicated. Pleasure is charged with danger, safety with regret.

For both male and female college students, the usual drive toward sexual experience collides with the powerful drive against it. No matter how you choose to behave when it comes down to it at midnight on a Saturday, the conflicting pressures and contemporary taboos are with you in one way or another.

These pressures and taboos leave their traces all over campuses, in conversations and classrooms, in meetings and on bathroom walls. In the women's bathroom in the basement of the Princeton library, someone has scribbled "Sex is death," and in another bathroom someone has written "Sex is rape." These extreme and dramatic aphorisms spring from a fierce suspicion of sex. For most seventeen-year-olds college opens up a whole realm of sexual possibility, and some of the attention lavished on the darker, violent side of sex comes from a deep ambivalence about what that freedom actually entails.

In another Princeton bathroom, someone has written "There is no such thing as safe sex," and underneath it someone has added in bold letters, "Isolation is the best protection." Another person asks the communal wall, "Are you scared walking around late at night?" Several scribblers have answered yes.

At Wesleyan, the bathroom walls are filled with written conversations about rape and sexual harassment. Some people have named names, and there are comments back and forth. At Carleton College, in the bathroom on the third floor of the library, there is a list of alleged date rapists, popularly referred to as the "castration list."[*] Brown has a similar list. These lists are intended to allow victims to voice their experience in a safe, anonymous space. They enable victims to accuse without confrontation and consequences. Several campuses have erected "Walls of Shame" with a similar, though more public purpose, and at Columbia, students have posted the names of alleged date rapists on pieces of paper all over campus.

From cynical truisms about sex to written exchanges about date rape, on these campus walls expressions of sexuality are mingled with fear. The message is about danger and safety, about the perceived conflict between sex and well-being. Students have lost their faith in the simplicity of the sexual encounter, in the do-what-you-want-and-don't-worry-about-it mentality. The proverbial locker room is cluttered with a whole new set of sexual anxieties. These graffiti writers aren't worried about enough freedom anymore; they are worried about too much danger.

1993

CRITICAL THINKING POINTS: *After you've read*

1. Wesleyan is an all-women university. Why might parents and students have been shocked or at least uneasy about the feminist student who interrupted the pre-college tour to offer warnings about rape?

2. Roiphe started college during the Reagan and the first Bush administrations. Why might the American public's perception of sexuality have changed since then?

3. Roiphe says, "We still hear stories from older brothers, sisters, cousins, and aunts about sleeping around and not caring, and feeling free and pretending to feel free." What do you think she means?

[*]*Chronicle of Higher Education,* 15 May 1991.

SOME POSSIBILITIES FOR WRITING

1. Imagine that Roiphe is visiting your campus as part of a lecture series. Write down five questions you'd like to ask her.

2. This essay does not mention the choices that male college students must make concerning sex. From the male point of view, write a letter to Roiphe describing what she has overlooked in her essay.

3. What are some of the causes of sex and fear being linked in this essay? What are some of the effects of sex and fear being linked?

Dear Concerned Mother

Jill Wolfson

Jill Wolfson is co-author of *Somebody Else's Children: The Courts, the Kids, and the Struggle to Save America's Troubled Families* (Crown, 1997), and she reviews books for the *San Jose Mercury News*. She lives in Northern California.

My writing students in juvenile hall—addicts, thieves, gang bangers—have great parenting advice. All you have to do is ask.

CRITICAL THINKING POINTS: *As you read*

1. What kinds of advice do the students give to their teacher about her son? Why do you think they offer what they do?
2. What do you think is the best and the worst advice they give? Why?
3. What kinds of things do you think this teacher is trying to teach to her class?

I t was a Friday evening, and my 15-year-old son and I were at each other's throats. Most of the time these days, he is what my Yiddish-speaking grandmother used to call "farbissen"—sharp and sulky. He can find fault with the sky just by looking up. Between us, nothing is not an issue: his room, his grades, his behavior around the house, his friends. I harangued him a little more, let him get in the last word and headed out the front door, fuming.

On Friday nights, I run a writing class at the local juvenile hall. Most weeks, I am unrelentingly earnest with the incarcerated boys. I sweep in with my papers and books, and commence acting like everybody's dotty but ultimately harmless aunt. I wax poetic about the healing powers of writing. I show them intriguing words in the dictionary as if I am pointing out jewels. I gush over their work, frequently some of the most funny, sad, troubling, surprising, insightful and silly bits of writing you can imagine. But when I was buzzed into the hall that night, I felt sapped. I had not one iota of patience left for mankind—especially mankind of the 15-year-old, wispy mustache, smart mouth, smelly feet variety.

"It's been a real full-moon day here," a weary-looking staffer said. Great, I thought, just what I need to cap off the week—a room full of moody, pissed off, sullen gang members, addicts and thieves. My class would be smaller than usual since many of the young men had had their evening privileges revoked and were locked down in their cells. Participation in my writing program is considered a privilege, though you wouldn't have known it by the response I got when I greeted the half-dozen writers-in-waiting.

"Oh no! I'm not gonna write. Why should I write?" said Josh, a handsome boy who likes to dabble in White Power philosophy.

A young man who calls himself J-Money greeted me in his usual taunting manner. "I'm gonna write about being down for my gang. I'm gonna write about bitches and pussy."

"I have nothing to write about!" complained a boy nicknamed Storm. Storm and I often joke about how I—as much as anyone in his life—have watched him grow up, from a scared and scrawny 14-year-old street kid to a broad and buff 17-year-old with a huge dagger tattooed on his forearm. Storm, who always claims to have nothing on his mind to write about, is scheduled to stand trial as an adult for a well-publicized murder.

Soft-spoken, pasty-faced Gabe is another boy I often worry about. That night, I noticed fresh white bandages wrapped around his wrists. In juvenile hall parlance, Gabe is what is referred to as a cutter. No matter how frequently and thoroughly the staff searches him and his cell, he always manages to squirrel away a razor, a staple, the point of a pen, anything capable of carving into his flesh. Gabe also happens to be a remarkable and prolific poet. But even he was now determined to put me through the wringer: "I'm not writing tonight. That's final."

Without comment, I passed out paper and pencil and announced the evening's topic: Fear.

"What is your definition of fear?" I asked. "What are you afraid of? How do you handle your fears?" I tried putting some oomph into my voice—"Be honest. Get real with your words"—but even to my own ears I sounded flat and uninspired.

They didn't even give the topic a halfhearted try. J-Money, the king of posturing, wrote, "I ain't afraid of nothin'." Storm dashed out one poorly spelled sentence, "I'm afraid of Ben Laden and Anthrix," before pushing his paper aside. For most everyone else in the country, this would be a perfectly valid answer. But for Storm, I knew it was bullshit. He knew I knew it was bullshit. When you are 17 years old and looking at the probability of spending the next 25 years in San Quentin, even terrorism is a comfortable abstraction, a way of running from the truth. Normally, I would have attempted to move the boys, word by word, into examining their past, present and future. But I just couldn't muster the energy to steamroll over any more adolescent negativity. When I threw up my hands, it was not just at them, but at all teenage boys, especially the one who lived in my house.

"So don't write," I said. "Just sit here and give me a lot of crap. Waste your time."

I couldn't believe I was saying this. I knew I sounded vaguely hysterical. They stared, trying to figure out whether this was some new kind of motivational trick that I had up my sleeve. Josh finally decided that my funk was for real. "Whooo! Mama! What's the matter with you today?"

"Nothing," I said. This time, I was the one who was petulant, slumped in my chair like I didn't have any bones.

"Something's bugging you. Come on."

"Problems with my son," I pouted. "You're not interested."

But I could tell by the sudden buzz of alertness in the room that they were, in fact, extremely interested. I have always made it a point to leave my own moods at the thick metal door when it slams behind me. I figure that these kids have enough problems of their own—heroin addiction, incompetent public defenders, raging hormones, girlfriends who don't write, homeboys who have ratted them out, staff members who are always on their case—without having to endure mine.

But now, why not? So I laid it all out, the full banquet of bad grades and self-destructive attitudes. I even mentioned that I had found a pipe in my son's room the week before and it scared me.

"That's what my fear is," I confessed. "I'm angry at him a lot, but I'm also afraid for him, the choices he's making."

A boy named Bobby smirked the entire time and I felt like smacking him. "Uh-oh," he said, "The Writing Lady's son be smoking the weed, doing the doob, getting high. He's gonna be in here before long. Don't worry, Writing Lady, we'll take good care of him."

"Thanks a million, Bobby," I said sarcastically. But then, Josh jumped to my defense. "Shut up, Bobby, what the fuck you saying? Don't you see this is serious?"

And then, in imitation of every psychologist who had ever interviewed him for court, Josh leaned in and looked at me with earnest, intelligent eyes: "Just don't go nagging him. Nag, nag, nag. That's what's drove me crazy with my mom."

"So what I am supposed to do?"

"Back off him like my mom finally did me. He'll get it on his own."

I mulled this over. "I don't mean any disrespect, Josh. But you've got a serious drug problem and your life isn't exactly doing so hot. I'd rather he doesn't wind up in here while he's figuring things out for himself."

A half-dozen voices joined in with comments. I had never seen all of them so charged up at once before. It dawned on me then how I am the one always dishing out advice to them, not just about synonyms, but about how to deal with drugs, how to do better in school, how to make productive use of the endless hours they spend alone in their cells. The pattern is the same with all the adults in their lives, from parents to probation officers.

But how often are these young men—so often scolded and lectured, so often in the wrong—asked for their advice? How often do guys with names like Storm and J-Money get asked what they think, what they know about the world? How often do they get to give their expertise? And on the subject of troubled, uncommunicative teens, they are definitely the experts.

"Let's scrap writing about fear," I suggested. "Instead, let's pretend you are all advice columnists in the newspaper and I have written to you with my problem. What would you tell me?"

With little coaxing, they got to work. A half hour later, they read their columns aloud. I sat in my chair and let their answers wash over me. Their opinions, like a lot of their writing, reflected a desperate eagerness to be heard and to help. I felt their support and their solace. I could see their pasts, so much of what was right and so much of what was wrong. In their words, I also got some meaningful and some seriously twisted parenting advice.

A quiet 15-year-old named Omar spoke for the first time ever in class: "Dear Concerned Mother. You got to do something with him. I used to think nobody should tell me nothing. But now that I'm a dad myself, I tell my girlfriend we got to draw some lines with my son. My mom never drew lines and look at me. Don't listen to what Josh says. You should take things away from him. Lock him in his room. Ground him. Slap him across the back of the head if you have to."

At that, Gabe shouted "No!" I don't know the details of Gabe's family life. He never writes directly about it, but I once asked a staff person who replied, "Anything awful you can think of has been done to that boy by his parents."

"Whatever you do," he read from his paper, "don't, don't, don't hit him. That's child abuse. Hitting will only make a kid more frustrated and scared. That's a reason kids run away."

Others continued:

Dear Concerned Mother,

I feel that your son can't talk to you because of the way you react. You must be judging him. Lecture him but don't ever hit him. At the same time, tell him that it's his life and he has to do what he wants. If he makes the right choice, let him know. If he makes the wrong choice, ask him what he has learned from it. His choices will be a learning experience. If he has to learn the hard way, so be it!

Dear Concerned Mother,

Treat your son with respect. Buy him anything he wants. Don't yell at him. Don't hit him.

Dear Concerned Mother,

It's not your fault that your teenager is like that. He's going through a state where he thinks he's this person, but he's not—if you know what I mean. You could try to help but he'll just turn it down. He probably doesn't feel comfortable talking to you because he thinks you don't understand. Get to know him. Study the way he is and then get him to trust you.

Dear Concerned Mother,

He's going to try drugs. That's just the way it is. You could put him in sports to occupy his time. When I was playing football, I didn't have time for drugs. That was before I messed up and landed here.

Dear Concerned Mother,

Don't take him to a therapist. God forbid! He'll just sit there. It'll go in one ear and out the other.

Dear Concerned Mother,

Don't lock him in his room and duck tape the door shut like my step-mother used to do.

When it was Storm's turn, he began:

Dear Concerned Mother,

Your kid probably has a lot of stress right now. In elementary school, he only had one teacher and one class, right? Now he's got six classes and six teachers who are on him all the time. That's hard on a kid. Give him some space. You need to point out when he's doing something good—not just when he's messing up or only if he gets straight A's or wins the whole damn science fair.

And don't throw him against a wall and then throw him out of the house. That's what my dad did and how I wound up on the streets.

Oh yeah, and take him places. Take him miniature golfing. Have fun with him. You don't want your kid to learn from other people because he'll learn to steal and do things like that. You want him to get as much fun from YOU as he can. Tell him to dress punk and then say, "Guess what? We're going to a concert, you and me." I would have liked my mom to do something like that.

When Storm got to the end of his advice, he looked away sheepishly, caught with his tough-guy demeanor down. "But that's just my opinion," he added.

The writing workshop was over. They handed in their papers and left me with a lot to think about. Josh stayed behind for a few minutes.

"Good luck with your son," he said. "Did it help?"

"I think so. Yes, it definitely did."

"I got one more question for you. Does your son have a dad?"

I nodded yes and recalled what Josh had told me about his own father, how he "runs a prison." I knew Josh didn't mean that his dad is the warden. A longtime con, his father is the one who calls all the shots—from drug dealing to revenge killings—among the prisoners.

"Is he like a regular dad who does stuff with him? Baseball and shit like that?"

"Yes," I say.

"Well, you don't have to worry then." He patted me lightly on the shoulder, a wise old soul reassuring someone just getting her feet wet in the teenage parenting business. "Maybe he's doing some wild shit now. But hang in. Anyone who's got you and a dad around is going to be OK."

2001

CRITICAL THINKING POINTS: *After you've read*

1. Teachers often have lots of advice for their students. What if the tables were turned? What kinds of advice would you give to teachers if you could? Why would you advise them the way you would?
2. What would be some of the challenges and/or rewards of teaching a class like this?
3. What do you think the students might have learned from this class? What about the teacher? Why?

SOME POSSIBILITIES FOR WRITING

1. What might be some of the problems and/or advantages of being a child of a teacher? Why do you think the way you do?
2. Recall a time when teachers shared something personal in class, perhaps a problem they were having or a joy. How did the class react? Why do you think this was so?
3. The "Writing Lady" has some "fears" for her son. What are some of the fears your parents have had or still have for you? Do you feel these fears were justified? Why or why not?

The Undeclared Major

FROM *A GRAVESTONE MADE OF WHEAT*   Will Weaver

Will Weaver was born in northern Minnesota and grew up on a dairy farm. He teaches writing at Bemidji State University in Minnesota.

"Well," Walter said. His mouth went dry. He swallowed twice. "Well," he said, "I think I'm going to major in English."

His father pursed his lips. He pulled off his work gloves one finger at a time. "English," he said.

"English," Walter nodded.

His father squinted. "Son, you already know English."

CRITICAL THINKING POINTS: *As you read*

1. Why is it so difficult for Walter to tell his father about his intended major?
2. Pay attention to the description of the farm and its surroundings. Why might the author offer so many concrete details?
3. Why does it feel to Walter like he's the only "twenty-year-old Undeclared Major on the whole campus"?

I n his gloomy periods Walter Hansen saw himself as one large contradiction. He was still twenty, yet his reddish hair was in full retreat from the white plain of his forehead. He had small and quick-moving blue eyes, eyes that tended skyward, eyes that noted every airplane that passed overhead; his hands and feet were great, heavy shovels. As Walter shambled between his classes at the University of Minnesota in Minneapolis, he sometimes caught unexpected sight of himself in a tall glass doorway or window. He always stopped to stare: there he was, the big farm kid with a small handful of books. Walter Hansen, the only twenty-year-old Undeclared Major on the whole campus.

But even that wasn't true. Walter Hansen had declared a major some time ago; he just hadn't felt up to telling anyone what it was.

At present Walter sat in the last, backward-facing seat of the Greyhound bus, reading *The Collected Stories of John Cheever*. Occasionally he looked up to stare at the blue-tinted fields, which in their passing pulled him, mile by mile, toward home. Toward his twenty-first birthday this very weekend.

By the third hour of the trip Walter had a headache from reading. He put away Cheever and began to watch the passing farms. It was a sunny, wet April in central Minnesota. Farmers were trying to spread manure. Their tractors left black ruts in the yellow corn stubble, and once Walter saw two tractors chained together straining, the big rear wheels spinning, throwing clods in the air, as they tried to pull free a third spreader sunk its hubs beneath an overenthusiastic load of dung.

At the end of the fourth hour Walter's hometown came onto the horizon. It was low and scattered, and soon began to flash by in the windows of the slowing bus like a family slide show that was putting to sleep even the projector operator. A junkyard with a line of shining hubcaps nailed on the fence. A combination deer farm and aquarium with its stuffed black bear wearing a hula skirt, and wheels that stood by the front door. Then the tall and narrow white wooden houses. The square red brick buildings of Main Street, where the bus sighed to a stop at the Shell station. Ducking his head, Walter clambered down the bus steps and stood squinting in the sunlight.

Main Street was three blocks long. Its two-story buildings were fronted with painted tin awnings or cedar shake shingles to disguise the brick and make the buildings look lower and more modern. At the end of Main Street was the taller, dull gray tower of the feed mill. A yellow drift of cornmeal lay on its roof. A blue wheel of pigeons turned overhead. At the stoplight a '57 Chevy chirped its tires, accelerated rapidly for half a block, then braked sharply to turn down Main Street.

Which Walter planned to avoid. On Main Street he would have to speak to people. They would ask him things.

"Walt—so how's the rat race?"

"Walt—where does a person park down there?"

"So Walt, what was it you're going into again? Business? Engineering? Vetinary?"

Carrying his small suitcase, and looking neither left nor right, Walter slipped undetected across Main Street. He walked two blocks to the railroad crossing where he set out east.

The iron rails shone blue. Between the rails, tiny agates glinted red from their bed of gravel, and the flat, sun-warmed railroad ties exhaled a faint breath of creosote. On Walter's right, a robin dug for worms on the sunny south embankment; on the north side, the dirty remnant of a snowbank leaked water downhill. Walter stopped to poke at the snowbank with a stick. Beneath a black crust of mud and leaves, the snow was freshly white and sparkling—but destined, of course, to join the muddy pond water below. Walter thought about that. About destiny. He stood with the chill on his face from the old snowbank and the sun warm on his neck and back. There was a poem buried somewhere in the snowbank. Walter waited, but the first line would not visit him. He walked on.

Walter was soon out of town and into woods and fields. Arms outstretched, suitcase balanced atop his head, he walked one rail for twenty-two ties, certainly a record of some sort. Crows called. A red-headed woodpecker flopped from east to west across the rails. The bird was ridiculously heavy for the length of its wings, a fact which made Walter think of Natural Science, Biology, Veterinary Medicine and other majors with names as solid and normal as fork handles.

Animal Husbandry.

Technical Illustration.

Mechanical Engineering.

Ahead on Walter's left was a twenty-acre field of new oat seeding, brown in the low spots, dusty chartreuse on the higher crowns of the field.

Plant Science.

He could tell people he was developing new wheat strains for Third World countries, like Norman Borlaug.

He walked on, slower now, for around a slight bend he could see, a half mile ahead, the gray dome of his father's silo and the red shine of the dairy barn. He neared the corner post of the west field, where his father's land began. Half the field was gray, the other half was freshly black. He slowed further. A meadowlark called from the fence post. Walter stopped to pitch a rock at the bird.

Then he heard a tractor. From behind a broad swell in the field rose his father's blue cap, tan face, brown shirt, then the red snout of the Massey-Ferguson. The Massey pulled their green four-row corn planter. His father stood upright on the platform of the tractor. He stood that way to sight down the tractor's nose, to keep its front tired on the line scuffed in the dirt by the corn planter's marker on the previous round. Intermittently Walter's father swiveled his neck for a glance back at the planter. He looked, Walter knew, for the flap of a white rag tied around the main shaft; if the white flag waved, the main shaft turned, the planter plates revolved, pink kernels fell—Walter knew all that stuff.

He stopped walking. There were bushes along the fencerow, and he stooped to lower his profile, certain that his father hadn't seen him. First Walter wanted to go home, talk to his mother, have a cup of coffee. Two cups, maybe. A cinnamon roll. A bowl of big cherries in sauce, with cream. Maybe one more splash of coffee. Then. Then he'd come back to the field to speak with his father.

Nearing the field's end, his father trailed back his right arm, found the cord, which he pulled at the same moment as he turned hard to left. Brakes croaked. Tripped, the marker arms rose, the Massey came hard around with its front wheels reaching for their new track, the planter straightened behind, the right arm with its shining disk fell, and his father, back to Walter, headed downfield.

Except that brakes croaked again and the tractor came to a stop. His father turned to Walter and held up a hand.

Walter waved once. He looked briefly behind him to the rails that led back toward town, then crossed the ditch and swung his suitcase over the barbed wire.

His father shut off the tractor. "Hey Walt—" his father called.

Walter waved again.

His father waited by the corn planter. He smiled, his teeth white against the tan skin, the dust. Walter came up to him.

"Walt," his father said.

They stood there grinning at each other. They didn't shake hands. Growing up, Walter believed people shook hands only in the movies or on used-car lots. None of his relatives ever shook hands. Their greeting was to stand and grin at each other and raise their eyebrows up and down. At the university Walter and his friends shook hands coming and going, European style.

"How's it going?" Walter said, touching his boot to the corn planter.

"She's rolling," his father said. He squinted at Walter, looked down at his clean clothes. "What would you do for a stuck disk?" he asked.

"I'd take out the grease zerk and run a piece of wire in there. That failing, I'd take off the whole disk and soak it in a pan of diesel fuel overnight," Walter said.

Father and son grinned at each other.

His father took off his hat. His forehead was white, his hair coppery.

"So how's the rat race, son?"

"Not so bad," Walter said.

His father paused a moment. "Any . . . decisions yet?" his father said.

Walter swallowed. He looked off toward town. "About . . . a major, you mean?" Walter said.

His father waited.

"Well," Walter said. His mouth went dry. He swallowed twice. "Well," he said, "I think I'm going to major in English."

His father pursed his lips. He pulled off his work gloves one finger at a time. "English," he said.

"English," Walter nodded.

His father squinted. "Son, you already know English."

Walter stared. "Well, yessir, that's true. I mean, I'm going to study literature. Books. See how they're written. Maybe write one of my own some day."

His father rubbed his brown neck and stared downfield.

Two white sea gulls floated low over the fresh planting.

"So what do you think?" Walter said.

His father's forehead wrinkled and he turned back to Walter. "What could a person be, I mean with that kind of major? An English major," his father said, testing the phrase on his tongue and his lips.

"Be," Walter said. He fell silent. "Well I don't know, I could be a . . . writer. A teacher maybe, though I don't think I want to teach. At least not for a while. I could be . . . " Then Walter's mind went blank. As blank and empty as the fields around him.

His father was silent. The meadowlark called again.

"I would just be myself, I guess." Walter said.

His father stared a moment at Walter. "Yourself, only smarter," he added.

"Yessir," Walter said quickly, "that's it."

His father squinted downfield at the gulls, then back at Walter. "Nobody talked you into this?"

Walter shook his head no.

"You like it when you are doing it?" his father asked. He glanced across his own field, at what he had planted.

Walter nodded.

His father looked back to Walter and thought another moment. "You think you can make a living at it?"

"Somehow," Walter said.

His father shrugged. "Then I can't see any trouble with it myself," he said. He glanced away, across the field to the next closest set of barns and silos. "Your uncles, your grampa, they're another story, I suppose."

"They wouldn't have to know," Walter said quickly.

His father looked back to Walter and narrowed his eyes. "They ask me, I'll tell them," he said.

Walter smiled at his father. He started to take a step closer, but at that moment his father looked up at the sun. "We better keep rolling here," he said. He tossed his gloves to Walter. "Take her around once or twice while I eat my sandwich."

Walter climbed onto the tractor and brought up the RPMs. In another minute he was headed downfield. He stood upright on the platform and held tightly to the wheel. The leather gloves were still warm and damp from his father's hands. He sighted the Massey's radiator cap on the thin line on the dirt ahead, and held it there. Halfway downfield he remembered to check the planter flag; in one backward glance he saw his father in straight brown silhouette against the chartreuse band of the fencerow bushes, saw the stripe of fresh dirt unrolling behind, the green seed canisters, and below, the white flag waving. He let out a breath.

After two rounds, Walter began to relax. He began to feel the warm thermals from the engine, the cool breath of the earth below. Gulls hovered close over the tractor, their heads cocked earthward as they waited for the disks to turn up yellow cutworms. A red agate passed underneath and was covered by dirt. The corn planter rolled behind, and through the trip rope, a cotton cord gone smoothly black from grease and dusty kernels dropping, the press wheel tamping the seed into four perfect rows.

Well, not entirely perfect rows.

Walter, by round four, had begun to think of other things. That whiteness beneath the old snowbank. The blue shine of the iron rails. The damp warmth of father's gloves. The heavy, chocolate-layer birthday cake that he knew, as certain as he knew the sun would set tonight and rise tomorrow, his mother had hidden in the pantry. Of being twenty-one and the limitless destiny, the endless prospects before him, Walter Hansen, English Major.

As he thought about these and other things, the tractor and its planter drifted a foot to the right, then a foot to the left, centered itself, then drifted again. At field's end his father stood up. He began to wave at Walter first with one hand, then both. But Walter drove on, downfield, smiling slightly to himself, puzzling over why it was he so seldom came home.

1989

CRITICAL THINKING POINTS: *After you've read*

1. What are some of the advantages and disadvantages of being undeclared?
2. Why do you think it takes the author so long to get Walter home? What are some of the things the author hopes to accomplish?
3. Walter is part of the group of students that universities label "first-generation," that is, his parents did not attend college. What risks or difficulties might first-generation students face that others may not?

SOME POSSIBILITIES FOR WRITING

1. Research and present a report to your class on "majors." What are the most and least popular? Why do you think this is? What percentage of first-year students are undeclared? How often do students change majors? Why?
2. Have you and your parents ever disagreed on an important decision affecting your life? How and why was it resolved the way it was?
3. Prepare a report on what kinds of services and aid are available to students who are the first in their families to go to college.

The Good Student Apologizes to His Professor and to the Girl in Room 303

Ron Watson

Ron Watson's poems have appeared in such journals as *Kansas Quarterly* and *South Dakota Review.* He is a teacher for the Gifted and Talented Program in Madisonville, Kentucky.

It was only as they say
A phase I was going through with a girl my age
Who chose to sit with me
And tune you out each afternoon.

CRITICAL THINKING POINTS: *As you read*

1. There are many vague recollections in the poem. Why do you think that is so? List some of them.

2. What qualities make a "good" student? Is the narrator a "good" student? Make note of what details in the poem lead you to believe what you do.

3. What might lead any student to write an apology to his teacher? Is this a sincere apology? Make note of what details in the poem lead you to believe this.

This is to apologize
For not learning my maps in World Civ I and II
Which you took personally
Being an uncommon teacher loving what you do,
But it had nothing to do with you.
It was only as they say
A phase I was going through with a girl my age
Who chose to sit with me
And tune you out each afternoon.
We failed your tests together, those maps
With blanks where the names of countries go,
Although she knew enough to list the continents
And I had no choice but to be creative.
I have forgotten her name

But not the coldness her leaving left me with.
I failed you by inattention
And her by indecision
In the murky chambers of the heart.

To repent
I have scratched the state of Alabama
On a table in Roy's Bar, and sketched a road
From Tuscaloosa where she lived
Back to Birmingham.
And on the bathroom wall
I have added to the thighs
Of a local Picasso's naked lady
The continents of Africa and South America
And shaded the ocean blue between her legs.

1988

CRITICAL THINKING POINTS: *After you've read*

1. How is this poem an apology to "the girl in Room 303"? Do you believe the narrator is sincerely apologizing to the girl? Why or why not? What else might he be trying to accomplish?

2. What might Watson mean when he says, "I failed you by inattention / And her by indecision"?

3. Why do you think the poem ends the way it does? Is that an appropriate image? Why or why not?

SOME POSSIBILITIES FOR WRITING

1. Write "A Day in the Life Of . . . " (similar to the poem by Greg Adams in Chapter 2) for this student, based on what you know of him from the poem. Use concrete details, most of which you'll have to make up.

2. Have you ever felt bad for a teacher because you did poorly on a paper or test or even the entire course? Write about your experience. Explore why you felt the way you did.

3. Recall a time when you were influenced by your peers in the classroom. Did you have a positive or negative experience? Explore why the experience was positive or negative.

Homeward Bond

Daisy Nguyen (b. 1976) was born in Di Linh, Vietnam. She graduated from the University of California at Davis with majors in sociology and French.

This is a new reality, one I did not expect to face when I came "home-home." Still, I call this place home because my family treats me as one of them when I am there. They share their world with me, even when they are sometimes harsh realities. It is something I am not exposed to behind the safe confines of the university.

CRITICAL THINKING POINTS: *As you read*

1. The author uses two home clichés: "Home is where the heart is" and "A house is not a home without love." What are some other sayings or clichés about home?

2. Think of your own definition of "home." What are some details that you associate with "home"?

3. In what ways do the author's home life and university life differ? Make a list.

For as long as I can recall, perhaps since the day I moved to college, I have had trouble defining the word "home." It is one of those vague terms that lead people to create metaphors or clichés of their own to define. You've heard it all before: "Home is where the heart is," or "A house is not a home without love."

Webster's Dictionary defines it as the region in which something is familiar or native. A friend of mine, when he chooses to visit his family on weekends, always says "I'm going home-home for the weekend." The place he stays at college is simply called "home."

Almost every weekend now, since I have returned to Northern California from a one-year hiatus in France, I go "home-home." After a week of study at school, I go back to visit my family and hang out with friends in San Francisco—basically doing a lot of catching up. Indeed, many things have changed since I've been away and I'm often struck by the oddities that should be familiar to me.

One Saturday, for example, I went over to my cousin May's house to help put together some cards. She rolled to the door, opened it and greeted me. "Daisy! Hurry up and come in here. I've been waiting all week to show you these cards!"

I am now getting used to seeing her look up at me when she opens the door. It didn't use to be that way. May and I used to ride our bikes around Golden Gate Park on Sundays when we were little girls, and as teeny boppers we sashayed through downtown's hippest streets in our best skirts.

Now she stays home more often and she is putting together a small business: selling homemade greeting cards. They include beautiful photos that her father has taken throughout his extensive travels around Asia and North America. We sat in the kitchen pasting photos onto countless cards, while gossiping about family affairs. May also told me her future plans and outlook on life, now that she is in a wheelchair.

This is a new reality, one I did not expect to face when I came "home-home." Still, I call this place home because my family treats me as one of them when I am there. They share their world with me, even when they are sometimes harsh realities. It is something I am not exposed to behind the safe confines of the university.

At home-home, they don't demand me to analyze every problem nor do they demand brilliant response to every question. At home-home, mom just asks me how I have spent my week and how I like her soup. At home-home, I just sit around and listen to the radio with May, recounting stories of our adventures in life and love.

Sometimes, May's mom passes by, in her loud voice, and asks "Is the show on yet?"

"It's time! It's time! Jelly Spring-uh is on! Come and see!"

"Jelly Spring-uh?" I asked myself. "How can she like that awful show?" Here is a woman who has lived in the United States for almost 20 years, who does not understand much English, yet she enjoys the Jerry Springer show. Guess I can't comprehend it all, not everything is familiar to me at home-home.

Andric, the son of my oldest cousin, is the most observant little two-year-old I have ever seen. When May and I sat by the radio chatting, he ran around the kitchen chasing a beach ball and giggling to himself. Occasionally, he came to us and looked inquisitively, wondering what we were doing. When he wanted an apple, he would lift his tiny hand and make a fist, then put it to his cheek, making a sign for "apple." May gave him the apple and lifted him up to her lap. Celine Dion's hit from the "Titanic" soundtrack, "My Heart Will Go On," played on the radio, once again.

"I love this song!" May squealed. We listened to the haunting melodies and May hugged Andric. "I love music," she sighed. "I don't think I can live without it in my life, and when I think about how Andric can't hear music, it makes me love him so much more."

I looked into his smiling eyes and understood even more the reason the whole family adores him, and will do everything to protect him. His big round eyes, with long feathery eyelashes, are so bright you can clearly see life happening inside of him. It was a moment so heartbreaking and so inexplicable, even I couldn't describe it in words.

Now on Sundays, many members of my family go to the Buddhist temple to meditate and pray. There's a nice temple on Van Ness Avenue that my grandma and aunts frequent, so does May and Andric. One rainy morning, I hopped into my aunt's van and tagged along with her and my grandma to the temple.

On the way, grandma told me her worries for everyone in the family and asked about my life. We were driving up Van Ness, a very congested street even on Sunday mornings, when the van stopped at a red light. We waited a moment and my grandma saw a homeless man in crutches standing at the island, asking for money. She quickly grabbed a dollar from her purse and told my aunt, at the drivers' seat, to give the money to him. I looked at the light about to change, the huge distance between the van and the island, and the helpless man who couldn't reach to grab the dollar bill. "No, no, Grandma!" I panicked. "You can't do that! He can't reach for it and we must go."

The light turned green long ago, and cars behind us were honking incessantly. My aunt also panicked and she tossed the bill out the window, hoping he'd catch it. The van sped off. I turned around, and saw through the back window the dollar bill flying away, disappearing in the sea of cars.

To my grandma's dismay, all she could say was "Ay-yah, in America it is even hard to give bums some money when you want to." I knew right then her remark couldn't have been more profound nor appropriate.

When we arrived at the temple, my grandma's face brightened as she saw the crowd sitting there peacefully, chanting ancient songs. Most of all, her daughters, grandchildren and great grandchild, Andric, were there too.

We sat down, I crossed my legs and positioned myself for the upcoming meditation exercise. One of the monks came by, gave me a book and turned to the page where I followed the songs. Of course, I hardly understood the characters on the page, and mimicked to my grandma's singing instead.

After a while, the singing stopped and we sat in a long moment of silence. I was told that during meditation, you're supposed to not think about anything at all. How radical of an idea! It was so strange to me, but I didn't mind. While everyone else were attempting to put this theory into practice, I was happy to listen to the rain drops on the roof and think about how wonderful it was to sit in a room with my family in complete silence.

1998

CRITICAL THINKING POINTS: *After you've read*

1. In what ways is a university life, as the author calls it, "a safe confine"? In what ways is going home often a "safe confine"?

2. Consider the following statement: "Knowledge without compassion is dangerous." How is this statement reflected in the story?

3. What might Nguyen mean when she says, "I'm often struck by the oddities that should be familiar to me"? What are some of these?

SOME POSSIBILITIES FOR WRITING

1. Recall a recent trip home from college. What made you feel most welcomed and at ease, and what made you feel like an outsider?

2. Even if you feel that college has not changed you, imagine ways in which it might. Write a scene that shows rather than tells some of those changes.

3. Compare and contrast this author's experience with that of Walter in "The Undeclared Major." How do the two students balance home differently?

Everyday Use

FROM *IN LOVE AND TROUBLE: STORIES OF BLACK WOMEN*   Alice Walker

Alice Walker (b. 1944) is the author of *The Color Purple,* which won the Pulitzer Prize in 1982. She was the eighth child of Georgia sharecroppers. After a childhood accident blinded her in one eye, she went on to become valedictorian of her local school, and attend Spelman College and Sarah Lawrence College on scholarships. After college she worked as a social worker, teacher, and lecturer. Among her numerous awards and honors are the Lillian Smith Award from the National Endowment for the Arts, the Rosenthal Award from the National Institute of Arts & Letters, a nomination for the National Book Award, a Radcliffe Institute Fellowship, a Merrill Fellowship, a Guggenheim Fellowship, and the Front Page Award for Best Magazine Criticism from the Newswoman's Club of New York.

I didn't want to bring up how I had offered Dee (Wangero) a quilt when she went away to college. Then she had told me they were old-fashioned, out of style. "But they're priceless!" she was saying now, furiously; for she has a temper. "Maggie would put them on the bed and in five years they'd be in rags. Less than that!"

CRITICAL THINKING POINTS: *As you read*

1. What kinds of people are each of the characters in this story? What in the story do you base that on?
2. Why do you think the characters do what they do?
3. Every few pages, take a moment to stop and imagine what might happen next.

for your grandmama

I will wait for her in the yard that Maggie and I made so clean and wavy yesterday afternoon. A yard like this is more comfortable than most people know. It is not just a yard. It is like an extended living room. When the hard clay is swept clean as a floor and the fine sand around the edges lined with tiny, irregular grooves, anyone can come and sit and look up into the elm tree and wait for the breezes that never come inside the house.

Maggie will be nervous until after her sister goes: she will stand hopelessly in corners, homely and ashamed of the burn scars down her arms and legs, eying her sister with a mixture of envy and awe. She thinks her sister has held life always in the palm of one hand, that "no" is a word the world never learned to say to her.

You've no doubt seen those TV shows where the child who has "made it" is confronted, as a surprise, by her own mother and father, tottering in weakly from backstage. (A pleasant surprise, of course: What would they do if parent and child came on the show only to curse out and insult each other?) On TV mother and child embrace and smile into each other's faces. Sometimes the mother and father weep, the child wraps them in her arms and leans across the table to tell how she would not have made it without their help. I have seen these programs.

Sometimes I dream a dream in which Dee and I are suddenly brought together on a TV program of this sort. Out of a dark and soft-seated limousine I am ushered into a bright room filled with many people. There I meet a smiling, gray, sporty man like Johnny Carson who shakes my hand and tells me what a fine girl I have. Then we are on the stage and Dee is embracing me with tears in her eyes. She pins on my dress a large orchid, even though she has told me once that she thinks orchids are tacky flowers.

In real life I am a large, big-boned woman with rough, man-working hands. In the winter I wear flannel nightgowns to bed and overalls during the day. I can kill and clean a hog as mercilessly as a man. My fat keeps me hot in zero degree weather. I can work outside all day, breaking ice to get water for washing; I can eat pork liver cooked over the open fire minutes after it comes steaming from the hog. One winter I knocked a bull calf straight in the brain between the eyes with a sledge hammer and had the meat hung up to chill before nightfall. But of course all this does not show on television. I am the way my daughter would want me to be: a hundred pounds lighter, my skin like an uncooked barley pancake. My hair glistens in the hot bright lights. Johnny Carson has much to do to keep up with my quick and witty tongue.

But that is a mistake. I know even before I wake up. Who ever knew a Johnson with a quick tongue? Who can even imagine me looking a strange white man in the eye? It seems to me I have talked to them always with one foot raised in flight, with my head turned in whichever way is farthest from them. Dee, though. She would always look anyone in the eye. Hesitation was no part of her nature.

"How do I look, Mama?" Maggie says, showing just enough of her thin body enveloped in pink skirt and red blouse for me to know she's there, almost hidden by the door.

"Come out into the yard," I say.

Have you ever seen a lame animal, perhaps a dog run over by some careless person rich enough to own a car, sidle up to someone who is ignorant enough to be kind to him? That is the way Maggie walks. She has been like this, chin on chest, eyes on ground, feet in shuffle, ever since the fire that burned the other house to the ground.

Dee is lighter than Maggie, with nicer hair and a fuller figure. She's a woman now, though sometimes I forget. How long ago was it that the other house burned? Ten, twelve years? Sometimes I can still hear the flames and feel Maggie's arms sticking to me, her hair smoking and her dress falling off her in little black papery flakes. Her eyes seemed stretched open, blazes open by the flames reflected in them. And Dee. I see her standing off under the sweet gum tree she used to dig gum out of; a look of concentration on her face as she watched the last dingy gray board of the house fall in toward the red-hot brick chimney. Why don't you do a dance around the ashes? I'd wanted to ask her. She had hated the house that much.

I used to think she hated Maggie, too. But that was before we raised the money, the church and me, to send her to Augusta to school. She used to read to us without pity; forcing words, lies, other folks' habits, whole lives upon us two, sitting trapped and ignorant underneath her voice. She washed us in a river of make-believe, burned us with a lot of knowledge we didn't necessarily need to know. Pressed us to her with the serious way she read, to shove us away at just the moment, like dimwits, we seemed about to understand.

Dee wanted nice things. A yellow organdy dress to wear to her graduation from high school; black pumps to match a green suit she'd made from an old suit somebody gave me. She was determined to stare down any disaster in her efforts. Her eyelids would not flicker for minutes at a time. Often I fought off the temptation to shake her. At sixteen she had a style of her own: and knew what style was.

I never had an education myself. After second grade the school was closed down. Don't ask me why: in 1927 colored asked fewer questions than they do now. Sometimes Maggie reads to me. She stumbles along good-naturedly but can't see well. She knows she is not bright. Like good looks and money, quickness passed her by. She will marry John Thomas (who has mossy teeth in an earnest face) and then I'll be free to sit here and I guess just sing church songs to myself. Although I never was a good singer. Never could carry a tune. I was always better at a man's job. I used to love to milk till I was hooked in the side in '49. Cows are soothing and slow and don't bother you unless you try to milk them the wrong way.

I have deliberately turned my back on the house. It is three rooms, just like the one that burned, except the roof is tin; they don't make shingle roofs any more. There are no real windows, just some holes cut in the sides, like the portholes in a ship, but not round and not square, with rawhide holding the shutters up on the outside. This house is in a pasture, too, like the other one. No doubt when Dee sees it she will want to tear it down. She wrote me once that no matter where we "choose" to live, she will manage to come see us. But she will never bring her friends. Maggie and I thought about this and Maggie asked me, "Mama, when did Dee ever have any friends?"

She had a few. Furtive boys in pink shirts hanging about on washday after school. Nervous girls who never laughed. Impressed with her they worshiped the well-turned phrase, the cute shape, the scalding humor that erupted like bubbles in lye. She read to them.

When she was courting Jimmy T she didn't have much time to pay to us, but turned all her faultfinding power on him. He flew to marry a cheap city girl from a family of ignorant flashy people. She hardly had time to recompose herself.

When she comes I will meet—but there they are!

Maggie attempts to make a dash for the house, in her shuffling way, but I stay her with my hand. "Come back here," I say. And she stops and tries to dig a well in the sand with her toe.

It is hard to see them clearly through the strong sun. But even the first glimpse of leg out of the car tells me it is Dee. Her feet were always neat-looking, as if God himself had shaped them with a certain style. From the other side of the car comes a short, stocky man. Hair is all over his head a foot long and hanging from his chin like a kinky mule tail. I hear Maggie suck in her breath. "Uhnnnh," is what it sounds like. Like when you see the wriggling end of a snake just in front of your foot on the road. "Uhnnnh."

Dee next. A dress down to the ground, in this hot weather. A dress so loud that it hurts my eyes. There are yellows and oranges enough to throw back the light of the sun. I feel my whole face warming from the heat waves it throws out. Earrings gold, too, and hanging down to her shoulders. Bracelets dangling and making noises when she moves her arm up to shake the folds of the dress out of her armpits. The dress is loose and flows, and as she walks closer, I like it. I hear Maggie go, "Uhnnnh" again. It is her sister's hair. It stands straight up like the wool on a sheep. It is black as night and around the edges are two long pigtails that rope about like small lizards disappearing behind her ears.

"Wa-su-zo-Tean-o!" she says, coming on in that gliding way the dress makes her move. The short stocky fellow with the hair to his navel is all grinning and he follows up with "Asalamalakim, my mother and sister!" He moves to hug Maggie but she falls back, right up against the back of my chair. I feel her trembling there and when I look up I see the perspiration falling off her chin.

"Don't get up," says Dee. Since I am stout it takes something of a push. You can see me trying to move a second or two before I make it. She turns, showing white heels through her sandals, and goes back to the car. Out she peeks next with a Polaroid. She stoops down quickly and lines up picture after picture of me sitting there in front of the house with Maggie cowering behind me. She never takes a shot without making sure the house is included. When a cow comes nibbling around the edge of the yard she snaps it and me and Maggie and the house. Then she puts the Polaroid in the back seat of the car, and comes up and kisses me on the forehead.

Meanwhile Asalamalakim is going through motions with Maggie's hand. Maggie's hand is as limp as a fish, and probably as cold, despite the sweat, and she keeps trying to shake hands but wants to do it fancy. Or maybe he don't know how people shake hands. Anyhow, he soon gives up on Maggie.

"Well," I say. "Dee."

"No, Mama," she says. "Not 'Dee,' Wangero Leewanika Kemanjo!"

"What happened to 'Dee'?" I wanted to know.

"She's dead," Wangero said. "I couldn't bear it any longer, being named after the people who oppress me."

"You know as well as me you was named after your aunt Dicie," I said. Dicie is my sister. She named Dee. We called her "Big Dee" after Dee was born.

"But who was she named after?" asked Wangero.

"Her mother," I said, and saw Wangero was getting tired. "That's about as far back as I can trace it," I said. Though, in fact, I probably could have carried it back beyond the Civil War through the branches.

"Well," said Asalamalakim, "there you are."

"Uhnnnd," I heard Maggie say.

"There I was not," I said, "before 'Dicie' cropped up in our family, so why should I try to trace it that far back?"

He just stood there grinning, looking down on me like somebody inspecting a Model A car. Every once in a while he and Wangero sent eye signals over my head.

"How do you pronounce this name?" I asked.

"You don't have to call me by it if you don't want to," said Wangero.

"Why shouldn't I?" I asked. "If that's what you want us to call you, we'll call you."

"I know it might sound awkward at first," said Wangero.

"I'll get used to it," I said. "Ream it out again."

Well, soon we got the name out of the way. Asalamalakim had a name twice as long and three times as hard. After I tripped over it two or three times he told me to just call him Hakim-a-barber. I wanted to ask him was he a barber, but I didn't really think he was, so I didn't ask.

"You must belong to those beef-cattle peoples down the road," I said. They said "Asalamalakim" when they met you, too, but they didn't shake hands. Always too busy: feeding cattle, fixing the fences, putting up salt-lick shelters, throwing down hay. When the white folks poisoned some of the herd the men stayed up all night with rifles in their hands. I walked a mile and a half just to see the sight.

Hakin-a-barber said, "I accept some of their doctrines, but farming and raising cattle is not my style." (They didn't tell me, and I didn't ask, whether Wangero [Dee] had really gone and married him.)

We sat down to eat and right away he said he didn't eat collards and pork was unclean. Wangero, though, went on through the chitlins and corn bread, the greens and everything else. She talked a blue streak over the sweet potatoes. Everything delighted her. Even the fact that we still used the benches her daddy made for the table when we couldn't afford to buy chairs.

"Oh, Mama!" she cried. Then turned to Hakim-a-barber. "I never knew how lovely these benches are. You can feel the rump prints," she said, running her hands underneath her and along the bench. Then she gave a sigh and her hand closed over Grandma Dee's butter dish. "That's it!" she said. "I knew there was something I wanted to ask you if I could have." She jumped up from the table and went over in the corner where the churn stood, the milk in it clabber by now. She looked at the churn and looked at it.

"This churn top is what I need," she said. "Didn't Uncle Buddy whittle it out of a tree you all used to have?"

"Yes," I said.

"Uh huh," she said happily. "And I want the dasher, too."

"Uncle Buddy whittle that, too?" asked the barber.

Dee (Wangero) looked up at me.

"Aunt Dee's first husband whittled the dash," said Maggie so low you almost couldn't hear her. "His name was Henry, but they called him Stash."

"Maggie's brain is like an elephant's," Wangero said, laughing. "I can use the churn top as a centerpiece for the alcove table," she said, sliding a plate over the churn, "and I'll think of something artistic to do with the dasher."

When she finished wrapping the dasher the handle stuck out. I took it for a moment in my hands. You didn't even have to look close to see where hands pushing the dasher up and down to make butter had left a kind of sink in the wood. In fact, there were a lot of small sinks; you could see where thumbs and fingers had sunk into the wood. It was beautiful light yellow wood, from a tree that grew in the yard where Big Dee and Stash had lived.

After dinner Dee (Wangero) went to the trunk at the foot of my bed and started rifling through it. Maggie hung back in the kitchen over the dishpan. Out came Wangero with two quilts. They had been pieced by Grandma Dee and then Big Dee and me had hung them on the quilt frames on the front porch and quilted them. One was in the Lone Star pattern. The other was Walk Around the Mountain. In both of them were scraps of dresses Grandma Dee had worn fifty or more years ago. Bits and pieces of Grandpa Jarrell's Paisley shirts. And one teeny faded blue piece, about the size of a penny matchbox, that was from Great Grandpa Ezra's uniform that he wore in the Civil War.

"Mama," Wangero said sweet as a bird. "Can I have these old quilts?"

I heard something fall in the kitchen, and a minute later the kitchen door slammed.

"Why don't you take one or two of the others?" I asked. "These old things was just done by me and Big Dee from some tops your grandma pieced before she died."

"No," said Wangero. "I don't want those. They are stitched around the borders by machine."

"That'll make them last better," I said.

"That's not the point," said Wangero. "These are all pieces of dresses Grandma used to wear. She did all this stitching by hand. Imagine!" She held the quilts securely in her arms, stroking them.

"Some of the pieces, like those lavender ones, come from old clothes her mother handed down to her," I said, moving up to touch the quilts. Dee (Wangero) moved back just enough so that I couldn't reach the quilts. They already belonged to her.

"Imagine!" she breathed again, clutching them closely to her bosom.

"The truth is," I said, "I promised to give them quilts to Maggie, for when she marries John Thomas."

She gasped like a bee had stung her.

"Maggie can't appreciate these quilts!" she said. "She'd probably be backward enough to put them to everyday use."

"I reckon she would," I said. "God knows I been saving 'em for long enough with nobody using 'em. I hope she will!" I didn't want to bring up how I had offered Dee (Wangero) a quilt when she went away to college. Then she had told me they were old-fashioned, out of style.

"But they're priceless!" she was saying now, furiously; for she has a temper. "Maggie would put them on the bed and in five years they'd be in rags. Less than that!"

"She can always make some more," I said. "Maggie knows how to quilt."

Dee (Wangero) looked at me with hatred. "You just will not understand. The point is these quilts, these quilts!"

"Well," I said, stumped. "What would you do with them?"

"Hang them," she said. As if that was the only thing you could do with quilts.

Maggie by now was standing in the door. I could almost hear the sound her feet made as they scraped over each other.

"She can have them, Mama," she said, like somebody used to never winning anything, or having anything reserved for her. "I can 'member Grandma Dee without the quilts."

I looked at her hard. She had filled her bottom lip with checkerberry snuff and it gave her face a kind of dopey, hangdog look. It was Grandma Dee and Big Dee who taught her how to quilt herself. She stood there with her scarred hands hidden in the folds of her skirt. She looked at her sister with something like fear but she wasn't mad at her. This was Maggie's portion. This was the way she knew God to work.

When I looked at her like that something hit me in the top of my head and ran down to the soles of my feet. Just like when I'm in church and the spirit of God touches me and I get happy and shout. I did something I never had done before: hugged Maggie to me, then dragged her on into the room, snatched the quilts out of Miss Wangero's hands and dumped them into Maggie's lap. Maggie just sat there on my bed with her mouth open.

"Take one or two of the others," I said to Dee.

But she turned without a word and went out to Hakim-a-barber.

"You just don't understand," she said, as Maggie and I came out to the car.

"What don't I understand?" I wanted to know.

"Your heritage," she said. And then she turned to Maggie, kissed her, and said, "You ought to try to make something of yourself, too, Maggie. It's really a new day for us. But from the way you and Mama still live you'd never know it."

She put on some sunglasses that hid everything above the tip of her nose and her chin.

Maggie smiled, maybe at the sunglasses. But a real smile. Not scared. After we watched the car dust settle I asked Maggie to bring me a dip of snuff. And then the two of us sat there just enjoying, until it was time to go in the house and go to bed.

1973

CRITICAL THINKING POINTS: *After you've read*

1. What do the quilts and butter churn seem to mean to Dee/Wangero? To the narrator and Maggie?

2. How important are the quilts to Maggie? What else seems at least as important if not more so?

3. Why do you think that until recently things like quilts weren't often considered "art"? Can you think of other similar items?

SOME POSSIBILITIES FOR WRITING

1. Does your family have objects like the quilts and butter churn? Write about at least one of them.

2. Choose a scene in the story and write it from a different character's point of view.

3. Choose one of the Critical Thinking Points following the story and develop your original responses further.

Further Suggestions for Writing—
"Student Relations"

1. What kinds of changes do you think your being away at college will make for your family and/or your friends at home? Write about some of them.

2. Write a letter to your parents titled "Ten Commandments for the Parents of a College Freshman." Include both do's and do not's.

3. As Shakespeare says, "The course of true love never runs smooth." Although this may be true of all people "in love," some pressures are particular to college students involved in romantic relationships. What are some of them, and how do they affect college relationships?

4. Many college students leave behind or are otherwise separated from a "significant other." What are some of the advantages and disadvantages of being in such a situation?

5. Organize a discussion between a group of male and female friends in which the subject is "College Men Are from Mars; College Women Are from Venus." Write a report of the "findings" of your discussion to present to your class.

6. Working in groups, compare and contrast some aspect of sexual behavior, love, romance, or dating at college.

7. Is it possible for a man and a woman to be "just friends"? Why do you think the way you do about this subject?

8. Describe an incident or pattern of gender discrimination that you have noticed since you arrived at college.

9. Evaluate your school's policies on sexual harassment. How well informed about these policies do first-year students seem to be?

10. Find a few recent issues of two different magazines that are popular among college students, one of which is directed primarily at women and the other at men. Compare and contrast the way these two publications reveal attitudes about gender. In what way(s) are gender stereotypes reinforced and/or challenged? What support do you have for your position?

11. Do you believe men and women communicate differently? Research this subject to find support for your opinion.

12. As an investigation of how the sexes view each other, compare and contrast some of the metaphors that men use for women at your school and that some women use for men. What kinds of insights does this lead you to?

13. Many of the pieces in this book depict males in unflattering terms. Working in groups, discuss the issue of "male bashing" on college campuses. Is it acceptable? Why or why not?

14. Recent studies show that more women are attending universities than men and are graduating at much higher rates. Why do you think this is so? Research this

relatively new phenomenon and report back to your class on some of the reasons traditional-age college women succeed at school more than men.

15. What kinds of influences do you think your religious and/or family upbringing have had on your attitudes about sex and sexuality and/or love, marriage, and divorce?

16. Some young men and women take pride in preserving their virginity until marriage. Write a dialogue between two men or two women in which one of them explains to the other why virginity is valued.

17. Research your university's policy on faculty and staff dating students. Do you agree with this policy? Why or why not?

18. Evaluate your school's program and policies concerning rape education, prevention, and intervention.

19. For an entire day, record the sexual images you see around campus. Watch for images on signs, posters, billboards, books, TV programs, or other private or public places. Did you notice these images without consciously looking for them? Why or why not? Write a composite of the kinds of images you found and the purpose of these images

20. Argue for or against co-ed dorms.

21. Music played a major part of the sexual revolution of the 1960s and 1970s. Compare and contrast some of those songs to some popular songs in recent years that promote sexuality.

22. Contact your Dean of Students Office or Residence Life Office to find out what types of support are available for gay, lesbian, or bisexual students on your campus. Research student organizations that offer an outlet for these students. Deliver a report to your class on your findings.

23. Research and write a paper about the changes, if any, in sexual behavior among college students pre- and post-AIDS. What surprises you about your findings? Why?

24. Interview an adult student. What caused that student to return to school? Are his or her motivations and/or methods for success the same as yours? Why or why not?

25. Read *Don't Come Back a Stranger* by James L. Summers (1970) and/or *A Hope in the Unseen: An American Odyssey from the Inner City to the Ivy League* by Ron Suskind (1998) and/or *Black Ice* by Lorene Cary (1992) and/or some other college-life memoir. How does the college experience portrayed in any or all of these books compare to your experience? Why do you think so?

26. Read *I'll Take You There: A Novel* by Joyce Carol Oates (2002) and/or *Move Over, Girl: A Novel* by Brian Peterson (2000) and/or *Better Than I Know Myself* by Donna Grant (2004) and/or *The Rules of Attraction* by Bret Easton Ellis (1998) and/or *Been Down So Long It Looks Like Up to Me* by Richard Farina (1983). How do the college relationships portrayed in any or all of these books compare to your experience? Why do you think so?

27. Choose at least three films from the list at the end of this chapter. What do they seem to say about student relationships? What support do you have for your position?

28. Choose one of your responses to the "Some possibilities for writing" topics in this chapter and do further research on some aspect of the topic you addressed in your narrative. Write about how and why this new information would have improved your previous effort.

29. Find the original text from which one of the selections in this chapter was taken. What led you to choose this particular text? How does reading more from the text affect your original reading? Is there more you would like to know about the text, its subject, or its author? Where might you find this further information?

30. Compare Robin and Malia's relationship in "50% Chance of Lightning" in Chapter 1 to that of Kate and Carmen in "Carmen" in this chapter.

Selected Films—"Student Relations"

American History X (1998, USA). A former neo-Nazi skinhead tries to prevent his younger brother from going down the same wrong path that he did. Drama. 119 min. R.

Boys (1996, USA). College student John Baker finds Patty Vare after she has fallen off a horse and takes her back to his dorm room, intending to nurse her back to health. Hiding Patty from the administration, as well as from fellow students, is more difficult than John anticipated. Mystery/Drama. 86 min. PG-13.

But I'm a Cheerleader (1999, USA). A naïve teenager is sent to rehab camp when her strait-laced parents and friends suspect her of being a lesbian. Comedy/Romance. 85 min. R.

Double Happiness (1994, Canada). A young Chinese-Canadian woman has a romance with an Anglo college student, against the wishes of her very traditional father. Comedy/Drama. 87 min. PG-13.

8 Mile (2002, USA). A young rapper (Eminem) in Detroit uses music to help him with his struggles with his anger. Drama. 110 min. R.

First Daughter (2004, USA). First daughter of the U.S. president heads off to college where she falls for a graduate student with a secret agenda. Forest Whitaker directs. Comedy/Romance. 90 min. PG.

First Love (1977, USA). An idealistic college student finds that neither his classmates nor his girlfriend take sex as seriously as he does. Based on Harold Brodkey's story "Sentimental Education." Romantic drama. 92 min. R.

The French Lesson (1986, Great Britain). A young English woman goes to Paris for a romantic education. Romantic comedy. 90 min. PG.

Ghost World (2000, USA). Best friends Enid and Rebecca graduate from high school and find themselves forced to enter the real world. They fear drifting apart when one considers moving across the country to attend college. Drama. 111 min. R.

Girl, Interrupted (1999, USA). Feeling adrift since graduation, Susanna "accidentally" overdoses on pills and booze and is accused of trying to commit suicide. Based on Susanna Kayson's autobiographical account of her stay in a mental hospital in the 1960s. Drama. 127 min. R.

How I Got into College (1989, USA). A second-rate student scratches his way into college to pursue his dream girl. Comedy. 89 min. PG-13.

Joy Luck Club (1993, USA). The life histories of four Asian women and their daughters reflect and guide each other. Drama. 139 min. R.

Les Cousins (1959, France). Within the milieu of Parisian student life, a decadent city boy and his pure country cousin vie for the affections of the same young woman. Drama. 112 min. N/R.

Lianna (1983, USA). Lianna, a faculty wife and mother in her early thirties, falls in love with Ruth, the visiting professor in a child psychology course she's taking at the college where her husband teaches. Drama. 110 min. R.

L.I.E. (2002, USA). A 15-year-old's mother is killed on the Long Island Expressway, and he soon becomes involved in a relationship with a much older man. Drama. 97 min. R.

A Little Stiff (1991, USA). A Gen-X UCLA film student pines hopelessly for his classmate. Written by and starring Caveh Zahedi. Romantic comedy. 85 min. N/R.

Lost and Delirious (2002, Canada). A newcomer to a girl's boarding school is befriended by her two new roommates and later discovers the others are lovers. Drama. 103 min. R.

Love and Basketball (2000, USA). Next-door neighbors since first grade, Quincy and Monica age into best friends and lovers. While Quincy plays college basketball on huge courts to cheering, sold-out crowds, we see Monica's sweat, tears, and sheer physical dedication in front of tiny audiences in small gyms and second-rate auditoriums. Drama/Romance. 124 min. PG-13.

Maurice (1987, Great Britain). Two male students feel they have to repress their mutual attraction, given the stifling sexual mores at Cambridge University in the Edwardian era. Based on E.M. Forster's novel of the same name. Drama. 140 min. R.

Mozart and the Whale (2005, USA). Tells the story of two people with Asperger's syndrome, a form of autism, whose emotional dysfunctions threaten to sabotage their budding romance. Romantic comedy. PG-13.

My Family, Mi Familia (1995, USA). Traces more than three generations of an immigrant family's tragedies and triumphs. Drama. 128 min. R.

My First Mister (2001, USA). A 17-year-old goth girl has a platonic relationship with a 49-year-old man who has no friends or family. He gives her a job, not to mention a real friendship. Drama. 108 min. R.

Pretty in Pink (1986, USA). Directed by "master of the eighties teen flick" John Hughes, this film follows the story of Andie Walsh, a girl from the wrong side of the tracks who catches the eye of one of the most popular high-school hunks. Comedy/Drama. 96 min. PG-13.

Real Women Have Curves (2003, USA). A Mexican-American teen is torn between accepting a full scholarship to Columbia University and working in her sister's dress factory close to home. Drama. 90 min. PG-13.

Smoke Signals (1998, USA). After not seeing his father for ten years, Victor hears his dad has died. Thomas, a nerd who tells stories no one wants to hear, offers Victor money for the trip to get his father's remains, but only if Thomas can go along. Comedy/Drama. 88 min. PG-13.

The Sterile Cuckoo (1969, USA). Liza Minnelli plays an aggressive college student pursuing a shy freshman boy. Comedy/Drama. 107 min. PG.

The Sure Thing (1985, USA). Spatting college students thrown together on a cross-country trip find love on the way. Romantic comedy. 94 min. PG-13.

When He's Not a Stranger (1989, USA). Intensely portrayed date-rape story. Made for TV. Drama. 100 min. N/R.

XX/XY (2002, USA). Three college friends begin a dangerous three-way relationship that spirals out of control, leading to dire consequences that haunt them ten years later. Drama/Romance. 91 min. R.

For critical thinking points on these films, see Appendix (p. 281).

Four

Teacher, Teacher

A teacher can affect an eternity or simply make a class period feel like one. The selections here present teachers in the roles of disciplinarian, mentor, instructor, scholar, and friend, but most of all as people facing many of the same challenges and fears as their students. This chapter will explore the lessons students and teachers give one another, and the inspiration—however misguided—of teachers on students' lives.

READING SELECTIONS

Did I Miss Anything?

Grading Your Professors

from *Tales Out of School*

No Immediate Danger

Teachers: A Primer

Open Admissions

What Teachers Make

Did I Miss Anything?

FROM *I'LL BE RIGHT BACK*   **Tom Wayman**

Tom Wayman (1945) is a poet, essayist, and teacher from British Columbia, Canada. He has published more than a dozen collections of his poems, most recently *I'll Be Right Back: Selected Poems 1980–96* (1997) in the United States and *My Father's Cup* (2002) in Canada. He teaches at the University of Calgary, Alberta.

When you are not present
how could something significant occur?

CRITICAL THINKING POINTS: *As you read*

1. What is the author's tone? How do you know? How does this contribute to your reading of the poem?

2. Why do you think the question, "Did I miss anything?" is such a pet peeve for teachers?

3. Often students ask a version of this question, "Did I miss anything *important?*" Or "Will I miss anything important?" How are these questions different than Wayman's question?

Did I Miss Anything?

Question frequently asked by students
after missing a class

Nothing. When we realized you weren't here
we sat with our hands folded on our desks
in silence, for the full two hours

    Everything. I gave an exam worth
    40 per cent of the grade for this term
    and assigned some reading due today
    on which I'm about to hand out a quiz
    worth 50 per cent

Nothing. None of the content of this course
has value or meaning
Take as many days off as you like:
any activities we undertake as a class

I assure you will not matter either to you or me
and are without purpose

Everything. A few minutes after we began last time
a shaft of light descended and an angel
or other heavenly being appeared
and revealed to us what each woman or man must do
to attain divine wisdom in this life and
the hereafter
This is the last time the class will meet
before we disperse to bring this good news to all
people on earth

Nothing. When you are not present
how could something significant occur?

Everything. Contained in this classroom
is a microcosm of human existence
assembled for you to query and examine and ponder
This is not the only place such an opportunity has
been gathered

but it was one place

And you weren't here

1993

CRITICAL THINKING POINTS: *After you've read*

1. How important is "attendance" when going to college?
2. Why is it that some classes/teachers are more difficult than others to "get the notes" for?
3. What other questions/statements have you discovered teachers find annoying?

SOME POSSIBILITIES FOR WRITING

1. Write a response to this poem called, perhaps, "What I Didn't Miss" or "Why I Wasn't Here."
2. Interview teachers and students about attendance policies for different classes. How do they feel about the worth of these policies and the reasons for them?
3. Choose one of your responses to the Critical Thinking Points above and develop it further.

Grading Your Professors

FROM *GRADING YOUR PROFESSORS AND OTHER UNEXPECTED ADVICE*

Jacob Neusner

Jewish scholar and author Jacob Neusner (b. 1932) has written nearly six hundred books on Judaism, including several multivolume works, textbooks for children and college students, and books for the general reader.

Since professors stand at the center of the student's encounter with college learning, students ought to ask what marks a good professor, what indicates a bad one.

CRITICAL THINKING POINTS: *As you read*

1. With which statements in this essay do you strongly agree or disagree? Which inspire you or make you angry?

2. While reading through this essay, recall teachers, classes, and/or experiences that illustrate what Neusner is talking about. What details in the essay remind you of those?

3. What makes a "scholar"? Are there specific qualifications for a person to become a scholar?

S ince professors stand at the center of the student's encounter with college learning, students ought to ask what marks a good professor, what indicates a bad one. The one who sets high standards and persists in demanding that students try to meet them provides the right experiences. The professor who gives praise cheaply or who pretends to a relationship that does not and cannot exist teaches the wrong lessons. True, the demanding and critical teacher does not trade in the currency students possess, which is their power to praise or reject teachers. The demanding professor knows that students will stumble. But the ones who pick themselves up and try again—whether in politics or music or art or sports—have learned a lesson that will save them for a lifetime: A single failure is not the measure of any person, and success comes hard. A banal truth, but a truth all the same.

The only teacher who taught me something beyond information, who gave me something to guide my life, was the only teacher who read my work carefully and criticized it in detail. To that point everyone had given me A's. After that I learned to criticize myself and not to believe the A's. The teacher who read my writing and corrected not so much the phrasing as the mode of thought—line by line, paragraph by paragraph, beginning to end—and who composed paragraphs as models for what I should be saying is the sole true teacher I ever had. But I did not need more than one, and neither do you.

I do not mean to suggest that for each one of us there is one perfect teacher who changes our lives and is the only teacher we need. We must learn from many teachers as we grow up and grow old; and we must learn to recognize the good ones. The impressive teacher of one's youth may want to continue to dominate—as teachers do—and may not want to let go. The great teacher is the one who wants to become obsolete in the life of the student. The good teacher is the one who teaches lessons and moves on, celebrating the student's growth. The Talmud relates the story of a disciple in an academy on high. The question is asked, "What happened in heaven that day?" The answer: "God clapped hands in joy saying, 'My children have vanquished me, my children have vanquished me.'" That is a model for the teacher—to enjoy losing an argument to a student, to recognize his or her contribution, to let the student surpass the teacher.

In the encounter with the teacher who takes you seriously, you learn to take yourself seriously. In the eyes of the one who sees what you can accomplish, you gain a vision of yourself as more than you thought you were. The ideal professor is the one who inspires you to dream of what you can be, to try for more than you ever have accomplished before. Everyone who succeeds in life can point to such a teacher, whether in the classroom or on the sports field. It may be a parent, a coach, employer, grade school or high school or art or music teacher. It is always the one who cared enough to criticize, and stayed around to praise.

But what about college professors? To define an ideal for their work, let me offer guidelines on how to treat professors the way we treat students: to give grades.

Professors grade students' work. The conscientious ones spend time reading and thinking about student papers, inscribing their comments and even discussing with students the strengths and weaknesses of their work. But no professor spends as much time on grading students' work as students spend on grading their professors as teachers and as people. For from the beginning of a course ("Shall I register?") through the middle ("It's boring . . . shall I stick it out?") to the very end ("This was a waste of time."), the students invest time and intellectual energy in deciding what they think, both about how the subject is studied and about the person who presents it. Since effective teaching requires capturing the students' imagination, and since sharp edges and colorful ways excite imagination, the professor who is a "character" is apt, whether liked or disliked, to make a profound impression and perhaps also to leave a mark on the students' minds. The drab professors, not gossiped about and not remembered except for what they taught, may find that even what they taught is forgotten. People in advertising and public relations, politics and merchandising, know that. A generation raised on television expects to be manipulated and entertained.

Yet the emphasis on striking characteristics is irrelevant. Many students have no more sophistication in evaluating professors than they do in evaluating deodorants. This should not be surprising, since they approach them both in the same manner. The one who is "new, different, improved," whether a professor or a bar of soap, wins attention. In this context people have no way of determining good from bad. I once asked an airline pilot, "What is the difference between a good landing and a bad one?" He replied, "A good landing is any landing you can pick yourself up and walk away from." To this pilot, the landing is judged solely by its ultimate goal—safely delivering the plane's passengers. Can we tell when a teacher has safely delivered the student for the next stage of the journey? Can we define the differences between a good teacher and a bad one?

Students have their own definitions of *good* and *bad,* and professors generally have a notion of the meaning of students' grades. Let us consider how students evaluate their teachers, examining in turn the *A, B,* and *C* professors. We will begin at the bottom of one scale and work our way up. Let us at the same time consider what kind of student seeks which grade.

Grade C Professors

The first type is the *C* professor. This is the professor who registers minimum expectations and adheres to the warm-body theory of grading. If a warm body fills a seat regularly and exhibits vital signs, such as breathing at regular intervals, occasionally reading, and turning in some legible writing on paper, then cosmic justice demands, and the professor must supply, the grade of *C* or *Satisfactory.* The effort needed to achieve *F* or *No Credit* is considerably greater. One must do no reading, attend few class sessions, and appear to the world to be something very like a corpse.

The professor who, by the present criteria, earns a *C* respects the students' rights and gives them their money's worth. He or she sells them a used car, so to speak, that they at least can drive off the lot. At the very least the professor does the following:

1. Attends all class sessions, reaches class on time, and ends class at the scheduled hour.

2. Prepares a syllabus for the course and either follows it or revises it, so that students always know what topic is under (even totally confused) discussion.

3. Announces and observes scheduled office hours, so that students have access to the professor without groveling or special pleading, heroic efforts at bird-dogging, or mounting week-long treasure hunts.

4. Makes certain that books assigned for a course are on reserve in the library and sees to it that the bookstore has ample time in which to order enough copies of the textbooks and ancillary reading for a course.

5. Comes to class with a clear educational plan, a well-prepared presentation, a concrete and specific intellectual agenda.

6. Reads examinations with the care invested in them (certainly no more, but also no less) and supplies intelligible grades and at least minimal comments; or keeps office hours for the discussion of the substance of the examination (but not the grade); and supplies course performance reports—all these as duty, not acts of grace.

These things constitute student rights. No student has to thank a professor for doing what he or she is paid to do, and these six items, at a minimum, are the prerequisites for professional behavior. They are matters of form, to be sure, but the grade C is deemed by (some) students to be a matter of good form alone; the warm-body theory of this grade applies to professors and students alike.

"Tell me my duty and I shall do it" are the words of the minimally prepared. Just as students of mediocre quality want to know the requirements and assume that if they meet them, they have fulfilled their whole obligation to the subject, so mediocre professors do what they are supposed to do. The subject is in hand; there are no problems. The C professor need not be entirely bored with the subject, but he or she is not apt to be deeply engaged by it.

Grade C professors may be entertaining, warm, and loving. Indeed, many of them must succeed on the basis of personality, because all they have to offer is the studied technology of attractive personalities. They may achieve huge followings among the students, keep students at the edge of their seats with jokes and banter, badger students to retain their interest, but in the end what they have sold, conveyed, or imparted to the students' minds is themselves, not their mode of thinking or analyzing. Why? Because C professors do not think much; they rely on the analysis of others.

Above all, the grade C professor has made no effort to take over and reshape the subject. This person is satisfied with the mere repetition, accurate and competent repetition to be sure, of what others have discovered and declared to be true. If this sort of professor sparks any vitality and interest in students, then he or she will remind students of their better high school teachers, the people who, at the very least, knew what they were talking about and wanted the students to know. At the end of a course, students should ask themselves, *Have I learned facts, or have I grasped how the subject works, its inner dynamic, its logic and structure?* If at the end students should be grateful—at least they have learned that much—but award the professor a polite C. For the professor has done little more than necessary.

Grade B Professors

A course constitutes a large and detailed statement on the nature of a small part of a larger subject, a practical judgment upon a particular field of study and how it is to be organized and interpreted. The grade of B is accorded to the student who has mastered the basic and fundamental modes of thought about, and facts contained within, the subject of a course.

The grade B professor is one who can present coherently the larger theory and logic of the subject, who will do more than is required to convey his or her ideas to the students and who will sincerely hope he or she is inspiring the minds of the students. B professors, as they continue to grow as scholars, are not very different from A professors; they might be described as teachers striving to become A professors. But they are definitely very different from C professors. Let us, then, move on to consider A professors, keeping in mind that B professors will probably become A professors.

Grade A Professors

Grade A professors are the scholar-teachers, a university's prized treasures among a faculty full of intangible riches. America has many faculties of excellence, groups of men and women who with exceptional intelligence take over a subject and make it their own, reshape it and hand it on, wholly changed but essentially unimpaired in tradition, to another generation.

The grade of A goes to student work that attends in some interesting way and with utmost seriousness to the center and whole of the subject of the course. Notice, I did not say that an A goes to the student who says something new and original. That is too much to hope, especially in studying a subject that for hundreds or thousands of years has appeared to the best minds as an intricate and difficult problem.

The grade A professors may have odd ideas about their subjects, but they are asking old-new questions, seeking fresh insight, trying to enter into the way in which the subject works, to uncover its logic and inner structure. What makes an effective high school teacher is confidence, even glibness. What makes an effective university teacher is doubt and dismay. The scholarly mind is marked by self-criticism and thirsty search; it is guided by an awareness of its own limitations and those of knowledge. The scholar–teacher, of whatever subject or discipline, teaches one thing: Knowledge is not sure but uncertain, scholarship is search, and to teach is to impart the lessons of doubt. What is taught is what we do not know.

On whom do you bestow a grade A? It is given to the professor who, stumbling and falling, yet again rising up and walking on, seeks both knowledge and the meaning of knowledge. It is to the one who always asks, *Why am I telling you these things? Why should you know them?* It is to the professor who demands ultimate seriousness for his or her subject because the subject must be known, who not only teaches but professes, stands for, represents, the thing taught. The grade A professor lives for the subject, needs to tell you about it, wants to share it. The Nobel Prize scientist who so loved biology that she gave her life to it even without encouragement and recognition for half a century of work, the literary critic who thinks getting inside a poem is entering Paradise, the historian who assumes the human issues of the thirteenth century live today—these exemplify the ones who are ultimately serious about a subject.

One who has made this commitment to a field of scholarship can be readily identified. This is the one full of concern, the one who commits upon the facts the act of advocacy, who deems compelling what others find merely interesting. The scholar–teacher is such because he or she conveys the self-evident, the obvious fact that facts bear meaning, constituting a whole that transcends the sum of the parts. True, to the world this sense of ultimate engagement with what is merely interesting or useful information marks the professor as demented, as are all those who march to a different drummer. What I mean to say is simple. Anybody who cares so much about what to the rest of the world is so little must be a bit daft. Why should such things matter so much—why, above all, things of the mind or the soul or the heart, things of nature and mathematics, things of structure and weight and stress, things of technology and science, society and mind? Professors often remember lonely childhoods (for my part, I don't). As adults, too, professors have to spend long hours by themselves in their offices, reading books, or in their laboratories or at their computers, or just thinking all by themselves. That is not ordinary and commonplace behavior. This is what it means to march to a different drummer. A student earns an *A* when he or she has mastered the larger theory of the course, entered into its logic and meaning, discovered a different way of seeing. Like a professor, the student who through accurate facts and careful, critical thought seeks meaning, the core and center of the subject, earns the grade *A*.

Yet matters cannot be left here. I do not mean to promote advocacy for its own sake. Students have rights too, and one of these is the right to be left alone, to grow and mature in their own distinctive ways. They have the right to seek their way, just as we professors find ours. The imperial intellect, the one that cannot allow autonomy, is a missionary, not a teacher. Many compare the imperial teacher with the *A* professor, but if you look closely at their different ways of teaching, you will see that this is an error. The teacher leads, says, "Follow me," without looking backward. The missionary pushes, imposes self upon another autonomous self. This is the opposite of teaching, and bears no relevance to learning or to scholarship. The teacher persuades; the missionary preaches. The teacher argues; the missionary shouts others to silence. The teacher wants the student to discover; the missionary decides what the student must discover. The teacher enters class with fear and trembling, not knowing where the discussion will lead. The missionary knows at the start of a class exactly what the students must cover by the end of the class.

Grade *A* professors teach, never indoctrinate. They educate rather than train. There is a fine line to be drawn, an invisible boundary, between great teaching and self-aggrandizing indoctrination.

Knowledge and even understanding do not bring salvation and therefore do not have to be, and should not be, forced upon another. And this brings me back to the earlier emphasis upon scholarship as the recognition of ignorance, the awareness not of what we know but of how we know and of what we do not know. The true scholar, who also is the true teacher, is drawn by self-criticism, compelled by doubting, skeptical curiosity, knows the limits of knowing. He or she cannot be confused with the imperial, the arrogant, and the proselytizing. By definition, we stand for humility before the unknown.

A good professor wants to answer the question, *Why am I telling you these things?* A good student wants to answer the question, *Why am I taking these courses? What do I hope to get out of them? Why are they important to me?* I have not put before you any unattainable ideals in these questions. Some of us realize them every day, and nearly all of us realize them on some days. Just as students' transcripts rarely present only *A*'s or *No Credits*, so professors rarely succeed all of the time. No one bears the indelible grade of *A*.

1984

CRITICAL THINKING POINTS: *After you've read*

1. What do you think Neusner means when he says, "The professor who gives praise cheaply or who pretends to a relationship that does not and cannot exist teaches the wrong lessons"? What are some of those lessons?

2. What do you think Neusner means when he says, "The only teacher who taught me something beyond information . . . "? What kinds of things can teachers teach that are "beyond" information, and how might they teach those things?

3. The lowest "grade" Neusner gives is the C professor. What is a professor who fails? Illustrate what constitutes a "failing" professor.

SOME POSSIBILITIES FOR WRITING

1. Compare and contrast the best and worst teacher and/or class you've had since starting college.

2. Many students spend nearly as much time devising ways to "con" or "suck up" to a professor as impressing one. Write an essay that compares and contrasts "sucking up" to "impressing" a teacher.

3. In his criteria for the C professor, Neusner establishes six minimum standards for what he calls "students' rights." Evaluate this list by considering how important to students each item on the list is. Would you add or subtract any items? Why?

Tales Out of School

AN EXCERPT **Susan Richards Shreve**

Susan Richards Shreve is the author of twelve novels, including *A Country of Strangers, The Train Home,* and *Plum and Jaggers.* She is an award-winning children's author and co-editor of *Tales Out of School: Contemporary Writers on Their Student Years.* In her thirty-five years as an educator, she has taught every level from kindergarten to graduate school.

"Why would you throw your life away?" my mother, the teacher, said to me the first year I taught school. "You could be anything and you choose to be a teacher."

CRITICAL THINKING POINTS: *As you read*

1. Watch for the author's role as student, parent, and teacher. How does her role impact each tale she tells?
2. What kind of student is the author/narrator? What kind of parent and teacher?
3. Can these tales be grouped or ordered in any way? If so, how?

1. The first day of first grade and I'm sitting in the front row, chewing off the collar of the dress my mother made me, a habit I had of eating the cotton collars of several outfits a year—a condition of general agitation that would be corrected today with regular doses of Ritalin. I'm watching Mrs. Comstock, soft, plump, weary, and very old, write on the blackboard.

"Who reads?" she asks.

I put up my hand. I don't read and wonder as I look around the room whether the other students with their hands up are telling the truth.

"Good," Mrs. Comstock says, satisfied that we're off to a fine start. "I'm going to write down the rules for First Grade, Section A, Mrs. Comstock's class."

1. NO lateness
2. NO impudence
3. NO speaking out in class
4. NO whispering

5. NO bathroom visits during class
6. NO morning recess unless classwork is completed
7. NO food in the classroom
8. NO temper tantrums
9. NO pushing or shoving when you line up
10. NO tears

I'm extremely pleased as I watch the list run down the blackboard. Although I can't read, do not even want to learn if it means, as I'm afraid it will, giving up the hours sitting next to my mother or father in my small bed while they read to me—I do recognize the word NO. I even count the number of NOs filling up the blackboard. There are ten.

"So," Mrs. Comstock says, turning around to face us. "Who can read me the rules?"

I don't raise my hand but there I am sitting directly in front of her and without a second's hesitation, she calls my name. I don't even stop to think.

"No, no, no, no, no, no, no, no, no, no," I say without taking a breath.

2. Checking the obituaries in the *Washington Post* as I have done forever, preferring the story of a whole life, pleased to fill in the missing spaces—I find on page three of the metro section the notice that my fifth grade teacher, age ninety-three, is dead of natural causes. Dead and I didn't know it. She slipped out of the world and I wasn't even aware of the sudden absence of danger when I woke up this morning.

I am a grown-up, forty-two with four children of my own, a responsible job as a teacher. A teacher of course, a teacher of all things.

"Why would you throw your life away?" my mother, the teacher, said to me the first year I taught school. "You could be anything and you choose to be a teacher."

I cut the obit and tape it on the refrigerator.

"My fifth grade teacher," I say when my children ask why the death of a stranger is noted on the fridge.

Friends School, Section 5-B on the first floor next to the library. I sat in the middle of the last row between Harry Slough, who smelled of old bananas, and God's perfect creation, Toni Brewer, with her loopy blond braids and straight A's.

"I never heard you mention your fifth grade teacher to us," one of my children says to me. "Are you *very* upset?"

"Not a bit," I reply. "Only that it took so long to happen."

They look at me in horror, knowing maybe for the first time, the full measure of revenge.

The story of my fifth grade teacher goes like this:

I was going to a Quaker school selective in its choice of students, no blacks, no learning disabilities, but willing to accept the occasional handicapped child that the public schools did not. I wasn't exactly handicapped but I had had polio and when I was young I wore metal braces and went around on crutches. Children like me used to be taught at home by drop-in tutors, our social lives accommodated by regular deliveries of turkeys and gumdrops and occasional coloring books from the local Kiwanas Club, which did nothing to compensate for the lonely life of home schooling.

It was late autumn before Thanksgiving and I had been in the habit of forgetting my math homework. Maybe I didn't do it and lied about it, maybe I never did my math homework—those details I have forgotten. But this morning the fifth grade teacher noted to the class that once again I had flunked my math test.

"But," she added with a show of enduring patience, folding her arms across her military chest, "we have to be nice to little Suzie Richards because she had polio."

3. In twelfth grade, with little distinction as a student but a belief, not commonly shared, that I was a promising writer, I had Mr. Forsythe as a teacher. We all did. We'd been waiting throughout high school for this extraordinary opportunity to write under his direction. The papers were long, analytic essays in response to questions about our readings in English literature. I had in mind to rescue my academic reputation in Mr. Forsythe's senior English and was stunned as paper after paper came back to me full of red pencil and paragraphs of criticism written in his tiny, crabbed hand with D+ and C− and D and D and D.

"I suppose you think I'm a terrible writer," I said when I finally went into his office.

He looked up under hooded eyes, an expression of unspeakable boredom on his face. "You make up your answers," he replied.

"These questions require research."

4. I am twenty-two living in England and I'm hired to teach what would be fourth grade at a school in a working-class community across the river from Liverpool. These students are hard-core tough, raised on cowboy movies where they've learned a new vocabulary—*ain't*, for example. There are forty of them and I have never taught school. The only thing I'm told before I walk into the makeshift classroom, two to a desk, is that caning in England is against the law. Of course, I think. I have a Dickensian view of caning, the craggy, long-faced wet-eyed master beating the child to smithereens with a heavy cane.

My despair as a teacher focuses on Lily Diamond, a small, plump, vacant child who has it in mind to drive me crazy. Maybe sixty times a day, she falls off her chair, turns upside down, her legs in the air, screaming, "Ain't, ain't, ain't, ain't," while the rest of the class goes wild with excitement. I have absolutely no control.

It has come to my attention that in the top drawer of my desk there is a small stick, not much longer than a pencil, the same width and hollow like a reed. I have begun to imagine this stick applied to the bottom of Lily Diamond. And one Wednesday during math, right in the middle of a chorus of "ain'ts" from the floor, I take out the stick, walk down the aisle—the children have gone dead silent—and carry out my fantasy. The rest of the school day is bliss. For the first time in weeks I can actually hear my own voice about theirs.

The following morning when I arrive at Birkenhead Elementary the police and the head of the school are standing on the front steps waiting for me. I'm ushered into the principal's office and there facedown on the principal's desk, her dress up, her pink panties pulled down so the full bottom is exposed, is Lily Diamond. Her mother is there with her arms folded across her chest, the officers of the law are examining Lily Diamond's bottom and Lily is screaming.

"I told the American that caning is against the law in England," the head of the school says to the police.

"I had thought a cane was an actual cane," I say, product of the sixties, against all punishment, certainly corporal, now a sudden criminal in my own court.

"A cane is a cane," the head of the school says coolly.

The police make their assessment, give Lily a friendly slap.

"No mark appears to be evident," they say.

Lily hops off the desk, pulls up her pants, shakes herself proudly, giving me a look of complete disdain.

"Ain't you terrible sorry," she says, drawing the word to its full length.

5. It is the summer of my younger son's freshman year in high school and thirty boys are in our living room planning an insurrection. One among them, Danny C, has been dismissed, voted out by the faculty, flunked, they say, unable to return to the Quaker school for his sophomore year.

"How come?" I ask.

"He's an artist," my son says.

"They think he's weird."

"Different."

"Bad."

"Learning disabled." The new catchphrase.

I have known this boy since he was five—a curious, ebullient boy, neither athletic, nor in a conventional sense academic, imaginative, impulsive, fearless.

The boys are examining reasons for his dismissal, studying the school handbook that outlines the rules, looking over Danny's report cards that he has brought to the meeting, as well as the letters the school has sent to his parents that he has slipped out of his mother's file cabinet. They spend all day.

The rules are specific. No drugs, no alcohol, no cheating, no failing grades. There are twenty-six reasons for dismissal and Danny C, as the boys discover, hasn't measured up to any of them.

"Wear coats and ties," my husband says as the boys organize their defense for the head of the school.

The mothers of these boys cannot imagine a reversal of the faculty decision, but cheerleaders always, we drive them to school on the morning of their meeting with Mr. Harrison—thirty adolescent boys with their argument in hand, point by point, all twenty-six reasons for dismissal addressed.

I wasn't at the meeting. The next I knew they were flooding into the house, shedding their ties, a victorious army, organizing their rule of the school for the next three years.

Mr. Harrison had reversed the decision.

"What happened?" I ask my son after everyone has gone home.

"Mr. Harrison is very brave," he says simply.

"How is that?" I ask.

"He listened to us."

6. When I am called to the nursery school where my oldest child is a student, one of twelve in a class of two teachers, Mrs. Nice and Mrs. Something Else, at the school where his father is head of the high school, I have a new baby and a two-year-old and no baby-sitter, so they come along. I have been called in to witness my son in action so I will understand why these two women in a small class are unable to manage him. So I sit in one of those little chairs with my finger in the new baby's mouth so he won't cry and wait for the drama to unfold.

"Po," Mrs. Nice is talking. "Please sit down at the table and get out your crayons."

No one else is sitting down but all around the room the other children turn to look at my son expectantly, a kind of pleasure in their attitude, waiting for something to happen.

My son doesn't sit down.

"Po," Mrs. Nice says again. "What did I tell you?"

He puts his hands over her ears and walks around the periphery of the room very quickly—dum dum dum dum de dum de dum de dum de dum. His hands are in his pockets now and the other children are giggling at him, glancing back and forth at each other. He gives them a knowing collaborator's look.

"You see?" Mrs. Nice says to me. She turns to my son as he passes her on his march.

"Your mother is here watching, Po," she says as if this news will come as a surprise to him. "So you better be good."

"He doesn't ever do what I ask him to do," Mrs. Nice says.

I am beginning to have that mother's sense of a temperature change in my son, an arriving decision, a moment of action. He has stopped his trip around the classroom and is listening to Mrs. Nice, an expression of bemusement on his face.

"Why haven't you told the other children to sit down?" I ask.

"Because they *will* sit down if I ask them to," she says. "So I don't need to ask them to, of course."

I am feeling homicidal.

Suddenly out of the corner of my eye, I see my son running across the room toward me, a maniacal smile on his face, leaping onto the table, racing around the edge of the circle with amazing speed and control, not even falling, his balance so perfect. All around the children are looking at him with something between admiration and envy.

Mrs. Nice is a picture of pure happiness.

"You see the problem, Mrs. Shreve?" she says. "Emotionally disturbed."

I pick up my two-year-old, grab Po by the hand, and we fly out of the room, down the corridor in which my four-year-old son spends hours sitting on a chair, into the parking lot, into the car and home.

"You see, Mom," Po says to me. "Mrs. Nice is crazy."

7. I am probably thirty-five, a teacher and administrator of an alternative school in Philadelphia called Our House for smart children in trouble, attending a conference of teachers in Atlanta where the major speaker will be Margaret Mead. I am sitting with my own children in the lobby of the hotel waiting for the speech when I notice a small, square woman, slightly hassled and bewildered, loaded down with bags and books and papers. I am in her line of vision and she stops.

"Do you know where the speech is?" she asks.

I know who this is, of course. These are the seventies, when Margaret Mead in many circles had the aura of a rock star. She was the mother of us all, accumulating weight from our acclamation.

I tell her this.

She is examining my children playing on the floor with Fisher-Price families and Legos and Matchbox cars.

"Are you coming to the speech?"

"Yes, I am," I reply, adding some compliment that she ignores.

"My speech is about the end of the family as we know it," she looks at me, assessing my role as mother. "Parents have abdicated their role and now the school must take over the family's job. In the next twenty years, they won't have time to educate." She brushes her small hands together, walks between a plastic Fisher-Price family and heads to the lectern.

8. I sit down in the office of the college guidance counselor, relieved that for the fourth and last time I am about to set out on the trip to look at colleges for a child. Especially with this child, this reader of *Anna Karenina* who has told me that she would prefer to be homeschooled or else to go to a fiercely strict Catholic school with nuns who carry rulers peering out of stiff white boards. Either freedom or confinement is what she's after. Not this wishy-washy middle of accommodation and concern and judgment, because no choice a child could possibly make in this atmosphere of freedom of choice will be the right one.

The college guidance counselor and my daughter are already seated and there is decision about the room.

"We are meeting to talk about Kate's college choices, which she should make by the end of her junior year," the counselor says.

Kate has been a good student in spite of her limited attendance, so I'm not worried, in fact almost comfortable this fourth time around.

"So what are you thinking, Kate?" the counselor asks, a conversation I can tell they have already had and are repeating for my benefit.

"I'm actually leaving high school," Kate says.

The counselor, a Quaker and therefore by definition nonconfrontational, looks at me with something close to fury.

"We have never had a student choose to drop out of high school in her junior year," she says.

"I didn't know this was happening," I say, immediately sorry that I hadn't said instead: "Of course. Kate and I discussed the subject last night and decided that high school was absolutely useless for her. Many better things to do with her time."

"I'm very sorry," Kate says, and always polite adds that she is quite fond of the school, admiring the college counselor, respectful of the values, but simply is no longer willing to spend her time there.

In the car coming home, trying to concentrate in order not to run a stop sign or red light or hyperventilate, I ask Kate what she plans to do.

"I haven't decided," she says. "I simply know that I'm not suited to high school."

I am reminded of a conversation I overheard when as a young mother I went to visit a friend whose daughter was in high school.

We were sitting in the living room when her daughter came home from school, dropped her books, her coat, and flopped down on the couch.

"I am miserable in high school," she said crossly to her mother.

"I'm so glad to hear that, darling," my friend said cheerfully. "All of the interesting people I know were miserable in high school."

9. Elizabeth is in fourth grade at a new school and I imagine that she's perfectly happy, since that's what she tells me. She is making new friends, although she doesn't want them to come over and never seems to be invited to their houses. She only misses her old school at night when I turn out the light in her room. So it comes as a terrible surprise when one of the fourth grade mothers asks me do I know about the I Hate Elizabeth Club. The mother has just discovered that her daughter belongs to it. Membership in the club costs a dollar, she tells me, and all the girls in the fourth grade have been asked to join or else to suffer exclusion if they refuse. The rules are simple. No one is allowed to speak to Elizabeth and members are rewarded for an imaginative punishment such as the sticking of straight pins in my daughter's back during Meetings for Worship.

"I thought it was my fault," Elizabeth says when I ask her why she never told me. She doesn't cry. She begs me not to tell the teacher or it will be worse for her.

"I have to," I tell her. "What they have done is terrible and your teacher has the right to know about it. She's in charge."

That night she tells me everything. Day after miserable day of the I Hate Elizabeth Club while I in my stupidity was thinking she was happy.

"What are you going to do then?" she asks me, lying next to me in the dark.

I have made a decision. Already what was done to my child is forming itself into a story in my mind.

"I'm going to write a book about them and call them each by name," I say.

"Maybe you'll be sued," she says.

"I won't be sued," I reply.

Sometime later, maybe three years, I am at lunch with Elizabeth and the former president of the I Hate Elizabeth Club. They aren't friends of course but the former president is trying. I can tell she wants to tell me something, has thought about it for a long time. She has apologized to Elizabeth, once when she had to because she was caught, and recently, just weeks before, when she meant it.

"You used my real name," she says finally.

"Yes I did."

"I read the book," she says. "I didn't realize what I'd done until I read about myself."

2000

CRITICAL THINKING POINTS: *After you've read*

1. Speculate why the narrator doesn't tell any positive stories about her teachers.
2. Does the narrator learn anything as a teacher from even so-called negative experiences with her own teachers or her children's?
3. As a mother, what qualities does the narrator seem to value in her children?

SOME POSSIBILITIES FOR WRITING

1. School rules often begin with "No . . . " Why is that? Research the ideology behind positive and negative rules.
2. Write one of your own "tales out of school."
3. Find and read Kendall Hailey's *The Day I Became an Autodidact* (Delacorte, 1988). How do Richards Shreve's tales compare?

No Immediate Danger

Mary McLaughlin Slëchta

Mary McLaughlin Slëchta (b. 1956) is a fiction writer and poet whose work has appeared in many journals and anthologies, including *New to North America* (1997) and *Identity Lessons: Learning American Style* (November 1998). She lives in Syracuse, New York, with her husband and two sons.

At the center of attention, I reposed like Play-Doh, forming and unforming itself at the pleasure and whim of the committee.

CRITICAL THINKING POINTS: *As you read*

1. A stark contrast exists between the narrator's life and the college where she interviews. What are some details in the story that show this?
2. Setting is very important in this story. Pay attention to all the different kinds of "times and places" represented in the story.
3. What pressure to succeed does the narrator feel? What kinds of things create that pressure?

On my fourth run through the kitchen, I remembered I'd made up my face but forgotten mascara, so I went to do that and the bacon burned. Fifty cents worth of smoking burnt pork and Hank screamed like it cost a week's paycheck. His week's paycheck. His empty stomach. "Don't even bother frying eggs if there's no bacon!"

"And did you finish feeding the baby?" he shouted as he slammed open windows. "I said, has the baby had her breakfast?"

When I rushed back to the kitchen, the baby was banging a spoon into a pool of cereal on the tray of the high chair. Her brown face and hair, like the nearest wall, were speckled with white flakes of oatmeal. She'd somehow broken the suction cup hold on her bowl and toppled it onto the floor. I quickly scraped the bacon pan into the trash and covered the steaming mess with newspaper. With a few quick sweeps of damp paper towels, I cleaned everything else: baby, spoon, chair, wall, and floor. Then I popped open a jar of pears and tried to coax the spoon from her hand. On top of the rude cleaning she'd received, this indignity was too much. She opened her mouth wide and howled.

"The smoke could have killed her!" Hank screeched from the outer limits of the apartment, still slamming open windows and doors. "Or were you planning a grease fire?"

I searched the utensil drawer and drain and then faced the sink where two days of breakfast, lunch, and dinner had crusted into a tottering mountain. There wasn't a spoon, clean or dirty, in sight and no dish detergent anyways. I'd known this. I'd known, been to the store more than once, and forgotten each time. There remained no choice but to wrestle the spoon from the baby's hand. She wailed even louder.

"See! See!" Hank shouted from the threshold. "You take care of your face and the baby goes hungry. Not to mention I gotta get up early to no breakfast and a stinking house that looks like a pigsty. What happens when you get a job?"

I spooned the runny pear into the baby's screaming mouth and caught it as it ran straight down her chin. Eat, eat, eat, stupid baby, I thought, and immediately promised to be kinder. It wasn't baby's fault. It wasn't Hank's either, though I'd like to think so. It's just that there's always too much to do. Like that morning, for instance. I had a 10:00 interview at a state college twenty miles out of Syracuse, and it was going to be tight.

Since morning, I'd given the apartment, baby included, what my mother would call "a lick and a promise." Only a Friday night never passes without her keeping those promises, mopping the kitchen floor at midnight if it comes to that. In the middle of the night, my promises hang before me like an unbalanced ledger. Specks of cereal on the wall would remain as reminders of one more unfinished job. A week later, I'd find traces of cereal matted in the coarse tangles of my daughter's hair. If I got to the dishes at all today, I'd have to use laundry detergent and rinse extra long.

Hank thrust the checkbook in my face. "You forgot to write in another check," he said with disgust.

"I wrote it down somewhere," I lied. "I'll put it in later."

"Later, later," he said. "Always later with you."

I'd coaxed the baby to take half of the pears before panic pushed against the bottom of my stomach. It felt dangerously late and traffic might be heavy. I wasn't exactly sure where I was going, where I'd park, and how far I'd have to walk or run.

"What's for her lunch, I'd like to know," Hank asked, breaking into my thoughts. I handed him the spoon.

To keep the peace, I bit my tongue at his nasty face twisted into a red knot and quietly relished small instruments of revenge: the baby bawling as I rummaged for keys; the phone ringing on my way out the door; Hank hollering "Mom!"

"Milk's in the freezer," I shouted over my shoulder. "Sweet potato, something else."

"You're gonna be late!" he screamed back accusingly, possibly shattering his mother's eardrum.

In my haste, I nearly tripped over the boy from upstairs curled pitifully on the front porch like a lost puppy. When I asked about school, he sank deeper inside his jacket and stared longingly at another boy in the street toting a boom box on his shoulder. The heavy bass and drive of the rapper clamped my chest like two tight fists pulling forward. But when the boy nodded towards us, I managed to smile and raise my arm hello. These boys needed to be in school or at least at home. I backed out the driveway and turned in a direction opposite from the teen hangout corner. I meant to avoid any more eyes of those whose mothers and grandmothers I knew.

Knowing I was a teacher, they expected more of me, some way of helping that they couldn't articulate and which I didn't want to bear.

With the late registration sticker on the car, I was careful not to speed within the city limits. Once on the highway, I made up time by keeping the needle quivering above sixty-five.

Now, plan for the interview, I ordered myself. In the same instant, I snapped on the radio for the time without realizing Hank had left the tape in play. The song that blasted through the speakers was one of our favorites back in college. A real funky dance beat like you don't hear anymore. My shoulders and head remembered how to swing to the beat. Hank and I were starting over again on the dance floor of the Student Union. No marriage, no baby—so little money that money wasn't a concern.

Eight years earlier, I'd waited in the car with the volume high like this, swinging my shoulders, fixing my hair, touching up my lipstick. Things I hadn't done with such ardor ever before in life—or since. Hank was my first boyfriend, and at twenty years old I was primping like a high school girl. Beyond the rearview mirror I watched Hank striding back from the supermarket, a bag of wine coolers under one arm. I could still count the number of times we'd kissed, and I was anticipating another within the next minute when I happened to turn my head towards the car beside ours. A bear of a man with mean little eyes raised his white fist with the thumb down.

"Let's get out of here," I told Hank when he dropped into the driver's seat and reached for that kiss.

I never got used to people staring at us like we'd offended them personally. Neither did Hank, I think. Having a child didn't legitimize our relationship either. People actually asked if it really was my baby. Eventually we found set patterns to follow that made isolation not only bearable but also indiscernible to the larger world. We found a word for our life together: "private." Dancing stopped. Holding his white hand against my brown one. We became simply ourselves, growing older and encased in a glass bubble with a baby. Safe enough, but never knowing when someone might turn a microscope on our very existence: *So how did you two meet? What did your parents think?* On the highway, the morning of the interview, I turned the music up like the boy in the street had done and sang louder.

I must have lost all sense of time and place because I was suddenly seeing signs for the exit in ten miles. Switching to the radio, I discovered I had ten minutes to be only five minutes late for a job interview—provided I was lucky with parking. Here it was again. Always when it counts the most, I'm running late. Drive and sheer luck usually cut the lateness to around five minutes. My twenty-four-hour-and-five-minute day. I imagine as time passes and old age and mental weariness take their toll, the time will increase proportionally. Ten minutes, twenty, thirty, forty—until I don't show up anywhere at all.

At this point in route, I passed a string of cars behind a semi when a girl in a bright red Trans Am raced behind me flashing her brights. As I slipped back into the right to the horn of the semi, she zoomed past like somebody leaving the scene of a crime. Almost immediately, I zigzagged around a blue sedan with a business-man yapping into a cell phone. For just an instant, my mouth wide open in song, our eyes met, and he gave me a disagreeable sneer. I set aside any possible meaning behind his features, snapped off the radio, and began to formulate my interview speech on setting up peer-group activities, very much in vogue in those days for Freshman Comp. Suddenly I noticed blue lights flashing in the rearview mirror. In the tension of the moment, my breasts stung with milk.

I instantly eased my pressure on the gas and moved back to the right lane, but there seemed to be no question. In a moment I would be sitting by the side of the road waiting for someone in a tall hat to finish writing a ticket. After a while, he would strut over and, barely looking at me, ask how fast I thought I was going. I would lie, of course. But then there would be other unpleasantries: the expired registration, previous points on my license. I prayed for divine intervention, promising that hereafter I would accept my destiny to arrive everywhere late and to do so without the pain of struggle. I must admit, I also began to see the fortu-ity of actually being stopped. Surely my interview could empathize with an all too human predicament.

Instead, nothing happened—to me, at least. In the mirror, I watched the blue sedan with the disagreeable businessman pull over, and my heart sank along with my adrenaline level. Someone else would be late somewhere for a legitimate reason. Sometime later this morning, a portly white man in a dark suit would stride into a meeting delayed for his convenience. Chances were he was right now phoning ahead while he waited for the opportunity to dispute the ticket. Afterwards he would hitch his pants up around his crotch and complain about the inequities of law enforcement. Not that anyone needed to know why he was late, but because it made a good story: how some black bitch passed him going seventy-five in a frig-gin heap of junk and he'd gotten screwed.

When I turned up thirteen minutes late to the English department office, the secretary glanced at the wall clock and let me pretend not to squirm while she fin-ished a phone conversation, distinctly personal in tone. Her upturned nose seemed to turn up a little higher at the sight of my face, shiny with sweat from running, and encircled by a frizzy halo of hair.

"They've been waiting for you," she whispered ominously as she finally ush-ered me into a conference.

"They?" I wondered with panic. Before I could bolt, eight very annoyed white faces stared up at me from a long narrow table. I apologized immediately, and some of the graying heads nodded politely. White people are never late, I thought, acknowledging their lukewarm greeting with a redemptive air of humility. I calcu-lated they'd been early and would meanly count that fact against me. I'd have to work harder to convince them of my abilities as a teacher.

I made a conscious effort not to let this inauspicious beginning injure my demeanor. I'd hung along the periphery of academic circles long enough to recog-nize that many who are prompt to a fault work far below 100-percent capability. Perhaps it's the prospect of free coffee and Danish that pulls them from the stagnant compartments of the university. Several of my interviewers were even now using the scattered copies of my resume as makeshift coasters and plates. What other small perks might they enjoy as members of an ad hoc hiring committee for adjuncts? Did they have a favorite pub in this provincial New York town where the locals, terrified of any threat to employment, pretended to be a soundless backdrop to their posturing eccentricities?

They went around the table with introductions and then around again with questions: B.A., M.A., thesis work, work experience, philosophy, method, approach. . . . The majority of questions I'd accurately predicted and actually planned for, although when and how I couldn't say. Maybe the night the baby kept me on the edge between sleep and wake with a racking, croupy cough. At any rate, now that I'd arrived and the issue of lateness had been handled with some finesse and the questions found to be manageable, I let my stiff back appreciate the cushions and began to critique the surroundings.

I found the formality of the setting particularly galling. Eight interrogators, coffee, Danish, and a pitcher of water for a low-paying, part-time, temporary position seemed superfluous, to say the least. The low pay compounded by a restrictive medical plan for the one-semester post—assuming I got it, which I figured I had a pretty good shot at doing since scuttlebutt had it the school was under legal pressure to hire more minorities and women—didn't warrant such extravagance. Was each candidate scrutinized so closely, I wondered, or did I appear to be a radical upstart in her last good jacket? One of that vast encroaching horde of minorities predicted to outnumber whites in the twenty-first century? There had been plenty of flags in my resume to sound off alarms.

As four or five of the interrogators forgot me and pursued a gentlemanly disagreement over the work of a well-known professor I'd used as a reference, I silently made prophesy. There would be no office space where I could meet my students during the required office hours. Two chairs in a corridor would have to do. The faculty would quickly come to know my name. Many of those not in attendance already did. At no point, however, would I have occasion to learn most of theirs. Some would be friendly at first, to a fault; some later; others never. Yet each would maintain a courteous air of detachment, much as they kept towards certain segments of their "diverse student body." I would be the subject of a story around the dinner table, part of an anecdote told at the next meeting of the hiring committee and the reason, if things did not go well with my "tenure," to resist hiring another minority. ("It never seems to work out!") I might perhaps be invited by marginal faculty members—the strident feminist at my right or the downstate transplant at my left whose every vowel made the others wince—to join them at that favorite pub. But having once stopped for lunch in a town like this one and been heckled by the locals back to my car, I had no intention of pushing my luck. I would truthfully say that my little girl needed me home. In fact, judging from one professor's surreptitious glances at my nursing mother's chest, I might enter the canon as a dusky paramour or the foil in a book about white angst. In my hoop earrings and fringed scarf, I could symbolize sensuous free expression in contrast to the cold analytical world of dust and doom around the table. At the center of attention, I reposed like Play-Doh, forming and unforming itself at the pleasure and whim of the committee.

The chairwoman at the head of the table called her chickens back to the yard. I hadn't understood this seat of control until she rapped firmly for attention and cleared her throat. She'd been in hiding among the others, and perhaps watching me watch them. The plain, matronly mask of indifference fell away and a fierce military expression took its place. The true guardian of the word, she meant to question me rigorously now, herself, and the others must be quiet and listen to a real expert. Each breath rattled in my gut before it came out my chest and throat and mouth a harmonic line of Standard English. Each word hung in the air as long as it took my interrogator to examine it top to bottom, inside to out. Sentence diagrams danced in the air above my head. You know this language, I reminded myself at intervals. But if you do too perfect a job, they'll doubt that you're a native speaker.

It was during my responses to the chairwoman, in fact, that I first became distracted by a barely perceptible but definitely rank odor. It was totally inconsistent with the paleness of the people, the walls, and the few impressionist paintings. I waited for the predictable allergy sufferer, frontline sufferer of sick building syndrome, to insist upon opening a window.

"We had a black adjunct a few years ago," the chairwoman told me later in her sunny office. "Things didn't work out," she added with a sad smile. "Are you sure you don't remember Professor W_____ at Amherst?"

Without a copy of my resume in hand, I was having great difficulty recalling names and places. I'd been accepted by a mysterious vote of approval around the table and now had secured the measly comp sections that would keep food on the table, Hank off my back, and my car on the road; yet, I was unable to satisfy the chairwoman's desire for small talk. My efforts to steer the conversation towards a more general topic proved futile. Already she was well into another story about the "very articulate Professor W_____ ," whom I assumed to be black.

Despite the tediousness of her chatter, or because of it, relief began to flood my entire body. A feeling of tenderness fluttered through my breasts and sent milk gushing into the pads of my bra. Over the course of a morning, this place had become comfortable. Here were a job and people, at least on the surface, who asked manageable questions and told anecdotes as they pleased. For whatever reason or reasons, they'd mutually decided to allow me some small entry into their private club. The fierce Germanic features of the chairwoman had taken on a cast of gentle Irish, and I forgave her her cultural insensitivity. The pale, well-manicured hand that reached across the desk and set a silver figurine swinging in perpetual motion would neither strike me nor point me towards the door. I was in no immediate danger.

When she stepped out a moment to check my paperwork with the secretary, I quickly straightened a trouser sock that had twisted like a child's in my shoe and gulped a cup of tepid coffee. As I grew sleepy watching the figurine swing back and forth between its narrow bars, only one nagging factor was left to concern me. The odd odor I'd detected in the meeting room was even more apparent in the office.

It was a rancid smell much like city children carry on them when they come indoors after heavy play. Clinging to their clothes and hair like nubby lint, it's an unwholesome mixture of exhaust fumes, sweat, fear, and greasy food. I wondered how such an odor had penetrated these walls and why the school hadn't removed it.

I found my answer waiting at home. A hungry daughter nestled at my breasts. I burrowed my nose into it. Burnt bacon.

1997

CRITICAL THINKING POINTS: *After you've read*

1. Why do you think the narrator gets the job? Did you expect her to? Why or why not? Why does she believe she gets the job? Do you agree with her? Why or why not?

2. After she finds out she has the job, the narrator says, "I was in no immediate danger." What impending or future danger is implied by her statement?

3. The narrator says to herself during the interview, "You know this language. . . . But if you do too perfect a job, they'll doubt that you're a native speaker." What might she mean?

SOME POSSIBILITIES FOR WRITING

1. Consciously or not, we all carry with us characteristics we have acquired from families, friends, neighborhoods, towns, or even larger geographic regions. Describe a time when your past or the place from which you came "followed" you to a new place. First recall a positive experience, then a negative one.

2. Write the scene in which the narrator tells Hank about her new position. What does she say? How does he react? What changes must be made in their life to deal with the new job?

3. The narrator is an outsider in many scenes in this story. What are some of them? What leads to her feeling this way in each of the scenes?

Teachers: A Primer

FROM *TIME'S FANCY*   **Ron Wallace**

Ron Wallace (b. 1945) is Felix Pollak Professor of Poetry and Halls-Bascom Professor of English at the University of Wisconsin–Madison and the author of many books of poetry including *Long for This World: New & Selected Poems* and *Quick Bright Things*.

She had a policy: A tattletale
or liar had to face the wall,
a tail pinned to his sorry ass,
and wear the laughter of the class.

CRITICAL THINKING POINTS: *As you read*

1. What is a "primer"?
2. What grades does Wallace cover in the poem? As you read, speculate about the grade level for each teacher and what subject he or she teaches.
3. Why do you think the poet chooses the names he does for the teachers he describes?

MRS. GOLDWASSER
Shimmered like butterscotch; the sun
had nothing on her. She bangled
when she walked. No one
did not love her. She shone,
she glowed, she lit up any room,
her every gesture jewelry.
And O, when she called us all by name
how we all performed!
Her string of little beads,
her pearls, her rough-cut
gemstones, diamonds, we hung
about her neck. And when
the future pressed her flat,
the world unclasped, and tarnished.

MRS. SANDS
Always dressed in tan. Her voice
abrasive as her name. What choice
did a second grader have? You got
what you got. Her room was hot
but she wore wool and heavy sweat
and worked our childhoods, short and sweet.
You didn't sass her or the school or
she'd rap your knuckles with a ruler.
She had a policy: A tattletale
or liar had to face the wall,
a tail pinned to his sorry ass,
and wear the laughter of the class.
So, to this day, my knuckles bent,
I tell the truth (but tell it slant).

MRS. ORTON
The perennial substitute, like some
obnoxious weed, a European interloper
in our native prairie, her instructions
full of nettles, her gestures parsnip
and burdock. Every day at 3:00 P.M.
we'd dig her out of our small lives,
and every morning she'd pop back.
We prayed she'd get the sack.
And to that end we taunted her—
tacks on her chair, a set-back clock—
as, weeping, she plodded through the week
turning, and turning the other cheek.
And every time we thought that we'd
eradicated her, she'd gone to seed.

MISS WILLINGHAM
A Southern Belle, she read *Huck Finn*
aloud to us, dropping her chin
to get the accent right. And me,
for some odd reason, she
singled out to learn the books
of the Bible and recite them back
to her in my high voice
I tried to measure lower. *Nice
boys go to Sunday school,* she said,
and made me promise, when I was grown,

to glorify our heavenly Lord
and take His teaching for my own.
And when she finished that dull story,
she lit out for the territory.

MR. AXT
The basketball coach. Short, tough.
Three days growth on his sharp chin.
Liked to see us all play rough,
and beat up on the stupid, thin,
weak kids who couldn't take it.
He wore white T-shirts, shoes, and slacks,
and taught us all to fake it
if we somehow naturally lacked
the mean competitive spirit.
Once a week he'd have us
bend over and spread our cheeks
for him and old Doc Moffett
who liked to slap us on the butt
and watch as we took leaks.

MRS. REPLOGLE
Her name forbidding, reptilian,
her reputation like a snake
around my expectations.
But then she played *Swan Lake*
and Ferde Grofe's *Grand Canyon Suite,*
a Bach chorale, a Beethoven quartet,
and when we were all back on the street
even the traffic kept a beat.
One day she had us close our eyes
and listen to a symphony
and write whatever image rose
in our small imagination's dark.
And what I saw was poetry,
each note a bird, a flower, a spark.

MR. GLUSENKAMP
His gray face was a trapezoid, his voice
droned on like an ellipse.
He hated students and their noise
and loved the full eclipse

of their faces at the end of the day.
No one could have been squarer,
and nothing could have been plainer
than his geometry.
He didn't go for newfangled
stuff—new math, the open classroom.
And yet he taught us angles
and how lines intersect and bloom,
and how infinity was no escape,
and how to give abstractions shape.

MR. WATTS
Sat cross-legged on his desk,
a pretzel of a man, and grinned
as if chemistry were some cosmic joke
and he'd been dealt a hand
of wild cards, all aces.
He drew for us a "ferrous" wheel
and showed when formic acid reverses
HCOOH becomes HOOCH, a peal
of laughter ringing from his nose.
He gave us Avogadro's number
and in his stained lab clothes
formulas for blowing the world asunder
or splitting genes. God knows
why he died shouting "No!" in thunder.

MISS GOFF
When Zack Pulanski brought the plastic vomit
and slid it slickly to the vinyl floor
and raised his hand, and her tired eyes fell on it
with horror, the heartless classroom lost in laughter
as the custodian slyly tossed his saw dust on it
and pushed it, grinning, through the door,
she reached into her ancient corner closet
and found some Emily Dickinson mimeos there
which she passed out. And then, herself
passed out on the cold circumference of her desk.
And everybody went their merry ways
but me, who chancing on one unexpected phrase
after another, sat transfixed until dusk.
Me and Miss Goff, the top of our heads taken off.

1989

CRITICAL THINKING POINTS: *After you've read*

1. What lessons does Wallace learn from each teacher? Make a list. How does he learn what he does?

2. How do these "lessons" reflect his becoming a poet? Do you think they helped make him a poet, or does his being a poet now simply make these lessons more memorable in retrospect?

3. What stereotypes of teachers are apparent in the poem?

SOME POSSIBILITIES FOR WRITING

1. Recall a teacher who stands out in your memory because of his or her personality, mannerisms, and so on. Write a one-page description of that teacher using specific details.

2. Choose another teacher from a work in this collection and compare him or her to one of Wallace's teachers.

3. Choose a teacher you did not understand or appreciate during the time you were in that teacher's class but learned to appreciate later. What happened to change your mind?

Open Admissions

Shirley Lauro

Shirley Lauro (b. 1933) is a former professor of speech. This play was selected for the *New York Times* "Ten Best Plays of the Year" list and was chosen as co-winner of the Fourth Annual Off-Off-Broadway Original Short Play Festival.

I'll 'ax' you how come I have been in this here college three months on this here Open Admissions and I don't know nothin more than when I came in here?

CRITICAL THINKING POINTS: *As you read*

1. What kind of person is the teacher? The student? Choose some adjectives that would describe each of them. What details in the play support your opinions?

2. Dialogue often depends as much on what goes unsaid as what is said. Pay attention throughout the play to what the characters don't really say but seem to be talking about. Why do you think that is so?

3. Pay attention to the words the teacher uses as examples of the student's "substandard urban patterns." Do you think that these words are chosen by the teacher (or the author) completely by accident?

The Characters

Professor Alice Miller: Professor of Speech Communications. Started out to be a Shakespearean scholar. Has been teaching Speech at a city college in New York for twelve years. She is overloaded with work and exhausted. Late thirties. Wears skirt, blouse, sweater, coat, gloves. Carries briefcases.

Calvin Jefferson: Eighteen, a Freshman in Open Admissions Program at the college. Black, powerfully built, handsome, big. At first glance a streetperson, but belied by his intensity. Wears jacket, jeans, cap, sneakers. Has been at the college three months, hoping it will work out.

The Place

A cubicle speech office at a city college in New York.

The Time

The present. Late fall. 6 o'clock in the evening.

The play begins on a very high level of tension and intensity and builds from there. The level of intensity is set by CALVIN who enters the play with a desperate urgency, as though he had arrived at the emergency room of a hospital, needing immediate help for a serious problem. He also enters in a state of rage and frustration but is containing these feelings at first. The high level of tension is set by both ALICE and CALVIN and occurs from the moment CALVIN enters. ALICE wants to leave. She does not want the scene to take place. The audience's experience from the start should be as if they had suddenly tuned in on the critical round of a boxing match.

CALVIN'S speech is "Street Speech" jargon. Run-on sentences and misspellings in the text are for the purpose of helping the actor with the pronunciations and rhythms of the language.

The speech office of Professor Alice Miller in a city college in New York. A small cubicle with partitions going three-quarters of the way up. Windowless, airless, with a cold antiseptic quality and a strong sense of impersonalness and transience. The cubicle has the contradictory feelings of claustrophobia and alienation at the same time. It is a space used by many teachers during every day of the week.

On the glass-windowed door it says:

SPEECH COMMUNICATIONS DEPT.
Prof. Alice Miller, B.A., M.A., Ph.D.

There are other names beneath that.

In the cubicle there is a desk with nothing on it except a phone, a chair with a rain coat on it, a swivel chair and a portable blackboard on which has been tacked a diagram of the "Speech Mechanism." Room is bare except for these things.

At Rise: *Cubicle is in darkness. Muted light filters through glass window on door from hallway. Eerie feeling. A shadow appears outside door. Someone enters, snapping on light.*

It is Alice. She carries a loose stack of essays, a booksack loaded with books and a grade book, one Shakespeare book, two speech books, and a portable cassette recorder. She closes the door, crosses to the desk, puts the keys in her purse, puts purse and booksack down and dials "0."

ALICE: Outside please. (*Waits for this, then dials a number.*) Debbie? Mommy, honey. . . . A "93"? Terrific! Listen, I just got through. I had to keep the class late to finish. . . . So, I can't stop home for dinner. I'm going right to the meeting . . . no, I'll be safe . . . don't worry. But you go put the double lock on, ok? And eat the cold meatloaf. (*She puts essays in booksack.*) See you later. Love you too. (*She kisses the receiver.*) Bye.

(She hangs up, puts on coat, picks up purse and booksack, crosses to door and snaps off light. Then opens door to go. CALVIN looms in doorway.)

ALICE: OOHH! You scared me!

CALVIN: Yes ma'am, I can see I scared you okay. I'm sorry.

ALICE: Calvin Washington? 10:30 section?

CALVIN: Calvin Jefferson. 9:30 section.

ALICE: Oh, right. Of course. Well, I was just leaving. Something you wanted?

CALVIN: Yes, Professor Miller. I came to talk to you about my grades. My grade on that Shakespeare project especially.

ALICE: Oh. Yes. Well. What did you get, Calvin? A *B* wasn't it? Something like that?

CALVIN: UMHMM. Thass right. Somethin like that . . .

ALICE: Yes. Well, look, I don't have office hours today at all. It's very dark already. I just stopped to make a call. But if you'd like to make an appointment for a conference, I'm not booked yet next month. Up 'till then, I'm just jammed.

CALVIN: Thass two weeks! I need to talk to you right now!

ALICE: Well what exactly is it about? I mean the grade is self-explanatory— "Good"—*B* work. And I gave you criticism in class the day of the project, didn't I? So what's the problem?

CALVIN: I wanna sit down and talk about *why* I got that grade! And all my grades in point of fact.

ALICE: But I don't have office hours today. It's very late and I have another commitment. Maybe tomor—*(She tries to leave.)*

CALVIN: *(voice rising)* I have to talk to you now!

ALICE: Look, tomorrow there's a faculty meeting. I can meet you here afterwards . . . around 12:30. Providing Professor Roth's not scheduled to use the desk.

CALVIN: I got a job tomorrow! Can't you talk to me right now?

ALICE: But what's it about? I don't see the emergen—

CALVIN: *(voice rising loudly)* I jiss *tole* you what it's about! My project and *my grades* is what it's about!

ALICE: *(glancing down the hall, not wanting a commotion overheard)* All right! Just stop shouting out here, will you? *(She snaps on light and crosses to desk.)* Come on in. I'll give you a few minutes now. *(He comes in)* *(She pulls purse and booksack down and sits at desk.)* Okay. Now then. What?

CALVIN: *(Closes door and crosses UC. Silent for a moment looking at her. Then—)* How come all I ever git from you is *B*?

ALICE: *(stunned)* What?

CALVIN: This is the third project I did for you. An all I ever git is *B*.

ALICE: Are you joking? This is what you wanted to talk about? *B* is an excellent grade!

CALVIN: No it's not! *A* is "excellent." *B* is "good."

ALICE: You don't think you deserved an *A* on those projects, do you?

CALVIN: No. But I got to know how to improve myself somehow, so maybe sometime I can try for a *A*. I wouldn't even mind on one of those projects if I got a *C*. Thass average—if you know what I mean? Or a *D*. But all I ever git from you is *B*. It don't matter what I do in that Speech Communications Class, seems like. I come in the beginnin a it three months ago? On the Open Admissions? Shoot, I didn't know which end was up. I stood up there and give this speech you assigned on "My Hobby." You remember that?

ALICE: *(Reads note on desk.)* About basketball?

CALVIN: Huh-uh. That was Franklin Perkins give that speech. Sits in the back row?

ALICE: *(Tosses note in wastebasket.)* Oh. Yes. Right. Franklin.

CALVIN: Umhmm. I give some dumb speech about "The Hobby a Makin Wooden Trays."

ALICE: Oh, yes. Right. I remember that.

CALVIN: Except I didn't have no hobby makin wooden trays, man. I made one in high school one time, thass all.

ALICE: *(Leafs through pages of speech books.)* Oh, well, that didn't matter. It was the speech that counted.

CALVIN: Umhmm? Well, that was the sorriest speech anybody ever heard in their lives! I was scared to death and couldn't put one word in front a the other any way I tried. Supposed to be five minutes. Lasted two! And you give me a *B!*

ALICE: *(Rises, crosses to DR table and puts speech books down.)* Well, it was your first time up in class, and you showed a lot of enthusiasm and effort. I remember that speech.

CALVIN: Everybody's firss time up in class, ain't it?

ALICE: Yes. Of course.

CALVIN: *(Crosses DR to ALICE)* That girl sits nex to me, that Judy Horowitz—firss time she was up in class too. She give that speech about "How to Play the Guitar?" And man, she brought in charts and taught us to read chords and played a piece herself an had memorized the whole speech by heart. An you give her a *B*.

ALICE: *(Crosses to desk, picks up booksack and puts it on desk.)* Well, Judy's organization and her outline was a little shaky as I recall.

CALVIN: *(Crosses end of desk.)* I didn't even turn no outline in.

ALICE: *(Picks up purse and puts it on desk.)* You didn't?

CALVIN: *(Leans in.)* Huh-uh. Didn't you notice?

ALICE: Of course! It's—just—well, it's been sometime—*(She quickly takes the gradebook from the booksack and looks up his name.)* Let me see, oh, yes. Right. Here, I see. You didn't hand it in . . .

CALVIN: Thass right, I didn'.

ALICE: You better do that before the end of the term.

CALVIN: I can't. Because I don' know which way to do no outline!

ALICE: *(Looks up name in gradebook and marks it with red pencil.)* Oh. Well . . . that's all right. Don't worry about it, okay? *(She puts gradebook away.)* Just work on improving yourself in other ways.

CALVIN: What other ways? Only thing you ever say about anything I ever done in there is how I have got to get rid of my "Substandard Urban Speech!"

ALICE: *(Picks up two files from desk and crosses UCR file cabinet.)* Well, yes, you do! You see, that's your real problem, Calvin! "Substandard Speech." It undercuts your "Positive Communicator's Image!" Remember how I gave a lecture about that? About how all of you here have Substandard Urban Speech because this is a Sub— an *Urban* College. *(She puts on gloves.)* Remember? But that's perfectly okay! It's okay! Just like I used to have Substandard Midwestern Speech when I was a student. Remember my explaining about that? How I used to say "crik" for "creek," and "kin" for "can" and "tin" for "ten"? *(She crosses in back of desk and chuckles at herself.)* Oh, and my breathiness! *(She picks up purse.)* That was just my biggest problem of all: Breathiness. I just about worked myself to death up at Northwestern U. getting it right straight out of my speech. Now, that's what you have to do too, Calvin. *(She picks up booksack and keys.)* Nothing to be ashamed of—but get it right straight out! *(She is ready to leave. She pats CALVIN on the shoulder and crosses UC.)*

CALVIN: *(Pause. Looks at her.)* Thass how come I keep on gittin B?

ALICE: "That's."

CALVIN: *(Steps in to ALICE.)* Huh?

ALICE: "That's." Not "Thass." Can't you hear the difference? "That's" one of the words in the Substandard Black Urban Pattern. No final "T's." Undermining your Positive Image . . . labeling you. It's "Street Speech." Harlemese. Don't you remember? I called everyone's attention to your particular syndrome in class the minute you started talking?
(He looks at her, not speaking.)

ALICE: It's "last," not "lass;" "first," not "firss." That's your friend, that good old "Final T!" Hear *it* when I talk?

CALVIN: Sometimes. When you say *it*, hitting *it* like that!

ALICE: Well, you should be going over the exercises on it in the speech book all the time, and recording yourself on your tape recorder. (*She pats booksack.*)

CALVIN: I don't got no tape recorder.

ALICE: Well, borrow one! (*She turns away.*)

CALVIN: (*Crosses in back of ALICE to her right.*) On that Shakespeare scene I jiss did? Thass why I got a *B*? Because of the "Final T's"?

ALICE: (*Backs DS a step.*) Well, you haven't improved your syndrome, have you?

CALVIN: How come you keep on answerin me by axin me something else?

ALICE: And that's the other one.

CALVIN: What "other one"?

ALICE: Other most prevalent deviation. You said: "axing" me something else.

CALVIN: Thass right. How come you keep axin somethin else?

ALICE: "Asking me," Calvin, "asking me!"

CALVIN: I jiss did!

ALICE: No, no. Look. That's classic Substandard Black! Textbook case. (*She puts purse and booksack down and crosses to diagram on blackboard.*) See, the jaw and teeth are in two different positions for the two sounds, and they make two completely different words! (*She writes "ass-king," and "axing" on the blackboard, pronouncing them in an exaggerated way for him to see.*) "ass-king" and "ax-ing." I am "assking" you the question. But, the woodcutter is "axing" down the tree. Can't you hear the difference? (*She picks up his speech book from desk.*) Here.
(*CALVIN follows her to desk.*)

ALICE: Go over to page 105. It's called a "Sharp S" problem with a medial position "sk" substitution. See? "skin, screw, scream"—those are "sk" sounds in the Primary Position. "Asking, risking, frisking"—that's medial position. And "flask, task, mask"—that's final position. Now you should be working on those, Calvin. Reading those exercises over and over again. I mean the way you did the Othello scene was just ludicrous: "Good gentlemen, I ax thee—" (*She crosses to the board and points to "ax-ing." She chuckles.*) That meant Othello was chopping the gentlemen down!

CALVIN: How come I had to do the Othello scene anyhow? Didn't git any choice. An Franklin Perkins an Sam Brown an Lester Washington they had to too.

ALICE: What do you mean?

CALVIN: An Claudette Jackson an Doreen Simpson an Melba Jones got themselves assigned to Cleopatra on the Nile?

ALICE: Everyone was assigned!

CALVIN: Uh-huh. But everybody else had a choice, you know what I mean? That Judy Horowitz, she said you told her she could pick outa five, six different characters. And that boy did his yesterday? That Nick Rizoli? Did the Gravedigger? He said he got three, four to choose off of too.

ALICE: (*Crosses to CALVIN.*) Well some of the students were "right" for several characters. And you know, Calvin, how we talked in class about Stanislavsky and the importance of "identifying" and "feeling" the part?

CALVIN: Well how Doreen Simpson "identify" herself some Queen sittin on a barge? How I supposed to "identify" some Othello? I don't!

ALICE: (*Crosses to blackboard, picks up fallen chalk.*) Oh, Calvin, don't be silly.

CALVIN: (*Crosses center.*) Well, I don'! I'm not no kind a jealous husband. I haven't got no wife. I don' even got no girlfriend, hardly! And thass what it's all about ain't it? So what's it I'm suppose to "identify" with anyhow?

ALICE: (*Turns to CALVIN.*) Oh, Calvin, what are you arguing about? You did a good job!

CALVIN: B job, right?

ALICE: Yes.

CALVIN: (*Crosses to ALICE.*) Well, what's that B standin for? Cause I'll tell you somethin you wanna know the truth: I stood up there didn' hardly know the sense a anythin I read, couldn't hardly even read it at all. Only you didn't notice. Wasn't even listenin, sittin there back a the room jiss thumbin through your book. (*ALICE crosses to desk.*)

CALVIN: So you know what I done? Skip one whole paragraph, tess you out—you jiss kep thumbin through your book! An then you give me a B! (*He has followed ALICE to desk.*)

ALICE: (*Puts papers in box and throws out old coffee cup.*) Well that just shows how well you did the part!

CALVIN: You wanna give me somethin I could "identify" with, how come you ain' let me do that other dude in the play . . .

ALICE: Iago?

CALVIN: Yeah. What is it they calls him? Othello's . . .

ALICE: Subordinate.

CALVIN: Go right along there with my speech syndrome, wouldn' it now? See, Iago has to work for the Man. I identifies with him! He gits jealous man. Know what I mean? Or that Gravedigger? Shovelin dirt for his day's work! How come you wouldn't let me do him? Thass the question I wanna ax you!

ALICE: (*Turns to CALVIN.*) "Ask me," Calvin, "Ask me!"

CALVIN: (*Steps SR.*) "Ax you?" Okay, man. (*Turns to ALICE.*) Miss Shakespeare, Speech Communications 1! (*Crosses US of ALICE.*) Know what I'll "ax" you right here in this room, this day, at this here desk right now? I'll "ax" you how come I have been in this here college three months on this here Open Admissions and I don't know nothin more than when I came in here? You know what I mean? This supposed to be some big break for me. This here is where all them smart Jewish boys has gone from the Bronx Science and went an become some Big Time Doctors at Bellevue. An some Big Time Judges in the Family Court an like that there. And now it's supposed to be my turn.

(ALICE looks away and CALVIN crosses R of ALICE.)

CALVIN: You know what I mean? *(He crosses UR.)* An my sister Jonelle took me out of foster care where I been in six homes and five school to give me my chance. *(He crosses DR.)* Livin with her an she workin three shifts in some "Ladies Restroom" give me my opportunity. An she say she gonna buss her ass git me this education I don't end up on the streets! *(Crosses on a diagonal to ALICE.)* Cause I have got brains!

(ALICE sits in student chair. CALVIN crosses in back, to her left.)

CALVIN: You understand what I am communicatin to you? My high school has tole me I got brains an can make somethin outta my life if I gets me the chance! And now this here's supposed to be my chance! High school says you folks gonna bring me up to date on my education and git me even. Only nothin is happenin to me in my head except I am getting more and more confused about what I knows and what I don't know! *(He sits in swivel chair.)* So what I wanna "ax" you is: How came you don't sit down with me and teach me which way to git my ideas down instead of givin me a B?

(ALICE rises and crosses UR.)

CALVIN: I don't even turn no outline in? Jiss give me a B. *(He rises and crosses R of ALICE.)* An Lester a B! An Melba a B! and Sam a B! What's that B standin for anyhow? Cause it surely ain't standin for no piece of work!

ALICE: Calvin don't blame me!

(CALVIN crosses DR.)

ALICE: I'm trying! God knows I'm trying! The times are rough for everyone. I'm a Shakespearean scholar, and they have me teaching beginning speech. I was supposed to have twelve graduate students a class, nine classes a week, and they gave me thirty-five freshman a class, twenty classes a week. I hear 157 speeches a week! You know what that's like? And I go home late on the subway scared to death! In Graduate School they told me I'd have a first-rate career. Then I started here and they said: "Hang on! Things will improve!" But they only got worse . . . and worse! Now I've been here for twelve years and I haven't written one word in my field! I haven't read five research books! I'm exhausted . . . and I'm finished! We all have to bend. I'm just hanging on now . . . supporting my little girl . . . earning a living . . . and that's all . . . *(She crosses to desk.)*

CALVIN: *(Faces ALICE.)* What I'm supposed to do, feel sorry for you? Least you can *earn* a livin! Clean office, private phone, name on the door with all them B.A.'s, M.A.'s, Ph.D.'s.

ALICE: You can have those too. (*She crosses DR to CALVIN.*) Look, last year we got ten black students into Ivy League Graduate Programs. And they were not better than you. They were just *perceived* (*Points to blackboard.*) as better. Now that's the whole key for you . . . to be perceived as better! So you can get good recommendations and do well on interviews. You're good looking and ambitious and you have a fine native intelligence. You can make it, Calvin. All we have to do is work on improving your Positive Communicator's Image . . . by getting rid of that Street Speech. Don't you see?

CALVIN: See what? What you axin *me* to see?

ALICE: "*Asking*" me to see, Calvin. "*Asking*" me to see!

CALVIN: (*Starts out of control at this, enraged, crosses UC and bangs on file cabinet.*) Ooooeee! Ooooeee! You wanna *see?* You wanna *see?* Ooooeee!

ALICE: Calvin stop it! STOP IT!

CALVIN: "Calvin stop it"? "Stop it"? (*Picks up school books from desk.*) There any black professors here?

ALICE: (*Crosses UR.*) No! They got cut . . . the budget's low . . . they got . . .

CALVIN: (*interrupting*) Cut? They got CUT? (*Crosses to ALICE and backs her to the DS edge of desk.*) Gonna *cut you,* lady! Gonna cut you, throw you out the fuckin' window, throw the fuckin' books out the fuckin' window, burn it all mother fuckin' down. FUCKIN' DOWN!!!

ALICE: Calvin! Stop it! STOP IT! YOU HEAR ME?

CALVIN: (*Turns away, center stage.*) I CAN'T!! *YOU* HEAR ME? I CAN'T! *YOU* HEAR *ME?* I CAN'T! YOU GOTTA GIVE ME MY EDUCATION! GOTTA TEACH ME! GIVE ME SOMETHING NOW! GIVE ME NOW! NOW! NOW! NOW! NOW! NOW! (*Calvin tears up textbook. He starts to pick up torn pages and drops them. He bursts into a wailing, bellowing cry in his anguish and despair, doubled over in pain and grief. It is a while before his sobs subside. Finally, ALICE speaks.*)

ALICE: Calvin . . . from the bottom of my heart . . . I want to help you . . .

CALVIN: (*barely able to speak*) By changin' my words? Thass nothin . . . nothin! I got to know them big ideas . . . and which way to git em down . . .

ALICE: But how can I teach you that? You can't write a paragraph, Calvin . . . or a sentence . . . you can't spell past fourth grade . . . the essay you wrote showed that . . . .

CALVIN: (*rises*) What essay?

ALICE: (*Crosses to UL files, gets essay and hands it to CALVIN.*) The autobiographical one . . . you did it the first day . . .

CALVIN: You said that was for *your* reference . . . didn't count . . .

ALICE: Here . . .

CALVIN: (*Opens it up. Stunned.*) F? Why didn't you tell me I failed?

ALICE: (*Crosses to desk, puts essay down.*) For what?

CALVIN: (*Still stunned.*) So you could teach me how to write.

ALICE: (*Crosses DL.*) In sixteen weeks?

CALVIN: (*Still can't believe this.*) You my teacher!

ALICE: That would take years! And speech is my job. You need a tutor.

CALVIN: I'm your job! They outa tutors!

ALICE: (*Turns to him.*) I can't do it, Calvin. And that's the real truth. I'm one person, in one job. And I can't. Do you understand? And even if I could, it wouldn't matter. All that matters is the budget . . . and the curriculum . . . and the grades . . . and how you look . . . and how you talk!

CALVIN: (*Pause. Absorbing this.*) Then I'm finished, man. (*There is a long pause. Finally—*)

ALICE: (*Gets essay from desk, refiles it and returns to desk.*) No, you're not. If you'll bend and take what I can give you, things will work out for you . . . Trust me . . . Let me help you Calvin . . . Please . . . I can teach you speech . . .

CALVIN: (*Crosses to UC file cabinet. Long pause.*) Okay . . . all right, man . . . (*Crosses to student chair and sits.*)

ALICE: (*Crosses to desk, takes off rain coat and sits in swivel chair.*) Now, then, we'll go through the exercise once then you do it at home . . . please, repeat after me, slowly . . . "asking" . . . "asking" . . . "asking" . . .

CALVIN: (*long pause*) Ax-ing . . .

ALICE: Ass-king . . .

CALVIN: (*During the following, he now turns from ALICE, faces front, and gazes out beyond the audience; on his fourth word, lights begin to fade to black*) Ax-ing . . . Aks-ing . . . ass-king . . . asking . . . asking . . . asking . . .

BLACKOUT

1983

CRITICAL THINKING POINTS: *After you've read*

1. What are some of the reasons the teacher offers the specific criticism she does? What other types of criticism might she have made? What are some of the reasons you think she did not make other types of criticism?

2. Why does the play end the way it does? What might have been some other possible endings? How would some of your imagined alternative endings change what you think and how you feel about the play?

3. It may seem obvious that Alice's job as a teacher requires her to help Calvin learn. Under what kinds of circumstances might that not be so? Why might Alice think that is not always so?

SOME POSSIBILITIES FOR WRITING

1. Write a brief report for your class on the procedures in place for contesting a grade at your school.
2. Is either character, or both, "right" in this play? What are some of the reasons you believe what you do?
3. Have you ever received a grade higher than you felt you deserved? Why do you think that happened? How did you feel about it?

What Teachers Make or You can always go to law school if things don't work out

Taylor Mali

Taylor Mali lives and writes in New York City. He wants to be the person responsible for an entire generation of college graduates considering teaching before business or law school. You can read more of his work at *www.taylormali.com* or hear him read this poem.

I make kids work harder than they ever thought they could.
I can make a C+ feel like a Congressional medal of honor
and an A− feel like a slap in the face.

CRITICAL THINKING POINTS: *As you read*

1. Which statements about teachers seem unrealistic and/or overly idealistic? Why?
2. What parts of this poem seem like things teachers shouldn't make? Why?
3. What parts of this poem would your parents particularly admire or be troubled by? Why?

He says the problem with teachers is, "What's a kid going to learn
from someone who decided his best option in life was to become a
teacher?"
He reminds the other dinner guests that it's true what they say about
teachers:
Those who can, do; those who can't, teach.

I decide to bite my tongue instead of his
and resist the temptation to remind the dinner guests
that it's also true what they say about lawyers.

Because we're eating, after all, and this is polite company.

"I mean, you're a teacher, Taylor," he says.
"Be honest. What do you make?"

And I wish he hadn't done that
(asked me to be honest)

because, you see, I have a policy
about honesty and ass-kicking:
if you ask for it, I have to let you have it.

You want to know what I make?

I make kids work harder than they ever thought they could.
I can make a C+ feel like a Congressional medal of honor
and an A− feel like a slap in the face.
How dare you waste my time with anything less than your very best.

I make kids sit through 40 minutes of study hall
in absolute silence. No, you may not work in groups.
No, you may not ask a question.
Why won't I let you get a drink of water?
Because you're not thirsty, you're bored, that's why.

I make parents tremble in fear when I call home:
I hope I haven't called at a bad time,
I just wanted to talk to you about something Billy said today.
Billy said, "Leave the kid alone. I still cry sometimes, don't you?"
And it was the noblest act of courage I have ever seen.

I make parents see their children for who they are
and what they can be.

You want to know what I make?

I make kids wonder,
I make them question.
I make them criticize.
I make them apologize and mean it.
I make them write.
I make them read, read, read.
I make them spell definitely beautiful, definitely beautiful,
definitely beautiful
over and over and over again until they will never misspell
either one of those words again.
I make them show all their work in math.
And hide it on their final drafts in English.
I make them understand that if you got this (brains)
then you follow this (heart) and if someone ever tries to judge you
by what you make, you give them this (the finger).

Let me break it down for you, so you know what I say is true:
I make a goddamn difference! What about you?

2002

CRITICAL THINKING POINTS: *After you've read*

1. This poem was meant primarily to be read out loud. What elements would contribute to it being presented that way? Why?

2. Do you agree with the statement, "Those who can, do; those who can't, teach"? Why or why not?

3. What might be some answers to "What's a kid going to learn from someone who decided his best option in life was to become a teacher?"

SOME POSSIBILITIES FOR WRITING

1. Write your own poem, maybe "What Lawyers Make," or choose a profession you are considering.

2. Given the often relatively low pay and social status, why would someone want to become a teacher?

3. What kinds of "differences," both good and bad, have teachers made in your own life?

Further Suggestions for Writing— "Teacher, Teacher"

1. Write an essay about "How to impress a professor."

2. Recall a time when you were entranced by a teacher. Write about the qualities you found attractive and why you respected or liked that teacher.

3. Write about a teacher you thought represented one thing but turned out to be much different—for example, the health teacher who is a smoker or the dull math teacher who is funny outside of class.

4. Do you expect your relationships with your college teachers to be similar to or different from your earlier relationships with teachers? Why or why not? In what ways?

5. Argue for or against a policy at your school banning or regulating romantic/sexual relationships between teachers and students.

6. Do you think that students are in the best position to be able to evaluate their teachers? Defend your answer.

7. Visit your college learning center and interview tutors or staff about the causes of test anxiety. Research some ways to alleviate test anxiety.

8. Interview your current teachers and ask them who were their greatest or most important teachers. After a number of interviews, write an essay on what makes a successful teacher.

9. Interview faculty about "success stories" of some of their students whom they have mentored. Can you come up with some generalizations (and support them) that teachers remember about students?

10. Taking into consideration all the inherent problems and shortcomings of the lecture format, what kinds of alternative teaching methods do you think could be put into place? Use classes you now have or have had in the past as examples.

11. Research and define the terms "passive learning" and "active learning." Which seems to be the way you have learned previously? Which seems to be the dominant style you have encountered so far at your current school? Why do you think that is so?

12. What are "Open Admissions" programs? What is the history of such programs? What schools have them? Write an essay in which you argue for or against such programs.

13. Determine the number of faculty and staff of color at your university. How does your university compare to other campuses in your state? How does it compare nationally? Why do you think that is so? Are there any policies in place at your school to recruit more multicultural professionals?

14. Given the generally low pay and social status, why would anyone want to teach at the college level? At any other level? Write an analysis of what might cause or inspire someone to become a teacher.

15. Many colleges have an honor system that requires students to sign a pledge not to cheat and to report others whom they observe cheating. Does your college have a similar system? Working in groups, consider the issue of an honor system at your college.

16. Students are often uncertain about what constitutes academic dishonesty and especially what qualifies as plagiarism. On what issues of academic dishonesty (definitions, policies, sanctions) do you think there is confusion or ambiguity?

17. Why do students cheat?

18. Can or should professors set out to "change the minds" of students? Why or why not?

19. Argue for or against tenure for professors.

20. Pick two or three teachers from "Teachers: A Primer." How do you think they would react to Calvin and his problems in "Open Admissions." Why do you think the way you do?

21. What grade do you think Jacob Neusner, author of "Grading Your Professors," would give to the teacher who is portrayed in Taylor Mali's poem "What Teachers Make"?

22. Choose at least three episodes from "Tales Out of School." How do you think the teacher in "No Immediate Danger" would react to these tales? What support do you have for your position?

23. Read *What the Best College Teachers Do* by Ken Bain (2004) and/or *Clueless in Academe: How Schooling Obscures the Life of the Mind* by Gerald Graff (2003) and/or *The Effective, Efficient Professor: Teaching Scholarship and Service* by Philip C. Wankat (2002) or some other examination of college teaching. What insights and/or new awareness have you learned regarding college teaching after considering these points of view?

24. Choose at least three films from the list at the end of this chapter. What do they seem to say about college teachers? What support do you have for your position?

25. Choose one of your responses to "Some possibilities for writing" in this chapter and do further research on some aspect of the topic you addressed. Write about how and why this new information would have improved your previous effort.

26. Find the original text from which one of the selections in this chapter was taken. What led you to choose the text you did? How does reading more from the text affect your original reading? Is there more you would like to know about the text, its subject, or its author? Where might you find this further information?

Selected Films—"Teacher, Teacher"

The Blackboard (1999, Iran). Set along the Iran–Iraq border in the mountainous area of Kurdistan, *The Blackboard* follows two teachers in search of students. With blackboards strapped to their backs, the teachers encounter groups of young children, their own backs strapped with contraband, and Kurdish refugees, all headed towards the border. Drama. 84 min. N/R.

The Blackboard Jungle (1955, USA). A middle-aged school teacher takes on inner-city kids and street thugs in this 1950s classic. Drama. 101 min. N/R.

Children of a Lesser God (1986, USA). A speech teacher at a school for the deaf finds himself drawn to a tough, headstrong, beautiful janitor. Adapted from the play by Mark Medoff. Romantic drama. 119 min. R.

Conrack (1974, USA). When Pat Conroy arrives on a small South Carolina island to take on his new teaching post, he finds that his students are illiterate and developmentally disabled. He takes matters into his own hands and turns his students' lives around. Drama. 106 min. PG.

The Corn Is Green (1945, USA). Schoolteacher Lilly Moffat (Bette Davis) is dismayed by conditions in a Welsh mining town. She sets up a school to teach basic education to the villagers. Drama. 115 min. N/R.

Dangerous Minds (1995, USA). A former marine takes a teaching position in an inner-city school and struggles to reach her intelligent but socially defiant students. Drama. 99 min. R.

Dead Poets Society (1989, USA). Unorthodox prep-school English teacher John Keating (Robin Williams) inspires his 1950s-era students to love literature. The film received an Oscar for best original screenplay. Drama. 128 min. PG.

Educating Rita (1983, Great Britain). A bright but unschooled hairdresser hires a dissolute, alcoholic tutor (Michael Caine) to expand her literary horizons. Drama. 110 min. PG-13.

Emperor's Club (2002, USA). An idealistic prep-school teacher attempts to redeem an incorrigible student. 108 min. PG-13.

The Freshman (1990, USA). Marlon Brando does a Godfather send-up as he gives a young film student (Matthew Broderick) an education in the school of life. Comedy. 102 min. PG.

Goodbye Mr. Chips (1939, Great Britain). A retired headmaster of a boys' boarding school reminisces about his career and personal life. Drama. 114 min. N/R.

Goodbye Mr. Chips (1969, USA). A spin on the classic tale: a shy and retiring Mr. Chips falls for a flashy showgirl. Drama/Musical. 155 min. N/R.

High School High (1996, USA). An over-the-top parody of the "High School Movie." Comedy. 86 min. PG-13.

Lean on Me (1989, USA). Morgan Freeman plays Joe Clark, an unorthodox, demanding, and sometimes overbearing principal who is devoted to the students of his inner-city high school—sometimes at the expense of his own job security and personal safety. Drama. 104 min. PG-13.

Lianna (1983, USA). Returning adult student Lianna falls for her visiting professor. Drama. 110 min. R.

Lucky Jim (1957, Great Britain). A lowly college lecturer bungles his attempts to impress his department head. Comedy. 95 min. N/R.

The Man Without a Face (1993, USA). The story of a relationship between a teacher and his troubled pupil. Mel Gibson stars and directs. Drama. 113. PG-13.

The Mirror Has Two Faces (1996, USA). A college math professor tired of sexual politics makes a deal with a dowdy colleague (Barbra Streisand) that they provide companionship for one another. She teaches him how to be a better teacher. Romantic comedy. 126 min. PG-13.

Mona Lisa Smile (2003, USA). A free-thinking art professor (Julia Roberts) teaches conservative 1950s Wellesley students to question their traditional societal roles as women. Drama/Comedy/Romance 103 min. PG-13.

Mr. Holland's Opus (1995, USA). Follows the career of Glen Holland, a frustrated composer who becomes a high school music teacher. He writes music and struggles to reach certain students, while neglecting to communicate with his deaf son. Drama. 143 min. PG.

Music of the Heart (1999, USA). A music teacher struggles to keep her violin program alive in a Harlem school. Drama. 124 min. PG.

Oleanna (1994, USA). David Mamet wrote and directed this adaptation of his controversial play about collegiate sexual harassment and sexual politics. Drama. 89 min. R.

The Paper Chase (1973, USA). First-year law students toughen up to survive the acid wit of their intimidating professor (John Houseman). Comedy/Drama. 111 min. PG.

Pay It Forward (2000, USA). Kevin Spacey plays a seventh-grade teacher whose class assignment puts into action an idea that could change the world. Drama. 123 min. PG-13.

The Prime of Miss Jean Brodie (1969, Great Britain). Based on the play by Jay Presson Allen. Between the two world wars, the unconventional Jean Brodie teaches her group of female students about love, life, and the rights and responsibilities of liberated women. Drama. 116 min. NR.

The Principal (1987, USA). A principal assigned to a crime-ridden high school struggles to turn things around. Drama/Crime. 109 min. R.

Remember the Titans (2000, USA). Denzel Washington stars as an African-American coach hired to take a high school football team through their first racially integrated season. Based on actual events in 1971 at Virginia's T.C. Williams High School. Drama. 113 min. PG.

Renaissance Man (1994, USA). A down-and-out ad executive is hired to teach "thinking skills" to Army recruits. Comedy. 128 min. PG.

Sarafina! (1992, USA). In a world where truth is forbidden, an inspiring teacher (Whoopi Goldberg) dares to instill in her students lessons not found in schoolbooks. In doing so, she challenges their freedom and hers. Drama. 119 min. PG-13.

School of Rock (2003, USA). Jack Black stars as a would-be rock star who pretends to be a substitute teacher at a prep school; he ends up turning his class into a rock band. Comedy. 108 min. PG-13.

Songcatcher (2000, USA). After being denied a promotion at the university where she teaches, Dr. Lily Penleric, a brilliant musicologist, impulsively visits her sister who runs a struggling rural school in Appalachia. There she stumbles upon the discovery of her life: a treasure trove of ancient Scots–Irish ballads, preserved intact by the seclusion of the mountains. Drama. 109 min. PG-13.

Stand and Deliver (1988, USA). A class from an East L.A. barrio commits to taking the Advance Placement Test in calculus, inspired by their dedicated, tough-love teacher (Edward James Olmos). Drama. 105 min. PG.

Surviving Desire (1991, USA). A neurotic English professor falls for his student, who, for her part, is using the affair as fuel for her writing. Romantic comedy. 86 min. N/R.

Teachers (1984, USA). A high school teacher, frustrated by class after class of "flunkies," goes to extremes to help his students and ends up in trouble with the school board. Comedy/Drama. 106 min. R.

To Sir with Love (1967, Great Britain). An inexperienced teacher takes matters into his own hands in order to teach his upstart, adolescent students. Drama. 105 min. N/R.

Up the Down Staircase (1967, USA). A young, naïve schoolteacher faces the reality of teaching young, not so naïve students at New York City's Calvin Coolidge High School. Based on the novel by Bel Kaufman. Drama. 124 min. N/R.

Wit (2001, USA). A fiercely demanding English literature professor deals with her cancer treatment. Drama. 98 min. PG-13.

Wonder Boys (2001, USA). A pot-smoking, aging writing teacher and his bizarre and brilliant student embark on a lost weekend that changes them both. Comedy/Drama. 120 min. R.

For Critical Thinking Points on these films, see Appendix (p. 281).

Five

Been There, Done That

LOOKING FORWARD, LOOKING BACK

Education can change some people or help them recognize how they have stayed the same. This chapter proves it is never too soon to look ahead, offering pieces that explore life after graduation and provide the advantage of hindsight when offered by those who have survived what today's students are trying to get through.

When I Heard the Learn'd Astronomer

Walt Whitman

In 1855, Walt Whitman (1819–1892) published the first of many editions of *Leaves of Grass*, a volume of poetry indisputably ranked among the greatest in American literature. Today, Whitman's poetry has been translated into every major language. It is widely recognized as a formative influence on the work of such American writers as Hart Crane, William Carlos Williams, Wallace Stevens, and Allen Ginsberg.

When I sitting heard the astronomer where he lectured with
*   much applause in the lecture room,*
How soon unaccountable I became tired and sick

CRITICAL THINKING POINTS: *As you read*

1. Exactly what is an "astronomer"? What kinds of people might be attracted to or successful in the field of astronomy?
2. Walt Whitman is famous for his sounds. As you read, write down phrases that strike you as particularly wonderful or odd arrangements of words. What makes these phrases "poetic"?
3. What makes the astronomer "learn'd"? In what ways is he or is he not "learn'd"?

When I heard the learn'd astronomer,
When the proofs, the figures, were ranged in columns before me,
When I was shown the charts and diagrams, to add, divide,
    and measure them,
When I sitting heard the astronomer where he lectured with
    much applause in the lecture room,
How soon unaccountable I became tired and sick,
Till rising and gliding out I wander'd off by myself,
In the mystical moist night-air, and from time to time,
Look'd up in perfect silence at the stars.

1892

CRITICAL THINKING POINTS: *After you've read*

1. Read or reread Antler's "Raising My Hand," later in this chapter. What common themes do the poems share?
2. What kinds of statements might the poet be making about formal education? What in the poem leads you to your opinions?
3. The poet Jack Gilbert wrote, "We must unlearn the constellations to see the stars." How is his statement a reflection of Whitman's poem?

SOME POSSIBILITIES FOR WRITING

1. Why might the speaker in this poem, at the very end, look up "in perfect silence at the stars"? Explore at least two different reasons.
2. Find Walt Whitman's "Song of Myself" and read Section 6, which begins "A child said, What is the grass?" The speaker of that poem, the poet, seems to be the "teacher" in that situation. How does reading this poem change your reading of "When I Heard the Learn'd Astronomer," if at all?
3. Write a scene in which Antler, the author of "Raising My Hand" or Calvin Jefferson in "Open Admissions" by Shirley Lauro (in Chapter 4) meets Walt Whitman. What do they talk about? How is each conversation a reflection of what you know about the author or character?

The Art of Regret

Jonathan Ritz

Jonathan Ritz's essays and stories have appeared in *Cimarron Review, Passages North,* and the *Chicago Tribune,* and they have been nominated for two Pushcart Prizes. He teaches writing at the University of Pittsburgh at Johnstown.

When I look back at the fall of 1989—the semester I started at Pitt after failing out of Penn State—I think of it as the first step up I took from the bleak years of high school and early college. It wasn't that I changed myself or my life drastically; I simply made a few small but precise turns of some inner emotional screw.

CRITICAL THINKING POINTS: *As you read*

1. What regrets does the narrator have? What regrets does he think his mother has?
2. Why do people sometimes contemplate "what if" or, as Ritz says, its remorseful cousin "if only"? Have you ever done this? About what?
3. How can negative experiences motivate a person?

AMANDA: You are the only young man I know who ignores the fact that the future becomes the present, the present the past, and the past turns into everlasting regret . . .

TOM: I will think that over and see what I can make of it.

— Tennessee Williams, *The Glass Menagerie*

In the summer of 1989 my mom and I made a car trip from her father's house in Florida back to our home in Pittsburgh. We took turns driving, and the first night of our trip we stayed in a Motel Six in Savannah, Georgia. It was early evening and we were still a little wound up from the road, but neither of us felt much like swimming or watching cable TV, so I talked her into buying us a bottle of wine at a nearby gas station. It took a bit of coaxing, though, because I was currently on a run of bad luck in which drinking had had some part, and my mom felt a little guilty about her complicity.

I was not quite twenty years old and had just failed out of Penn State, the All-American college of my father's salad days. A week later I'd gotten busted for underage drinking at a friend's party, which resulted in a two-hundred dollar fine and a ninety-day suspension of my driver's license, due to start the day we returned home. The suspension would last the entire summer, ending just in time for me to begin commuting to classes at the University of Pittsburgh in the fall.

We sat at the table in our motel room and drank the wine, with ice, out of plastic cups. We talked some about the car and the trip. In two days we would be back home, back in Pittsburgh, and it would be time for Mom to return to work. My mother had graduated from college with a triple major in art history, English, and French (the world's three most practical disciplines, she'd joke), then gone on to teach high school in Detroit. A few years later she met and married my father, and when my older brother was born she left her teaching job to stay home full time. When she re-entered the working world two kids and twenty years later, what was awaiting her was a secretarial job in a suburban financial planning firm. Her boss was a homely, humorless man who condescended to her, even as she was fixing up his incompetently written correspondences before mailing them.

I was listening to her familiar complaints sympathetically, when suddenly we were talking, for some reason, about Charleston, West Virginia, a city we'd be passing through the next day.

"You know we almost lived in Charleston," she told me.

We'd moved several times as I was growing up, and I had some dim recollection of Charleston being a possible destination at one time. "When was that?"

"When we were living in Cincinnati. Your father was in the running for a job in Charleston. We even went down one weekend to price houses."

"I guess I remember that."

"That was a good job," my mother said, somewhat dreamily. "Partner in charge of the Charleston office." At the time my father was an accountant working for a national firm.

"Charleston," I said. "I wonder what that would have been like."

"Well, we would have been . . . wealthy." She laughed a little at the word, like it was some kind of happy accident that might have befallen our family. "It was quite a good job. And it's a small city, Charleston," she continued. "It's where Governor Rockefeller and his wife live. There's probably only one good private school and country club. I imagine we would have gotten to know the Rockefellers eventually." She stirred the ice in her glass with a finger. "They might have become friends."

It was unusual to hear this kind of talk coming from my mom. A running source of amusement for our family was the bourgeois pretensions of our fellow suburbanites: the neighbors across the street with a mailbox which was a bronze replica of their house; the family next door with the $2,000 pure-bred German husky my mother described as "Aryan;" the neighbors who each Christmas put up an array of lights so vast and blinding that it was inadvisable to look directly at it. I had seen my mother look at all these people with ridicule, even scorn, and yet here she was, waxing wistfully about lost chances for big money, missed opportunities to befriend the aristocracy.

But I knew what she was doing. She had just visited her eighty-year-old father, my grandfather, who looked healthy, but eighty. His home was full of reminders of her mother, who had died the year before. And here she was drinking wine from a gas station with her twenty-year-old son, who was basically a good kid but seemed to be going nowhere fast. And on Monday it was back to work, back to the job where no one cared that she was a triple-major in college, or that she spoke French pretty well, or that she had a racy sense of humor. This was her life, her reality, so she was, for a few minutes, allowing herself to imagine another one.

I poured the last of the wine into our glasses. "So, I would have gone to a private school, you said?" I wanted to hear more about it. I thought of the factory-like high school I'd attended in suburban Pittsburgh. My graduating class had been almost 700 kids; my name was misspelled on my diploma.

"If you'd wanted. It would be your choice." She touched me on the shoulder. "You would have been a lot happier there."

I was quiet a moment, thinking about there. After all, my current situation was this: I had failed out of college after two semesters, and soon I'd be back home to spend the summer working some mindless job, some mindless job my parents would have to drive me to. And there was more. The girl I'd been seeing at Penn State had moved back to New Jersey for the summer, and out of my picture for good, and I had more or less decided that it was impossible I'd be meeting anyone new for awhile. Of course, you could also add to that list that I was a white, middle-class American male, with two parents who invariably put my needs before their own, but this, needless to say, didn't seem to count for much at the time. My disappointments and failures seemed much more significant.

So we sat there together, mother and son, both of us indulging in the same thoughts, both of us, I knew, speaking silently to ourselves the same words. Different. Wealthy. What if . . .

What if my family had made that move? What if we'd joined a country club with an Olympic-sized swimming pool, where all summer I was given privileged access to the tanned daughters of the town's elite? What if I'd gone to a private high school where I simply wasn't permitted to be an anonymous under-achiever?

What if, Charleston?

The memoir of adolescence generally narrates the author's passage into self-understanding; in contemporary memoirs, this understanding often involves a coming-to-terms with a bizarrely dysfunctional family, with parents and other relations in the throes of dramatic maladies. As a memoirist, I have no such luck; I have only that most pedestrian of human proclivities to explore: regret. Like most kids, I grew up assuming that my family was normal, so I figured that regret was a common indulgence, a sort of benign national pastime. It was a given that the reality of our lives was something we viewed with disappointment, always weighing it against some expansive, unrealized alternative. For my mother and me, this took the form of reveries like our Charleston one: What if things had been done differently?

For my father, it manifested itself in his professional wanderlust. By the time I was seventeen and preparing to go to college, my family had moved four times in order for my father to change jobs. My dad seemed to be in a constant state of dissatisfaction with his current occupation; by the time we had relocated and he'd settled into a new job, he was already starting to assemble a list of grievances, already starting to plan the possibility and occasion of his escape. It was certainly not the principle of work he had a problem with—he held religiously to the Protestant ethos that hard work is by its very nature virtuous. Instead, it was the type of work that it had become his lot to do—answering to bosses who were deceitful and political, dealing in abstract financial principles that seemed to have no relevance to anything truly useful. Surely, he must have figured, there is a better alternative. And every few years our family would pack up and pursue one.

In contrast to my dad's grocery list of complaints—the alcoholic co-worker, the carping client—my mom composed lyrical ballads of regret. Dad's sorrows were generally aired at the evening meal, as we dispatched the family pot roast, but mom tended to wax wistfully before dinner, as she was out in the kitchen preparing the roast. With a glass of wine in one hand and an oven thermometer in the other, she'd sing along with a weepy Sinatra album playing a bit too loudly in the living room (last night, when we were young). Some nights I'd wander in and she'd tell me about different moments from her past, things which only later in life did I come to recognize as her touchstones of regret. She talked about boys she had dated in high school, a journalism contest she won as a teenager, her acceptance (eventually declined) to Bennington, the teaching she had done in Detroit before getting married. When I was little I would listen in awe as my mother described the rich potential of her past. Then my father would get home, and we'd eat.

As for me, I exhibited my parents' tendencies in equal measure. I was certainly my father's son, losing interest in my various adolescent pursuits with impressive swiftness. In sports, I went from rabid interest in baseball to obsession with soccer in one season. In school, I would spend the fall quarter enchanted with history, only to be fully out of love with it by Christmas (in just about every subject I'd run the entire spectrum of grades over the course of a year, finishing with my inevitable C+). Even with friends I jumped around a lot, moving between whichever social cliques would have me like some kind of high school double agent.

But I was also—probably even more so—my mother's son. Even at fifteen I had racked up an impressive list of regrets, and figured that I had already made several irreparably wrong turns on the road of life. Friday nights I would gather with my friends at a hang out spot in the woods and pass along pilfered bottles of beer. For awhile I would joke and gossip with everyone else, but soon the booze would soak in and I would start indulging in the joys of "what if," and its remorseful cousin, "if only." Even surrounded by friends, reeling pleasantly from an illicit buzz, I was deeply dissatisfied. I longed for things I didn't have. I wanted new friends to hang out with on

Friday nights. I wanted a girlfriend. I wanted to be recognized as extraordinary, or at least special, for something. As a teenager, I could drink and get as morose as a balding middle-age divorced guy.

One day in late spring, during my final semester of high school, my dad took the day off work and the two of us drove up to the "Happy Valley" of State College, Pennsylvania, so I could see the campus. There was a certain absurdity to the trip because I was currently failing Senior English, a class required for graduation, and I was undecided about college in general, but I could tell my dad was looking forward to it, so I tried to act interested. At the time, the only thing I had any real interest in was writing self-absorbed songs on a cheap electric guitar laden with heavy, wet distortion (a style of music Seattle would make popular, but not for another few years). My parents understood that writing and playing music was my dream, but they also wanted me to go to college, so we made a deal: I would go to Penn State to study classical guitar, an instrumental style I didn't know the first thing about, but I could also join a rock band and play in bars at night instead of getting a part-time job.

We began our visit with a brief sweep around the campus, my dad animatedly describing his alma mater's various attractions: Beaver Stadium (where he only missed three home games in four years); the ivy-covered brick building where most of his business courses met; the diner (now a bar) on College Avenue where he'd worked as a short order cook. It was unusual for the two of us to take a trip together, even more unusual to see my dad so excited, and I tried to muster some enthusiasm on his behalf.

"Sounds like you really loved college," I said.

"Well," he started, and paused. We were at an intersection, and he watched as a group of students crossed in front of us. "I guess I did."

"It's supposed to be the best years of your life."

My dad looked over at me and smiled, which surprised me; he was generally distrustful of such overblown statements.

Later we met with a music professor, who shook my dad's hand and gave us a pile of forms to fill out. Paunchy and non-descript, the professor looked depressingly like the band teacher at my high school. He asked me what my instrument was, and when I said "guitar" he looked briefly to my dad, who nodded.

By the time we left the building I was already depressed, my adolescent hopes already meeting head on with the unappealing realities. I pictured myself on the first day of class, walking into a room full of other music students. They would all be warming up their polished acoustic guitars, running expertly through arpeggio scales, and I would get out my dented electric and start banging out the opening bar chords of "Cinnamon Girl," slightly out of tune.

"Wrong room," they would all say at once. "Wrong room."

We left the music building and walked the several blocks into downtown. The day was clear and cool; the students were wearing shorts and heavier tops, mostly sweatshirts turned inside out. We must have been instantly recognizable as a father and son prospecting the campus, and that transparency made me uncomfortable as it would any teenager, but I was still glad to have him with me. Not only because he knew his way around, but because this was really his day, and I was glad to have the attention off me, glad to be excused from the obligation of acting ambitious and optimistic. We ate lunch at a fast food restaurant right across from the diner-turned-bar, where 30 years earlier my father had wielded lard and spatula to earn money for his undoubtedly modest living expenses.

Maybe ghosts aren't just the spirits of the dead, but also the traces of ourselves that we leave in the past. About a year later, as I was completing the fiery descent of my final semester at Penn State, I'd have this strange notion that the ghost of my dad as a young man, a shadow from his best years long past, was with me, watching, helplessly.

Many of us, I think, try to make sense of our lives by constructing them as narratives: we're the protagonist in a story we read by living through it. There are supporting characters, conflicts and tension, recurring themes and motifs, and, if we're lucky, occasional periods of climax and resolution. When I look back at the fall of 1989—the semester I started at Pitt after failing out of Penn State—I think of it as the first step up I took from the bleak years of high school and early college. It wasn't that I changed myself or my life drastically; I simply made a few small but precise turns of some inner emotional screw. Part of this was a result of a creative writing course I took, the first class I signed up for at Pitt.

The class was called "Introduction to Fiction," and I wasn't sure if it was a writing course or a literature one; I took it because it met in the late afternoon and it filled a general Humanities requirement (unnerving, sometimes, to consider how many of my life's paths were decided arbitrarily). Our first assignment was to complete a short story. My mind turned quickly to the most clearly identifiable "short stories" I could think of—the half-hour Twilight Zone episodes I had collected on video as a kid. The day the story was due I sat down and typed out eight-pages: one Christmas Eve a hopeless drunken man who has squandered all his life's possibilities is given a gift-wrapped box by a mysterious Santa on a street corner. The man unwraps the box and is instantly transported into an alternate version of his life, all sober and shining, complete with house, wife, kids. The story was titled, inscrutably, "The Present," and I thought it had a certain eerie redemptive quality to it, but the day it was work-shopped the other students called it "unbelievable" and "predictable." Then the instructor, pronouncing the final judgment, called my story "genre."

The mass rejection stung, but I caught on quickly. The other students—most of them English majors—were handing in stories that seemed to me simply typed pages from their diaries, but those stories met with steady praise from the other students and the professor. There were stories about smoking pot and drinking in bars and having sex on seedy futons, all of them in first-person. After workshopping several of these stories the class seemed to arrive at the conclusion that the writers were their narrator–protagonists, which everyone found exciting. It was certainly a new experience for me, looking around at my classmates and thinking, "there's the one who was molested by his uncle," and, "there's the one whose boyfriend is probably gay." I still couldn't remember most of their first names.

By the time I began working on my second story I was determined to gain admittance to the fold. The problem was, I didn't have the same things the others did to draw upon; my defeats and failures were significant, but hardly interesting. I began a draft—switching to the de rigueur first-person—about a college student who is failing out after his first year. I put him in his spartan dorm room on the last day of the semester, his roommate and friends already packed and gone for the summer. I had him gather together his "few lonely possessions": Kerouac paperbacks and Grateful Dead bootlegs, his journals. I had him smoke a joint and listen to Dylan's Blood on the Tracks and reflect on the seemingly inevitable nature of his failures. I was on page three.

Now what? I couldn't keep the character (his name was Jake, a pseudonym I assumed in many daydreams) in the dorm room, sitting on his bed, the entire story. Should I have him move back home, only to get an underage drinking citation and lose his driver's license? Should I have him confront his father, who sees in Jake's failures an extension of his own? Should I have his mother show up, and have the two of them move to West Virginia? I was hacking away at the story, trying out different possibilities, when it came to me.

I would let Jake escape—not only his immediate circumstances, but himself.

He finishes his joint and throws the Dylan CD into his traveling bag. He walks a mile to the Greyhound station and buys a ticket. No one knows anything about his plans (doesn't Jake have a family? Parents who will be worried sick when they don't hear from him?). He travels two days and arrives in a city where an old buddy lives. The friend gives Jake a place to live, sets him up with a job, introduces him to girls who see Jake as the beguilingly formless creature that he is. The friend becomes a brother—all the family Jake needs. I titled the story, "Homeward, and then Home."

The day it was workshopped the other students interrupted each other with praise. They looked at me as if for the first time, as if they hadn't before noticed me sitting at the table with them. At the bottom of the professor's typed comments— just above his signed name—he'd written, You've shown some real talent here. It was the first time in ten years I had received any kind of praise from a teacher. I left class with my head spinning. The acclaim had flushed my face, and made me so grateful I almost felt guilty.

For close to an hour I walked dreamily up and down Forbes Avenue, thinking about the possibilities. I thought about the thousand episodes from my own life that I was going to rewrite; the thousand different daydreams I was going to flesh out in words and step right into. After lunch I went over and signed the forms to declare myself an English major, then went to my professor to share the news of my conversion.

I knocked lightly on his open door and stepped in. He was sitting back in his chair, feet up on his desk, reading a book called Dreams of Distant Lives. I thought, yes, exactly.

Later that evening—the one we spent at the Motel Six during our trip back from Florida—my mother and I finished up our wine, then walked to a diner across the street. We didn't say much as we ate, both of us sliding deeper into our what-might-have-been, Charleston lives. I started thinking about how high school could have been different for me there. Perhaps I would have been a better student and a more disciplined athlete. Editor of the literary magazine and, say, captain of the soccer team. I saw myself saying heartfelt and final farewells to teachers and friends at the end of my senior year. After a stellar high school career I'd been accepted to Yale University, where I'd be starting classes in the fall.

The waitress refills my water glass, and I look up at my mother, who is quietly finishing a chicken salad sandwich. I know the look on her face; she is also elsewhere. Maybe she is having dinner with Jay Rockefeller, the Governor of West Virginia and a friend of the family.

Julie, he's saying between bites of pheasant, *I was wondering if you'd be interested in running the local wing of my re-election campaign.*

My mother considers this for a moment and asks a few pointed questions.

Oh, yes, one thing, the Governor interjects, *the job will require someone with a good command of French.*

They discuss details for a moment. Then my mom makes a slightly off-color but very funny joke, and it's a done deal.

1999

CRITICAL THINKING POINTS: *After you've read*

1. Why does praise for his second story affect the narrator so greatly? Have you experienced anything like this? Is this internal or external motivation?
2. What does the narrator learn from his parents' regrets?
3. How might this essay have been different if it had been written the semester after Ritz failed out of college rather than ten years afterward?

SOME POSSIBILITIES FOR WRITING

1. Ritz says, "Maybe ghosts aren't just the spirits of the dead, but also the traces of ourselves that we leave in the past." What prompts him to say this? Do you agree? Why or why not?
2. How do the narrator's parents' regrets differ from his? From each other's? Why do you think this is?
3. The narrator writes that it's "unnerving, sometimes, to consider how many of my life's paths were decided arbitrarily." Is this true for you? For people you know? How?

Raising My Hand

FROM *LAST WORDS*   **Antler**

Antler (b. 1946) is the author of *Factory* (City Lights) and *Last Words* (Ballantine), winner of the Walt
Whitman Award and a Pushcart Prize. He has poems in more than eighty anthologies, including *Earth
Prayers, A New Geography of Poets; Reclaiming the Heartland: Lesbian & Gay Voices from the Midwest;*
and *American Poets Say Goodbye to the 20th Century.*

> *How often I knew the answer*
> *And the teacher (knowing I knew)*
> *Called on others I knew (and she knew)*
> *had it wrong!*

CRITICAL THINKING POINTS: *As you read*

1. Think of a time when you knew the answer and the teacher called on someone else. How did you feel? Did this situation affect you differently when you
   were younger?

2. How would you characterize this teacher's attitude toward her students?
   What details in the poem led you to think this?

3. In what ways does this piece work as a poem? Could it have been written as
   a story? What changes would have to be made?

One of the first things we learn in school is
if we know the answer to a question
We must raise our hand and be called on
before we can speak.
How strange it seemed to me then,
raising my hand to be called on,
How at first I just blurted out,
but that was not permitted.
How often I knew the answer
and the teacher (knowing I knew)
Called on others I knew (and she knew)
had it wrong!

How I'd stretch my arm
as if it would break free
and shoot through the roof
like a rocket!
How I'd wave and groan and sigh,
Even hold up my aching arm
with my other hand
Begging to be called on,
Please, me, I know the answer!
Almost leaping from my seat
hoping to hear my name.

Twenty-nine now, alone in the wilds,
Seated on some rocky outcrop
under all the stars,
I find myself raising my hand
as I did in first grade
Mimicking the excitement
and expectancy felt then,
No one calls on me
but the wind.

1990

CRITICAL THINKING POINTS: *After you've read*

1. Have you ever known a student like the narrator? What were some of your reactions to him or her? Were you ever such a student? How did your classmates react to you?
2. What are some of the reasons a teacher might not call on a student with a raised hand? Have you ever known the answer to a question but did not raise your hand? What were some of the reasons you didn't?
3. Antler talks about one of the basic "rules" of formal education—raising one's hand to speak. Make a list of other rules you've learned, from elementary school through high school or college. What rules now seem silly and outdated?

SOME POSSIBILITIES FOR WRITING

1. Speculate about what questions the narrator is thinking of answering when he raises his hand at the end of the poem.
2. Choose one of the rules you've listed above. Write at least a page about how you continue to use that rule or how you never use that rule now.

For instance, in fourth grade you had to ask to use the bathroom, but you don't usually need to do that as an adult.

3. Read or reread Walt Whitman's "When I Heard the Learn'd Astronomer," earlier in this chapter. Compare and contrast it to Antler's poem. What does each seem to be suggesting about teaching? What does each seem to be suggesting about learning?

The Eighty-Yard Run

FROM *SHORT STORIES : FIVE DECADES*   Irwin Shaw

Irwin Shaw (1913–1984) was a Brooklyn-born writer whose works are marked by dramatic intensity and social awareness. His stories are collected in *Five Decades* (1978).

How long ago? It was autumn then and the ground was getting hard because the nights were cold and leaves from the maples around the stadium blew across the practice fields in gusts of wind and the girls were beginning to put polo coats over their sweaters when they came to watch practice in the afternoons. . . . Fifteen years.

CRITICAL THINKING POINTS: *As you read*

1. What do you associate with the name "Christian Darling"?
2. Why does Christian Darling hold on to the memory of the eighty-yard run? What details in the story reveal that this was a pivotal moment in his life?
3. What are some stereotypes associated with student athletes, particularly football players? Does Christian conform to any of these?

The pass was high and wide and he jumped for it, feeling it slap flatly against his hands, as he shook his hips to throw off the halfback who was diving at him. The center floated by, his hands desperately brushing Darling's knee as Darling picked his feet up high and delicately ran over a blocker and an opposing linesman in a jumble on the ground near the scrimmage line. He had ten yards in the clear and picked up speed, breathing easily, feeling his thigh pads rising and falling against his legs, listening to the sound of cleats behind him, pulling away from them, watching the other backs heading him off toward the sideline, the whole picture, the men closing in on him, the blockers fighting for position, the ground he had to cross, all suddenly clear in his head, for the first time in his life not a meaningless confusion of men, sounds, speed. He smiled a little to himself as he ran, holding the ball lightly in front of him with his two hands, his knees pumping high, his hips twisting in the almost-girlish run of a back in a broken field. The first halfback came at him and he fed him his leg, then swung at the last moment, took the shock of the man's shoulder without breaking stride, ran right through him, his cleats biting securely into the turf.

There was only the safety man now, coming warily at him, his arms crooked, hands spread. Darling tucked the ball in, spurted at him, driving hard, hurling himself along, his legs pounding, knees high, all two hundred pounds bunched into controlled attack. He was sure he was going to get past the safety man, stiff-armed him, feeling blood spurt instantaneously from the man's nose onto his hand, seeing his face go awry, head turned, mouth pulled to one side. He pivoted away, keeping the arm locked, dropping the safety man as he ran easily toward the goal line, with the drumming of cleats diminishing behind him.

How long ago? It was autumn then and the ground was getting hard because the nights were cold and leaves from the maples around the stadium blew across the practice fields in gusts of wind and the girls were beginning to put polo coats over their sweaters when they came to watch practice in the afternoons. . . . Fifteen years. Darling walked slowly over the same ground in the spring twilight, in his neat shoes, a man of thirty-five dressed in a double-breasted suit, ten pounds heavier in the fifteen years, but not fat, with the years between 1925 and 1940 showing in his face.

The coach was smiling quietly to himself and the assistant coaches were looking at each other with pleasure the way they always did when one of the second stringers suddenly did something fine, bringing credit to them, making their $2,000 a year a tiny bit more secure.

Darling trotted back, smiling, breathing deeply but easily, feeling wonderful, not tired, though this was the tail end of practice and he'd run eighty yards. The sweat poured off his face and soaked his jersey and he liked the feeling, the warm moistness lubricating his skin like oil. Off in a corner of the field some players were punting and the smack of leather against the ball came pleasantly through the afternoon air. The freshmen were running signals on the next field and the quarterback's sharp voice, the pound of the eleven pairs of cleats, the "Dig, now, *dig!*" of the coaches, the laughter of the players all somehow made him feel happy as he trotted back to midfield, listening to the applause and shouts of the students along the sidelines, knowing that after that run the coach would have to start him Saturday against Illinois.

Fifteen years, Darling thought, remembering the shower after the workout, the hot water steaming off his skin and the deep soapsuds and all the young voices singing with the water streaming down and towels going and managers running in and out and the sharp sweet smell of oil of wintergreen and everybody clapping him on the back as he dressed and Packard, the captain, who took being captain very seriously, coming over to him and shaking his hand and saying, "Darling, you're going to go places in the next two years."

The assistant manager fussed over him, wiping a cut on his leg with alcohol and iodine, the little sting making him realize suddenly how fresh and whole and solid his body felt. The manager slapped a piece of adhesive tape over the cut and Darling noticed the sharp clean white of the tape against the ruddiness of the skin, fresh from the shower.

He dressed slowly, the softness of his shirt and the soft warmth of his wool socks and his flannel trousers a reward against his skin after the harsh pressure of the shoulder harness and thigh and hip pads. He drank three glasses of cold water, the liquid reaching down coldly inside of him, soothing the harsh dry places in his throat and belly left by the sweat and running and shouting of practice.

Fifteen years.

The sun had gone down and the sky was green behind the stadium and he laughed quietly to himself as he looked at the stadium, rearing above the trees, and knew that on Saturday when the 70,000 voices roared as the team came running out onto the field, part of that enormous salute would be for him. He walked slowly, listening to the gravel crunch satisfactorily under his shoes in the still twilight, feeling his clothes swing lightly against his skin, breathing the thin evening air, feeling the wind move softly in his damp hair, wonderfully cool behind his ears and at the nape of his neck.

Louise was waiting for him at the road, in her car. The top was down and he noticed all over again, as he always did when he saw her, how pretty she was, the rough blonde hair and the large, inquiring eyes and the bright mouth, smiling now.

She threw the door open. "Were you good today?" she asked.

"Pretty good," he said. He climbed in, sank luxuriously into the soft leather, stretched his legs far out. He smiled, thinking of the eighty yards. "Pretty damn good."

She looked at him seriously for a moment, then scrambled around, like a little girl, kneeling on the seat next to him, grabbed him, her hands along his ears, and kissed him as he sprawled, head back, on the seat cushion. She let go of him, but kept her head close to his, over his. Darling reached up slowly and rubbed the back of his hand against her cheek, lit softly by a street lamp a hundred feet away. They looked at each other, smiling.

Louise drove down to the lake and they sat there silently, watching the moon rise behind the hills on the other side. Finally he reached over, pulled her gently to him, kissed her. Her lips grew soft, her body sank into his, tears formed slowly in her eyes. He knew, for the first time, that he could do whatever he wanted with her.

"Tonight," he said. "I'll call for you at seven-thirty. Can you get out?"

She looked at him. She was smiling, but the tears were still full in her eyes. "All right," she said. "I'll get out. How about you? Won't the coach raise hell?"

Darling grinned. "I got the coach in the palm of my hand," he said. "Can you wait till seven-thirty?"

She grinned back at him. "No," she said.

They kissed and she started the car and they went back to town for dinner. He sang on the way home.

Christian Darling, thirty-five years old, sat on the frail spring grass, greener now than it ever would be again on the practice field, looked thoughtfully up at the stadium, a deserted ruin in the twilight. He had started on the first team that Saturday and every Saturday after that for the next two years, but it had never been as satisfactory as it should have been. He never had broken away, the longest run he'd ever made was thirty-five yards, and that in a game that was already won, and then that kid had come up from the third team, Diederich, a blank-faced German kid from Wisconsin, who ran like a bull, ripping lines to pieces Saturday after Saturday, plowing through, never getting hurt, never changing expression, scoring more points, gaining more ground than all the rest of the team put together, making everybody's All-American, carrying the ball three times out of four, keeping everybody else out of the headlines. Darling was a good blocker and he spent his Saturday afternoon working on the big Swedes and Polacks who played tackle and end for Michigan, Illinois, Purdue, hurling into huge pileups, bobbing his head wildly to elude the great raw hands swinging like meat cleavers at him as he went charging in to open up holes for Diederich coming through like a locomotive behind him. Still, it wasn't so bad. Everybody liked him and he did his job and he was pointed out on the campus and boys always felt important when they introduced their girls to him at their proms, and Louise loved him and watched him faithfully in the games, even in the mud, when your own mother wouldn't know you, and drove him around in her car keeping the top down because she was proud of him and wanted to show everybody that she was Christian Darling's girl. She bought him crazy presents because her father was rich, watches, pipes, humidors, an icebox for beer in his room, curtains, wallets, a fifty-dollar dictionary.

"You'll spend every cent your old man owns," Darling protested once when she showed up at his rooms with seven different packages in her arms and tossed them onto the couch.

"Kiss me," Louise said, "and shut up."

"Do you want to break your poor old man?"

"I don't mind. I want to buy you presents."

"Why?"

"It makes me feel good. Kiss me. I don't know why. Did you know that you're an important figure?"

"Yes," Darling said gravely.

"When I was waiting for you at the library yesterday two girls saw you coming and one of them said to the other, 'That's Christian Darling. He's an important figure.'"

"You're a liar."

"I'm in love with an important figure."

"Still, why the hell did you have to give me a forty-pound dictionary?"

"I wanted to make sure," Louise said, "that you had a token of my esteem. I want to smother you in tokens of my esteem."

Fifteen years ago.

They'd married when they got out of college. There'd been other women for him, but all casual and secret, more for curiosity's sake, and vanity, women who'd thrown themselves at him and flattered him, a pretty mother at a summer camp for boys, an old girl from his hometown who'd suddenly blossomed into a coquette, a friend of Louise's who had dogged him grimly for six months and had taken advantage of the two weeks when Louise went home when her mother died. Perhaps Louise had known, but she'd kept quiet, loving him completely, filling his rooms with presents, religiously watching him battling with the big Swedes and Polacks on the line of scrimmage on Saturday afternoons, making plans for marrying him and living with him in New York and going with him there to the nightclubs, the theatres, the good restaurants, being proud of him in advance, tall, white-teethed, smiling, large, yet moving lightly, with an athlete's grace, dressed in evening clothes, approvingly eyed by magnificently dressed and famous women in theatre lobbies, with Louise adoringly at his side.

Her father, who manufactured inks, set up a New York office for Darling to manage and presented him with three hundred accounts and they lived on Beekman Place with a view of the river with fifteen thousand dollars a year between them, because everybody was buying everything in those days, including ink. They saw all the shows and went to all the speakeasies and spent their fifteen thousand dollars a year and in the afternoons Louise went to the art galleries and the matinees of the more serious plays that Darling didn't like to sit through and Darling slept with a girl who danced in the chorus of *Rosalie* and with the wife of a man who owned three copper mines. Darling played squash three times a week and remained as solid as a stone barn and Louise never took her eyes off him when they were in the same room together, watching him with a secret, miser's smile, with a trick of coming over to him in the middle of a crowded room and saying gravely, in a low voice, "You are the handsomest man I've ever seen in my whole life. Want a drink?"

Nineteen twenty-nine came to Darling and to his wife and father-in-law, the maker of inks, just as it came to everyone else. The father-in-law waited until 1933 and then blew his brains out and when Darling went to Chicago to see what the books of the firm looked like he found out all that was left were debts and three or four gallons of unbought ink.

"Please, Christian," Louise said, sitting in their neat Beekman Place apartment, with a view of the river and prints of paintings by Dufy and Braque and Picasso on the wall, "please, why do you want to start drinking at two o'clock in the afternoon?"

"I have nothing else to do," Darling said, putting down his glass, emptied of its fourth drink. "Please pass the whiskey."

Louise filled his glass. "Come take a walk with me," she said. "We'll walk along the river."

"I don't want to walk along the river," Darling said, squinting intensely at the prints of paintings by Dufy, Braque, and Picasso.

"We'll walk along Fifth Avenue."

"I don't want to walk along Fifth Avenue."

"Maybe," Louise said gently, "you'd like to come with me to some art galleries. There's an exhibition by a man named Klee—"

"I don't want to go to any art galleries. I want to sit here and drink Scotch whiskey," Darling said. "Who the hell hung those goddamn pictures up on the wall?"

"I did," Louise said.

"I hate them."

"I'll take them down," Louise said.

"Leave them there. It gives me something to do in the afternoon. I can hate them." Darling took a long swallow. "Is that the way people paint these days?"

"Yes, Christian. Please don't drink any more."

"Do you like painting like that?"

"Yes, dear."

"Really?"

"Really."

Darling looked carefully at the prints once more. "Little Louise Tucker. The Middle-Western beauty. I like pictures with horses in them. Why should you like pictures like that?"

"I just happen to have gone to a lot of galleries in the last few years. . . . "

"Is that what you do in the afternoon?"

"That's what I do in the afternoon," Louise said.

"I drink in the afternoon."

Louise kissed him lightly on the top of his head as he sat there squinting at the pictures on the wall, the glass of whiskey held firmly in his hand. She put on her coat and went out without saying another word. When she came back in the early evening, she had a job on a woman's fashion magazine.

They moved downtown and Louise went out to work every morning and Darling sat home and drank and Louise paid the bills as they came up. She made believe she was going to quit work as soon as Darling found a job, even though she was taking over more responsibility day by day at the magazine, interviewing authors, picking painters for the illustrations and covers, getting actresses to pose for pictures, going out for drinks with the right people, making a thousand new friends whom she loyally introduced to Darling.

"I don't like your hat," Darling said, once, when she came in in the evening and kissed him, her breath rich with Martinis.

"What's the matter with my hat, Baby?" she asked, running her fingers through his hair. "Everybody says it's very smart."

"It's too damned smart," he said. "It's not for you. It's for a rich sophisticated woman of thirty-five with admirers."

Louise laughed. "I'm practicing to be a rich, sophisticated woman of thirty-five with admirers," she said. He stared soberly at her. "Now, don't look so grim, Baby. It's still the same simple little wife under the hat." She took the hat off, threw it into a corner, sat on his lap. "See? Homebody Number One."

"Your breath could run a train," Darling said, not wanting to be mean, but talking out of boredom, and sudden shock at seeing his wife curiously a stranger in a new hat, with a new expression in her eyes under the little brim, secret, confident, knowing.

Louise tucked her head under her chin so he couldn't smell her breath. "I had to take an author out for cocktails," she said. "He's a boy from the Ozark mountains and he drinks like a fish. He's a Communist."

"What the hell is a Communist from the Ozarks doing writing for a woman's fashion magazine?"

Louise chuckled. "The magazine business is getting all mixed up these days. The publishers want to have a foot in every camp. And anyway, you can't find an author under seventy these days who isn't a Communist."

"I don't think I like you to associate with all those people, Louise," Darling said. "Drinking with them."

"He's a very nice, gentle boy," Louise said. "He reads Ernest Dobson."

"Who's Ernest Dobson?"

Louise patted his arm, stood up, fixed her hair. "He's an English poet."

Darling felt that somehow he had disappointed her. "Am I supposed to know who Ernest Dobson is?"

"No, dear. I'd better go in and take a bath."

After she had gone, Darling went over to the corner where the hat was lying and picked it up. It was nothing, a scrap of straw, a red flower, a veil, meaningless on his big hand, but on his wife's head a signal of something . . . big city, smart and knowing women drinking and dining with men other than their husbands, conversation about things a normal man wouldn't know much about, Frenchmen who painted as though they used their elbows instead of brushes, composers who wrote whole symphonies without a single melody in them, writers who knew all about politics and women who knew all about writers, the movement of the proletariat, Marx, somehow mixed up with five-dollar dinners and the best looking women in America and fairies who made them laugh and half-sentences immediately understood and secretly hilarious and wives who called their husbands "Baby." He put the hat down, a scrap of straw and a red flower, and a little veil. He drank some whiskey straight and went into the bathroom where his wife was lying deep in her bath, singing to herself and smiling from time to time like a little girl, paddling the water gently with her hands, sending up a slight spicy fragrance from the bath salts she used.

He stood over her, looking down at her. She smiled up at him, her eyes half closed, her body pink and shimmering in the warm, scented water. All over again, with all the old suddenness, he was hit deep inside him with the knowledge of how beautiful she was, how much he needed her.

"I came in here," he said, "to tell you I wish you wouldn't call me 'Baby.'"

She looked up at him from the bath, her eyes quickly full of sorrow, half-understanding what he meant. He knelt and put his arms around her, his sleeves plunged heedlessly in the water, his shirt and jacket soaking wet as he clutched her wordlessly, holding her crazily tight, crushing her breath from her, kissing her desperately, searchingly, regretfully.

He got jobs after that, selling real estate and automobiles, but somehow, although he had a desk with his name on a wooden wedge on it, and he went to the office religiously at nine each morning, he never managed to sell anything and he never made any money.

Louise was made assistant editor and the house was always full of strange men and women who talked fast and got angry on abstract subjects like mural painting, novelists, labor unions. Negro short-story writers drank Louise's liquor, and a lot of Jews, and big solemn men with scarred faces and knotted hands who talked slowly but clearly about picket lines and battles with guns and lead pipe at mine-shaft heads and in front of factory gates. And Louise moved among them all, confidently, knowing what they were talking about, with opinions that they listened to and argued about just as though she were a man. She knew everybody, condescended to no one, devoured books that Darling had never heard of, walked along the streets of the city, excited, at home, soaking in all the million tides of New York without fear, with constant wonder.

Her friends liked Darling and sometimes he found a man who wanted to get off in the corner and talk about the new boy who played fullback for Princeton, and the decline of the double wingback, or even the state of the stock market, but for the most part he sat on the edge of things, solid and quiet in the high storm of words. "The dialectics of the situation . . . the theatre has been given over to the expert jugglers . . . Picasso? What man has a right to paint old bones and collect ten thousand dollars for them? . . . I stand firmly behind Trotsky . . . Poe was the last American critic. When he died they put lilies on the grave of American criticism. I don't say this because they panned my last book, but . . . "

Once in a while he caught Louise looking soberly and consideringly at him through the cigarette smoke and the noise and he avoided her eyes and found an excuse to get up and go into the kitchen for more ice or to open another bottle.

"Come on," Cathal Flaherty was saying, standing at the door with a girl, "you've got to come down and see this. It's down on Fourteenth Street, in the old Civic Repertory, and you can only see it on Sunday nights and I guarantee you'll come out of the theatre singing." Flaherty was a big young Irishman with a broken nose who was the lawyer for a longshoreman's union, and he had been hanging around the house for six months on and off, roaring and shutting everybody else up when he got in an argument. "It's a new play, *Waiting for Lefty*, it's about taxi drivers."

"Odets," the girl with Flaherty said. "It's by a guy named Odets."

"I never heard of him," Darling said.

"He's a new one," the girl said.

"It's like watching a bombardment," Flaherty said. "I saw it last Sunday night. You've got to see it."

"Come on, Baby," Louise said to Darling, excitement in her eyes already. "We've been sitting in the Sunday *Times* all day, this'll be a great change."

"I see enough taxi drivers every day," Darling said, not because he meant it, but because he didn't like to be around Flaherty, who said things that made Louise laugh a lot and whose judgment she accepted on almost every subject. "Let's go to the movies."

"You've never seen anything like this before," Flaherty said. "He wrote this play with a baseball bat."

"Come on," Louise coaxed, "I bet it's wonderful."

"He has long hair," the girl with Flaherty said. "Odets. I met him at a party. He's an actor. He's didn't say a goddamn thing all night."

"I don't feel like going down to Fourteenth Street," Darling said, wishing Flaherty and his girl would get out. "It's gloomy."

"Oh, hell!" Louise said loudly. She looked coolly at Darling, as though she'd just been introduced to him and was making up her mind about him, and not very favorably. He saw her looking at him, knowing there was something new and dangerous in her face and he wanted to say something, but Flaherty was there and his damned girl, and anyway, he didn't know what to say.

"I'm going," Louise said, getting her coat. "I don't think Fourteenth Street is gloomy."

"I'm telling you," Flaherty was saying, helping her on with her coat, "it's the Battle of Gettysburg, in Brooklynese."

"Nobody could get a word out of him," Flaherty's girl was saying as they went through the door. "He just sat there all night."

The door closed. Louise hadn't said good-night to him. Darling walked around the room four times, then sprawled out on the sofa, on top of the Sunday *Times*. He lay there for five minutes looking at the ceiling, thinking of Flaherty walking down the street talking in the booming voice, between the girls, holding their arms.

Louise had looked wonderful. She'd washed her hair in the afternoon and it had been very soft and light and clung close to her head as she stood there angrily putting her coat on. Louise was getting prettier every year, partly because she knew by now how pretty she was, and made the most of it.

"Nuts," Darling said, standing up. "Oh, nuts."

He put on his coat and went down to the nearest bar and had five drinks off by himself in a corner before his money ran out.

The years since then had been foggy and downhill. Louise had been nice to him, and in a way, loving and kind, and they'd fought only once, when he said he was going to vote for Landon. ("Oh, Christ," she'd said, "doesn't anything happen inside your head? Don't you read the papers? The penniless Republican!") She'd been sorry later and apologized for hurting him, but apologized as she might to a child. He'd tried hard, had gone grimly to the art galleries, the concert halls, the bookshops, trying to gain on the trail of his wife, but it was no use. He was bored, and none of what he saw or heard or dutifully read made much sense to him and finally he gave it up. He had thought, many nights as he ate dinner alone, knowing that Louise would come home late and drop silently into bed without explanation, of getting a divorce, but he knew the loneliness, the hopelessness, of not seeing her again would be too much to take. So he was good, completely devoted, ready at all times to go anyplace with her, do anything she wanted. He even got a small job, in a broker's office and paid his own way, bought his own liquor.

Then he'd been offered the job of going from college to college as a tailor's representative. "We want a man," Mr. Rosenberg had said, "who as soon as you look at him, you say 'There's a university man.'" Rosenberg had looked approvingly at Darling's broad shoulders and well-kept waist, at his carefully brushed hair and his honest, wrinkleless face. "Frankly, Mr. Darling, I am willing to make you a proposition. I have inquired about you, you are favorably known on your old campus, I understand you were in the backfield with Alfred Diederich."

Darling nodded. "Whatever happened to him?"

"He is walking around in a cast for seven years now. An iron brace. He played professional football and they broke his neck for him."

Darling smiled. That, at least, had turned out well.

"Our suits are an easy product to sell, Mr. Darling," Rosenberg said. "We have a handsome, custom-made garment. What has Brooks Brothers got that we haven't got? A name. No more."

"I can make fifty, sixty dollars a week," Darling told Louise that night. "And expenses. I can save some money and then come back to New York and really get started here."

"Yes, Baby," Louise said.

"As it is," Darling said carefully, "I can make it back here once a month, and holidays and the summer. We can see each other often."

"Yes, Baby." He looked at her face, lovelier now at thirty-five than it had ever been before, but fogged over now as it had been for five years with a kind of patient, kindly, remote boredom.

"What do you say?" he asked. "Should I take it?" Deep within him he hoped fiercely, longingly, for her to say, "No, Baby, you stay right here," but she said, as he knew she'd say, "I think you'd better take it."

He nodded. He had to get up and stand with his back to her, looking out the window, because there were things plain on his face that she had never seen in the fifteen years she'd known him. "Fifty dollars is a lot of money," he said. "I never thought I'd ever see fifty dollars again." He laughed. Louise laughed, too.

Christian Darling sat on the frail green grass of the practice field. The shadow of the stadium had reached out and covered him. In the distance the lights of the university shone a little mistily in the light haze of evening. Fifteen years. Flaherty even now was calling for his wife, buying her a drink, filling whatever bar they were in with that voice of his and that easy laugh. Darling half-closed his eyes, almost saw the boy fifteen years ago reach for the pass, slip the halfback, go skittering lightly down the field, his knees high and fast and graceful, smiling to himself because he knew he was going to get past the safety man. That was the high point, Darling thought, fifteen years ago, on an autumn afternoon twenty years old and far from death, with the air coming easily into his lungs, and feeling deep inside him that he could do anything, knock over anybody, outrun whatever had to be outrun. And the shower after and the three glasses of water and cool night air on his damp head and Louise sitting hatless in the open car with a smile and the first kiss she ever really meant. The high point, an eighty-yard run in the practice, and a girl's kiss and everything after that a decline. Darling laughed. He had practiced the wrong thing, perhaps. He hadn't practiced for 1929 and New York City and a girl who would turn into a woman.

Somewhere, he thought, there must have been a point where she moved up to me, was even with me for a moment, when I could have held her hand, if I'd known, held tight, gone with her. Well, he'd never known. Here he was on a playing field that was fifteen years away and his wife was in another city having dinner with another and better man, speaking with him a different, new language, a language nobody had ever taught him.

Darling stood up, smiled a little, because if he didn't smile he knew the tears would come. He looked around him. This was the spot. O'Connor's pass has come sliding out just to here . . . the high point. Darling put up his hands, felt all over again the flat slap of the ball. He shook his hips to throw off the halfback, cut back inside the center, picked his knees high as he ran gracefully over two men jumbled on the ground at the line of scrimmage, ran easily, gaining speed, for ten yards, holding the ball lightly in his two hands, swung away from the halfback diving at him, ran, swinging his hips in the almost girlish manner of a back in a broken field, tore into the safety man, his shoes drumming heavily on the turf, stiff-armed, elbow locked, pivoted, raced lightly and exultantly for the goal line. It was only after he had sped over the goal line and slowed to a trot that he saw the boy and girl sitting together on the turf, looking at him wonderingly.

He stopped short, dropping his arms. "I . . . Once I played here."

The boy and the girl said nothing. Darling laughed embarrassedly, looked hard at them sitting there, close to each other, shrugged, turned and went toward his hotel, the sweat breaking out on his face and running down his collar.

1942

CRITICAL THINKING POINTS: *After you've read*

1. Why is it important to the story that Darling's memorable run occurred during practice? What implications does this have on his life? Compare Darling's first eighty-yard run to the one he re-creates fifteen years later. What has changed?

2. Does Darling's role as a Big Ten football player prepare him in any way for his life after college? Why or why not?

3. Why is the scene in the bathtub, when Darling says to Louise, "I wish you wouldn't call me 'Baby,'" a turning point in the story? What might Darling mean by his statement? Louise continues to call her husband "Baby," but he doesn't seem to mind after this scene. Why?

SOME POSSIBILITIES FOR WRITING

1. Write the next scene between the young couple who witnessed Darling's run as a 35-year-old. What do they talk about as they walk home from the stadium? Does seeing Christian Darling, a middle-aged man bolting down the football field, affect these two in any way?

2. The traditional male/female roles for this era are reversed in the story. Why do you think this is so?

3. Shaw says of Darling, "He had practiced the wrong thing, perhaps. He hadn't practiced for 1929 and New York City and a girl who would turn into a woman." How might Darling have "practiced" for such events? Was "practicing" even a possibility for him? Why or why not? What in his character supports your opinion?

Reunion

Dawn Karima Pettigrew

Reverend Dawn Karima Pettigrew (b. 1970) holds a degree in Social Studies, with a focus on Popular Culture and Media, from Harvard University as well as a Master of Fine Arts degree in Creative Writing from Ohio State University. An ordained minister of Cherokee, Creek, Chickasaw, Choctaw, and other Native descent, she directs Wells of Victory Ministries, Inc., which serves the people of North Carolina's Qualla Boundary Cherokee Reservation.

I see Ollie Panther in the grandmother's cheekbones,
and that young guy might as well be Thomas Crow.
Probably could see the whole Cherokee nation,
if I sit here and study them all long enough.

CRITICAL THINKING POINTS: *As you read*

1. Why might the title be read as ironic? Is it sarcastic? If so, to whom?
2. How does Jane Gisgi "reinvest," if at all, in Qualla Boundary Reservation?
3. What are some details that represent the narrator's past life on the Qualla Boundary Reservation? What are some details that represent her current life as an Ivy League student?

Jane Gisgi, Ivy League student, reinvests in
*   Qualla Boundary Reservation*

I endure the air-kisses,
avoid the cellular phones,
wend my way through the basil and hypocrisy
in the brunch-hour air.

Painted and powdered,
white-washed and well-read,
I slide into my seat
boy-girl-boy-girl.
Three pairs of sky-colored eyes
blink back at me.

I forget to remember to thank the waiter.
My eyes find,
at one table made from two,
earthen hands, clay-colored faces.
Men swing hair they can sit on.
Women balance babies between their knees and the table.

I see Ollie Panther in the grandmother's cheekbones,
and that young guy might as well be Thomas Crow.
Probably could see the whole Cherokee nation,
if I sit here and study them all long enough.

Higher education might hurt less if I know them,
it's no threat to my diploma if I wave.

"Look at that."
My undecided boyfriend sounds like anthro stirred with psych.
I was born in the dark, but it wasn't last night.
I've read enough textbooks to know what's coming.
"Looks like they brought the whole tribe with them."
He might love me, he's so mean without malice.

I should shout,
make a scene,
right out of drama class,
chant or cry,
"We do bring everyone with us.
No one is left behind.
We do not warehouse old people for profit,
or eat without children or raise them in boxes."
That's not what comes out.
After all, I left the mountains.
Tired of tourists, bored with bears,
embarrassed everytime Cousin Jess went chiefing,
I ran to college,
ran from drums,
ran from dulcimers.
It's amazing what'll make you go foolish.

I lift my head,
meet each pair of eyes in pale faces,
"Those people are my family."
My smile is wet sugar.

The eyes across the table drop,
fingers pinch the hearts from artichokes.
Soft "sorry" mixing with talk of Sartre
makes everything in me miss the mountains.

1998

CRITICAL THINKING POINTS: *After you've read*

1. How does the narrator's life in the mountains conflict with the life she adapted to at college? What details in the poem lead you to your conclusions?

2. In what ways do Native American students often leave a way of life behind when they go to college? How might this be similar to or different from the kinds of changes other students go through?

3. What might Pettigrew be feeling when she says, "Higher education might hurt less if I know them, / it's no threat to my diploma if I wave"?

SOME POSSIBILITIES FOR WRITING

1. Write about a time when you were with a group of peers or classmates and you were embarrassed to see someone from your past, such as an ex-boyfriend or ex-girlfriend, a friend from grammar school, or a family member.

2. Create the next scene for Jane and her boyfriend as they leave the restaurant. What might their conversation be like? How might the episode in the restaurant affect their future relationship?

3. Why does the narrator say, "Those people are my family"? Support your conclusions with details from the poem.

Scarlet Ribbons

Michael Perry

Michael Perry (b. 1964) is the author of *Population 485* (Perennial, 2003) and *Off Main Street* (Perennial, 2005). He lives and writes in rural Wisconsin. His essays have appeared in *Esquire, The Utne Reader, Orion Magazine,* and *Salon.*

It's one thing to speak of the heart as a center of emotion, quite another to see it lurching between the lungs like a spasmodic grey slug.

CRITICAL THINKING POINTS: *As you read*

1. What makes a "liberal arts" education?
2. What skills do writers and nurses share?
3. Would you prefer to have a nurse or doctor who was also knowledgeable and interested in fields such as music, art, and literature? Why or not?

The man in the small room with me is a convicted murderer. He is immense and simple, looks as if he was raised on potatoes and homemade biscuits. I'd lay money that before he wound up here, his clothes smelled of bacon grease. He knows I am uneasy. I know he knows, because he looked me square in the eye, grinned, and told me so. Still, *The New York Times Magazine* has given me an assignment, and although I may be edgy in this prison, in this room with concrete blocks close all around, with this bulky killer two feet away, I must complete it.

I am to determine if the prisoner is happy.

The first person to whom I ever administered an intramuscular injection was a cheery wee granny. I see her still, seated on a hospital chair, flannel gown hiked up to expose her left quadriceps, head fluffed with a blessing of fine white curls, smile as sweet and warm as a batch of sugar cookies. The steel needle is cocked an inch from her skin, and she chirps: "Have you ever done this before?"

"Oh yes," I lie. Brightly. Smoothly. Never breaking eye contact.

Heraclitus said you can never step in the same river twice. Jorge Luis Borges said time is forever dividing itself toward innumerable futures—that we choose one alternative at the expense of all others. We can never be who we set out to be, but will always be who we were. I went to college to become a nurse. I became a writer. We spring from a thicket of tangents. I remember the exact moment I decided to become a nurse. I was reading *Sports Illustrated* in the high school library. I was supposed to be in World Literature, but the university recruiter was in town, and we were allowed to skip class to catch her pitch. I signed up, but once in the library, headed straight for the magazine rack, lolling through *People* and *Newsweek* while the rest of the students joined the recruiter at a long table. Late in her presentation, I overheard her reciting a list of majors: "Biology. Business. Economics. History. Nursing."

"Nursing," I thought. "That sounds interesting."

I filled out the necessary paperwork, and reported for class in the fall.

Nursing is so easily caricatured by white skirts and chilly bed pans. Pills and needles. Shots. But this is like saying painting is about paint. Practiced at its best, nursing is humane art, arisen from intimate observation and expressed through care. Again and again our instructors reminded us that every patient is a point of convergence, an intersection of body, mind and spirit. We were trained to obtain quantifiable data with stethoscopes and sphygmomanometers, but we were also warned not to ignore intuition. We learned to change sheets without removing a bedridden patient, we learned how to prevent decubitus ulcers by monitoring pressure points, we learned to stick lubricated feeding tubes up noses, but we also learned to seek eye contact, percept nonverbal communication, and establish trust so rapidly that within five minutes of meeting a stranger we could quite comfortably inquire after his bowel habits. Facilitate, reflect, and clarify. Employ empathic response. These are the interviewing tools of the nurse. Also eminently functional, as it turns out, in the service of interviewing murderers for *The New York Times*. Every time I filled a syringe, I was filling my writer's pen with ink.

Heraclitus also said we are never being, but becoming, and in between clinical rotations and classes on skin disease, all nursing students were required to enroll in humanity courses. This rankled me. I have never been taken with the concept of a liberal arts education. The idea of lounging around dissecting Tom Jones when I should have been dissecting piglets always struck me as mark-time dawdling along the road to employability. I'd change out of surgical scrubs and hustle off to badminton class, Econ 110, or The United States Since 1877, or Introduction to Film, or Introduction to Creative Writing, or Folk Music in America. I expected the Chemistry 210, the General Zoology, the Developmental Psych and the Survey of Biochemistry, and willingly submitted to the Minnesota Multiphasic Personality Inventory assessment designed to reassure the beehived matron at the helm of the nursing school that I was unlikely to bite my patients or develop perverse affections for iodine swabs, but a .5 credit course in relaxation? What did these things have to do with nursing? Peering into the thicket of tangents, I saw nothing but obstruction.

Early one morning during a summer O.R. rotation, long before most people had finished their first cup of coffee, a surgeon inflated and deflated a lung for me. It pressed out of the patient's bisected chest like a greasy trick balloon, then shrunk back and retreated into a cheesy lump beside the patient's writhing heart. The mechanics were fascinating. Here was the corporeal gristle revealed. We tote our organs around not even knowing them. There is nothing abstract about a glistening length of intestine. But by drawing back the curtain, the surgeon managed to reframe the mystery. Now that I had peeked behind the liver, eyed the discrete lumps of organ, I wondered where the spirit might lie. It's one thing to speak of the heart as a center of emotion, quite another to see it lurching between the lungs like a spasmodic grey slug. We were as deep in the body as you can get—exactly where did they keep the soul? The finite, meaty nature of it all blunted my ability to imagine the body as a place for spirits.

When I was a child, my father, a quietly eccentric farmer, would sometimes come in the house after the evening milking, rustle up his blighted trumpet, and play "A Trumpeter's Lullaby." We sat at his feet, and he swayed above us, an overalled gnome, eyes closed, gently triple-tonguing the wistful passages. The notes twined from the brass bell in liquescent amber, settling over our hearts and shoulders, wreathing us in warm, golden light. Many years later I found myself standing at a meds cart in a surgical ward, sorting pills into cups, chafing in my polyester student nurse smock, short of sleep and overwhelmed by my patient care assignments, desperately trying to sort out the drug interactions before my instructor arrived to grill me on the same, when "A Trumpeter's Lullaby" came seeping from the speaker in the ceiling. I was swept with a desperate melancholy. I have never been so lonely. And try as I might, I could not see how the path on which I stood could be backtracked to the feet of my trumpeting father. In more dramatic circumstances, I might have stripped off my smock, gobbled the meds, and run off to join an agrarian brass band, but my instructor appeared and began to ask me if there was any danger in administering Diazepam and Clonidine in tandem. I fidgeted, answered hopefully, and resumed forward motion.

After four years, I took my nursing boards, convinced I'd fail, and passed just fine. Worked as a nurse for a while and liked it. But I kept having trouble remembering all the numbers, and how Demerol interacted with Elavil, and just what it was phagocytes did, and yet I could remember the poem the stunted guy behind me in creative writing wrote about electrical highlines, and what the professor said it lacked, and how I believed the highline guy could have done better, and how I remembered the way the folk music professor crossed his legs and fingered his guitar when he explained that the scarlet ribbons in "Scarlet Ribbons" weren't ribbons at all, but bright blood on a child's fractured head, and I thought of the lung puffing and falling, and I said if I can conjure these things so easily while I stumble over drug interactions and hematocrits, perhaps I ought to write instead. I took to talking about this. Overfrequently, apparently, because one day my girlfriend said, "Why don't you stop talking about it and do it?"

And so I did.

There was much to learn, but much less to unlearn.

I wonder if Heraclitus would dare tell the prisoner he was not stepping in the same river twice. A lifetime of days between those tan concrete blocks? Sounds like the same old river to me. Still, our little visit must have been a diversion. I imagine he chuckled with his roomie later when he described catching me in my unease. It was a fair cop. But as he leaned in and grinned, I slid the needle in and drew out what I needed. When I stepped out of the prison, it was cold and windy, but the waning light seemed to propose an answer.

1999

CRITICAL THINKING POINTS: *After you've read*

1. Why do you think humanities courses are required of nursing or other "technical" majors?

2. What might Perry mean when he says about changing careers, "There was much to learn, but much less to unlearn"?

3. The last few words seem to leave the essay quite open ended. Why do you think Perry chose to close his essay this way? What answer do you think is proposed?

SOME POSSIBILITIES FOR WRITING

1. Do you know people in jobs or careers they hate? Speculate about what kinds of things make them stay.

2. Many college faculty and administrators would like to think that the first year of college is one of exploration. Argue for or against first-year students declaring a major.

3. Which type of degree do you think is more valuable, a technical degree that teaches a specific skill or a liberal arts degree that offers exposure to many different areas of education? Why do you answer the way you do?

Signed, Grateful

Kate Boyes

Kate Boyes's poems and essays have been published in several anthologies including *American Nature Writing*. She teaches at Southern Utah University.

But thanks, especially, for not changing my life. Thanks for giving me the chance to talk myself into changing.

CRITICAL THINKING POINTS: *As you read*

1. This essay is written in the form of a letter. How does that form contribute to your reading of the text?
2. Boyes finds a college catalog in a dumpster, which leads her to apply to college. Why did you apply to and decide to enroll at the college you are currently attending?
3. How does Boyes change throughout the essay? Map the stages of her progress.

D ear Professor,
    I didn't belong in college. I should have told you that when we first met. My father had dropped out of school after third grade. My mother had finished high school, but her family thought she was a little uppity for doing that. I clerked parttime nights in a food store and worked days as a baby-sitter. My combined salaries from those two jobs fell far below the poverty level, where I'd lived for much of my life. Statisticians said I didn't belong in college. Who was I to argue?

And I came to college for the wrong reason. My health. I needed health insurance, but neither of my jobs included benefits. Every time one of my kids came down with a cold, every time I felt dizzy with flu, I wondered what would happen to us if we were really sick. How could I tell my kids that they would just have to suffer because I couldn't afford to take them to a doctor? How many extra part-time jobs would I need to take on if the kids or I ever rang up an emergency room bill?

One night when I was emptying the trash at the end of my shift, I noticed a brightly colored catalog in the dumpster behind the store. I fished the catalog out, wiped off the mustard and ketchup drips on the front cover, and took it home. Flipping through the catalog later, I discovered it advertised all the courses available at the local college.

And I discovered something else—taking only one course would make me eligible to sign up for student health insurance. I did some careful calculations. If I took one course each semester for a year, the cost of tuition, books, and fees would still be far lower than the cost for six months of private insurance. My kids would be covered by the student policy, too. What a deal!

Becoming a student was a great scheme. But I knew, when I took my first course from you, that I was an impostor.

We were both coming to college after a long break. You came from a decade of social work. I came from a decade and a half of post–high school marriage, kids, divorce, and minimum-wage jobs. Neither of us had spoken in a classroom for years.

Perhaps you wondered, that first day you taught, if anything you said affected your students. Well, here's how something you said affected me. You announced that each student must give an oral presentation at the end of the semester. When I came home, my youngest daughter, mimicking my voice and posing the same question I asked her every afternoon, said, "How was school today, Honey?" I couldn't answer. Your announcement of the oral presentation had made me so nervous that I rushed past her to the bathroom, where I lost my lunch.

Weeks passed before I sat through class without nausea. I came early each day to claim the only safe seat—the seat on the aisle in the back row. Close to the door. Just in case. Back with the whisperers and the snoozers. I crouched behind the tall man who always read the student newspaper during class, and I chewed the fingernails on one hand while I took notes with the other hand. I talked myself into going to class each day by telling myself, over and over again, that I was doing this for my kids.

I needed three credits. I didn't need the agony of a presentation. Dropping your course and signing up for something—anything—else made sense. But I stayed, even though I didn't know why. Your lectures certainly weren't polished; you gripped the lectern like a shield and your voice sometimes stopped completely in the middle of a sentence.

I think I stayed because your enthusiasm for the subject left me longing to know more. I looked forward to those few quiet hours each week—those rare times when the store was empty or when the babies were napping—that I spent reading, writing, and thinking about what I'd heard in your class.

And one day, while I was thinking, I recalled a fascinating lecture you gave on the importance of defining terms. I noticed on your syllabus that you hadn't defined "oral presentation." I decided oral meant spoken—in any form—rather than written. When the time came for my presentation at the end of the semester, I carried a tape recorder to the front of the room, pushed "play," and returned to my seat, where I listened with the other students to the oral presentation I'd taped the night before.

When I signed up for the next course you taught—a course on women who had shaped American culture and history—I knew you would require another oral presentation. But I figured a little agony while I started a tape recorder wouldn't be so bad. In this second course, you came out from behind the lectern and paced the aisles as you spoke. You often stood at the back of the room when you made an important point, and all heads turned in your direction. Whispering and sleeping ended when you did that, and newspapers dropped to the floor. Your voice stopped only when you asked a question, and you called on us by name.

I was so caught up in the class that a few weeks passed before I read the syllabus carefully. Then I found your long and precise definition of "oral presentation," a definition that excluded the use of tape recorders. To be sure I understood the definition, you stopped by my desk one day after class and said, "This time, I want it *live!*"

Taking college classes was beginning to sharpen my critical thinking skills, and I put those skills to work when choosing the subject for my presentation. I chose to speak about Lucretia Mott, an early Quaker. Why her? At the end of the semester, when my turn came to present, I walked to the front of the room dressed as Lucretia had dressed, in a long skirt and shawl, and with a black bonnet that covered most of my face. I spoke in the first person. Although I was the person standing in front of the other students and moving my lips, it felt to me as if someone else gave that presentation.

By the time we met again in the classroom, I had had to admit to myself that I was in college for more than my health. I'd scraped together enough credits to be one quarter away from graduation. I had an advisor, a major, and a lean program of study that included no frills, no fluff—just the courses I absolutely needed for my degree. They were all I thought I could afford. Your course didn't fit my program, but I decided to take it anyway, and I skipped lunch for weeks to pay for the extra credits.

When you handed back our first exam, mine had a note scribbled alongside the grade. You said you wanted *me* to give the presentation for this course. Not a tape recorder. Not a persona. The same panic that had gripped me during the first course I took from you returned, and I felt my stomach churn with anxiety. My only comfort came from knowing that by the time I fainted—or worse—during my presentation, the quarter would be over and I would have my degree.

You didn't lecture in this course. You pushed the lectern into a corner and arranged our chairs in a circle. You sat with us, your voice one among many. You gave direction to discussions that we carried on long after class periods officially ended. I came early, not to claim an escape seat but to share ideas with other students. I stayed late to be part of the dialogue.

Three can be a magic number, even in real life. At the end of that third course, I stood in front of the class. I spoke in my own voice, just as I had spoken during our discussion circles. You had erased the distinction between the front of the room and the back, between teacher and student, between those who have knowledge and those who seek to gain knowledge. And I remember thinking, as I walked back to my seat, that I wasn't an impostor in the classroom any more. I had just as much right to be in that room as any of the other students.

I was happy when you stopped to speak with me after class. Happy to belong. Happy to have survived the presentation. Happy to know I never had to do anything like that again. I thought you might congratulate me on surviving the presentation or on finishing course work for my bachelors degree. Instead, you asked where I planned to go to graduate school.

You were doing it again! Every time I crept over the line between the familiar and the fearful, you pushed the line a little farther away. I don't remember how I answered your question, but I remember how I felt when I left the room. Miffed. Okay, angry. I steamed out thinking that you'd already forced me to talk in front of people, to grapple with large concepts, to care about ideas. And now you wanted more?

Weeks later—after graduation, after I'd read all the mindless magazines on the rack at work, after I'd thought about life without the stimulation of classes—I cooled down. And applied to graduate school.

I'm sure you knew the only way I could finance my graduate degree would be by teaching classes as a graduate assistant. You knew I would need to stand in front of a class. Day after day. And speak. I'm also sure—now—that your motives were good and pure when you suggested I continue my education. But for a while, when I couldn't sleep nights before I lectured, when I couldn't eat on days I taught, when I couldn't stand in front of the room without feeling dizzy, I wondered if your motives had something to do with revenge.

Perhaps you wonder now if anything you've done as an instructor has affected your students. Here's how something you did affected me. The first time my voice gave out in the middle of a lecture, I remembered you. I realized then that you had felt as nervous while teaching as I had felt while being taught. Every time you'd pushed me, you were also pushing yourself.

I looked over the lectern at a room full of people who felt, more or less, the same way. Nervous, unsure, but anxious to learn. And I stopped the lecture, arranged the chairs in a circle, and gave everyone the opportunity to speak, to add more voices to the dialogue of education.

So . . . I write this letter to say thanks. My graduate degree opened up a great job for me. Yes, you guessed it—I'm teaching at a university. With health insurance.

But thanks, especially, for not changing my life. Thanks for giving me the chance to talk myself into changing.

1998

CRITICAL THINKING POINTS: *After you've read*

1. How does the narrator, as she says, talk herself into changing?

2. Why does Boyes say, "Statisticians said I didn't belong in college. Who was I to argue?" Who, if anyone, does not "belong" in college? What kinds of statistics might she be talking about?

3. How does the professor's teaching style transform as her student transforms? What evidence in the letter supports this?

SOME POSSIBILITIES FOR WRITING

1. Imagine you are Boyes's professor. Write a response to her in the form of a letter.

2. Read or reread Booker T. Washington's excerpt from *Up from Slavery*, in Chapter 1. In what way is Boyes's story similar to Washington's?

3. Read or reread Jacob Neusner's "Grading Your Professors," in Chapter 4, and speculate about what grade he might give Boyes's professor. What in the letter leads you to offer that grade?

Passion

Monica Coleman

Monica Coleman, of Ann Arbor, Michigan, is a 1995 magna cum laude graduate of Harvard–Radcliffe College, where she earned a Bachelor of Arts degree in Afro-American Studies. In 1998, she earned a Master of Divinity degree with honors and a Certificate in the Study of Religion, Gender and Sexuality from Vanderbilt Divinity School.

Sometimes I think it was easier before I surrendered . . .
accepted.

CRITICAL THINKING POINTS: *As you read*

1. What is Coleman's definition of a calling? Can it be only religious in nature?
2. Do you typically think of the word "passion" when you think of a career? Why or why not?
3. What kinds of "callings" have you experienced or do you know that others have experienced?

P assion. Something in your heart that you can't let go of. Or more importantly, that won't let go of you. Something that makes your eyes sparkle and the pace of your words increase whenever someone asks you about it. That thing that keeps you up at night. Thinking and wrestling. That thing you do senseless activities for—like turn down good-paying jobs. That thing, that without, you are convinced you will die.

For me, that passion has always been books. I can not remember my life without books. My mother was a reading teacher, so I grew up believing that every room in a house was supposed to have a bookshelf, and every book on it should have been read . . . a couple times. I have been punished for reading—when I stayed up late with a flashlight under the covers instead of going to sleep—but I was usually rewarded. Summer book clubs at the local library, book reviews for the elementary school paper, payment of five dollars for every book I read during the summer—and ten dollars if my father chose the book. When my classmates spent the last weeks of their senior year traveling, gardening, building cars and robots, I read a book and made my first attempt at literary criticism by comparing the folk legend of the flying Africans to Toni Morrison's *Song of Solomon*. In trudging through the stacks at the local university library and sitting for hours in the PS 153 section, I discovered my passion—books.

My craving quickly became particular. After spending an entire high school summer reading through the works of James Baldwin and finding myself depressed, angry, and still inspired, I found my first heroines: Alice Walker, Toni Morrison, Zora Neale Hurston. I read quickly, and absorbed their stories like they were my own. I lived in the bodies of several women, I cursed at my blond-haired dolls, and I walked down the streets of Eatonville, Florida [home of Zora Neale Hurston]. Soon, my literary journeys became my committed cause: I berated my high school teachers for teaching only the "major works." I demanded more reading of literary criticism. I wanted course credit for writing on Gloria Naylor. I instituted a book club.

So it was like going to heaven the day I changed my economics and mathematics major to African American Studies. No one had ever told me that I could major in that which I loved. I had discovered that I could spend four years of my time and energy reading more, writing about reading, reading more, and writing about reading. The day I met Henry Louis Gates, Jr. was like finding the pot of gold at the end of my rainbow. Not only could I major in African American Studies (focusing on literature), but I could study with the man whose criticisms I read in my spare time. I could learn directly from the mind of someone who had previously been a name I had seen in everyone's bibliography. It's the same feeling I got when I met Nellie McKay, Toni Morrison, Hazel Carby, Deborah McDowell and Arnold Rampersad. They would never remember me, but I put their faces with their names, and my world had suddenly and swiftly become not only real, but attainable. I fell in love with books, their authors, their critics, and I fell in love with academia.

Of course I wanted to write. Don't all lovers of literature secretly want to write?! But the deeper passion was for teaching. I wanted less to become a Nella [Larsen], Jessie [Fauset], Gloria [Naylor], Gayl [Jones], Ntozake [Shange] or Octavia [Butler], than I wanted to nurture others into the love affair I had found with them. I had no desire to write a novel. In fact, I am still certain that I would fail if I tried. I just wanted to see the light in someone else's eyes. I wanted to see the marked up books in the hands of my students. I wanted to be the harsh midwife that Maryemma, Thadious and Jamaica were to me as they watched me labor through thirty-page papers, and still insisted I could do better. Most importantly, I wanted to be paid to spend hours in the libraries, at the computer and know that I was not crazy.

I remember trying to explain to my parents that academia is a career, a job, a joy, even. They sat blank-eyed, as do all from the generation that believes you go to school to get a job. Wanting to be a professor is like never leaving school. It is like never graduating. To them, it was some quirky license I had invented to become "a professional student." I won numerous grants that allowed me to research full time during my summers. I found fellowships that supported term-time research. I bonded with the stacks on campus, in small public libraries and in The Library of Congress. The more I researched without affecting my parents' checkbooks, and the more I convinced them that people do this—that Black people do this—the more supportive they became. So I was just as surprised as my parents when I found another passion. One I tried to ignore, but could not. One that I tried to escape, but could not. One that meant death, if I did not. It was ministry.

Unlike my passion for books, I had no role models. In my hometown, I had never seen a preacher under the age of 35, let alone a female minister. I didn't even know that there were young ministers or female ministers until I went to college. I came to know many as surrogate mothers and sisters. I simply assumed that I had my passion and they had theirs. I lived for Black women's books, and their authors, while they lived for "The Book" and its Author. I had prayed, and considered academia my calling.

Yet there was another calling on my life. When I had stopped paying attention, the time I once spent reading Barbara Christian and Mary Helen Washington, became time I spent on the train to church. The nights that were reserved for reading yet-another-unassigned novel, were spent on my knees, praying for the members of the Bible Study I now led. The courses that I once took in the Department of English, became graduate courses in the Divinity School. My friends were still the aspiring politicians and professors, but some were now aspiring preachers. These things made me a devoted Christian, I told myself, not a minister.

I knew it immediately, and I was outraged. One day my Bible opened to the book of Amos and I read, "But neither was I a prophet, nor was I a prophet's son, but I was a herdsman and a gatherer of sycamore fruit, and the Lord took me as I followed the flock and said, 'Go prophesy unto my people.' " I immediately called my best friend, and said to her, "Guess what God had the nerve to tell me!" I knew what it meant because I had read it, "But I was not a preacher, nor a preacher's kid, but a student, a scholar-in-training, and the Lord took me . . . " Instantly I knew it was a calling to preach—a calling towards ordained ministry—and I didn't want it. I was perfectly happy on my life plan to B.A. by twenty, Ph.D. by twenty-five, book by twenty-nine, tenure by thirty-two—and sometime fall in love, get married, have children. Everyone has dreams. This was mine.

Quiet as it's kept, I didn't want the hassle of being a young woman in the ministry in the Black church. My new exposure to seminaries, young preachers, and female preachers had quickly informed me of the disbelief and disrespect I would encounter if I woke up one day and said, "I've been called to preach." I didn't want to fight a system that seemed to respect age and male ego just as much as, if not more than, the calling itself. I didn't want to wear the tired look of carrying the burdens of your family, friends and congregation. I didn't want to stand behind a pulpit and be expected to say something important or holy. My disdain quickly became fear when I declared to myself that I would not do this "preaching thing." I heard wrong. I was called to academia. Period.

I soon learned that fighting the culture of ministry, and fighting God were two very different things. They both seemed impossible. I didn't want to do the former, even though victory was possible; and I consistently did the latter when defeat was inevitable. I didn't consciously hear myself asking other ministers about their callings. I didn't really even notice when I applied for scholarships and listed "ministry" as an interest. I didn't realize that I was writing sermons in my head. I was completely caught off guard the morning I prayed, "Okay God, I give up. I'll do this because I love You."

Sometimes I think it was easier before I surrendered . . . accepted. I was happy leading seminars, teaching Bible Study, receiving calls in the middle of the night by friends who would say, "I thought you could get a prayer through." No one really noticed me, and there were no expectations on my personal life—what kind of men I should date, what length of skirts I must wear, what style of hair I must choose. Now, two months before my senior year, I was entering a world about which I knew nothing except "Christ and Him crucified." That didn't seem like enough when I had three months to apply to seminaries, pursue ordination, explain to my professors, mentors, family and friends that "the plan had changed." I barely left time to do my own personal mourning over the dismantling of the dream.

I began to feel how it was actually harder to live without my passion. Everytime I heard a sermon, I secretly wanted to preach—even though I didn't know what to do. Everytime I prayed, something seemed to be blocking communication between God and myself. Everytime I tried to find a Ph.D. program that would fit my needs, something didn't work out. The day I preached my first sermon, I found a comfort in sitting in the pulpit that I had previously only known when sitting down in the African American Studies section of Harvard Book Store. Once again, I was in love.

With the clarity of hindsight, I recognize ministry as a life-long passion as well. I remember the things that I said to family members about my interest in studying the Bible. I recall the times that I spent more time in church than at home or in school. I reminisce about the summer workshops I held for the children at my home church. It was all so natural, I didn't even notice it. I didn't know the passion was there, until it bubbled up inside me and threatened to erupt if I did not acknowledge it.

I went to seminary at Vanderbilt Divinity School. Attending seminary is known as a painful process because it causes one to consider your faith under the microscope of your professors. Sometimes it seems like they take their tools and try to chisel away at your inner core of beliefs. Everything that isn't stone, will fall away. I have discovered the parts of me that are stone, and the parts that are not. I feel a mixture of joy and anguish when I walk into a bookstore. I am reminded that I have left the plan that so quickly became part of my soul. I see the new books, and yearn to buy and read them all. I realize that I am out of the academic loop that once sustained me—I haven't been to conferences, I haven't read the Op-Ed page of *The New York Times*, I haven't seen a "Call for Papers" since I graduated from undergrad. In my core, I ache for Octavia and J. California—or sometimes, just the thrill of library research and the anticipation of instruction. In the height of those painful moments, I found that both my passions are true. I have discovered a way to have my cake and eat it too.

I first tasted the cake the year I convinced the director of field education at Vanderbilt that teaching can be considered ministry. I arranged to perform a grossly underpaid internship at a local university. As a "teaching assistant" in the department of Africana Studies, I returned to my first love. Every week, I taught twenty-five students about Martin Luther King, Malcolm X and contemporary issues in Black manhood. The class content was more political and sociological than literary, but the educational process was the same. I used excerpts from my favorite poets. I taught my students how to improve their writing and research techniques. I learned that religious questions arose no matter the official nature of the topic. Much to my surprise, I could respond to their inquiries. When their eyes lit up with recognition and understanding after class discussion, I did not feel like a thorough scholar. I felt like a successful minister.

I learned to change "the plan." I still intend to apply to Ph.D. programs, and I make more time to read and write between preaching engagements and seminary assignments. In the delay of one passion, I found joy in another. I have come to enjoy preaching, and the way the spoken word can reach another person. I have fallen in love with my denomination's liturgy, and I revel in small opportunities to read scripture, pray, or line a hymn. I bring my three years of theological education into every church Bible study I attend. I also believe that teaching college students is a valid branch of ministry. After all, it was my professors who ministered to me.

I also found ministry in being a graduate student. My friends in other graduate schools often asked me to pray for them, to find scriptures for them, to tell them something about God, and everything about my calling. The joy comes in telling them about both my callings, and saying, "Well, there are plans and passions. Sometimes they diverge, but sometimes they come together too."

1997

CRITICAL THINKING POINTS: *After you've read*

1. What books or movies have inspired you in the same way Coleman was inspired by African-American writers?

2. Are there some careers for which passion is a "requirement" more than others? What makes that so?

3. College students are often "forced" into an area of study by their parents or even their peers. How is Coleman's struggle different from that situation?

SOME POSSIBILITIES FOR WRITING

1. Write a definition of passion as it pertains to a career. Use concrete details to describe this abstract concept.

2. Coleman says, "Well, there are plans and passions. Sometimes they diverge, but sometimes they come together too." Write about a time when a plan you had came together perfectly with one of your passions. Now describe a time when the two did not come together.

3. Recall a time when your life plans changed significantly. What led to that change? Was the outcome positive because of or in spite of that change? Was the outcome negative? What made it so?

On the Radio

FROM *COMING LATE TO RACHMANINOFF*   **Richard Terrill**

Richard Terrill (b. 1953) is the author of *Coming Late to Rachmaninoff,* winner of the Minnesota Book Award for poetry, and several books of creative nonfiction, including *Fakebook: Improvisations on a Journey Back to Jazz* and *Saturday Night in Baoding: A China Memoir.* He teaches creative writing in the MFA program at Minnesota State University, Mankato.

In eighty years or less, describe
one unimaginable sorrow.

CRITICAL THINKING POINTS: *As you read*

1. What is a GED? Who generally gets one?
2. How does the speaker of the poem feel about the interviewer? How do you know that?
3. What makes a "good" test question?

"I wrote my answer about my parents dying in the same year,
one in the spring and one in the fall."
   —Cecil Smith, age 94, oldest known recipient of a GED

I wonder what the question was,
and what those in charge,
suits and ties in Central Office,
those who studied education hard but hated
to teach and couldn't say so,
what they expected the young people to answer;

1. In 500 words, why did you quit school?
2. What is the worst thing that can happen to someone?
3. What did you learn from experience
you could not have learned in school?

The inflection of the interviewer rises and falls,
peaks and valleys of condescension.
She talks as if he understood
a different language
(he does, though not the one she speaks).

It was the kind of feature they run ten minutes
before the news, public radio
finding novelty, reaching
beyond New York to the provinces.
Her voice climbs the ladder of the slide
then starts down the waxed way

"What's next for you, Mr. Smith, a dorm room at UCLA?"
"Well, keeping good health, I imagine."

*4. In eighty years or less, describe
one unimaginable sorrow. Be vague,
general, and philosophical. Cite examples
only from your own experience, feeling free
to ignore the reading selections from your test packet.
5. Have you ever felt bad about an experience
and later realized you shouldn't have?
If not, explain.*

2003

CRITICAL THINKING POINTS: *After you've read*

1. What are some other answers Mr. Smith might have given to the interviewer?
2. Why do you think the narrator might have come up with questions four and five? Are they "good" questions?
3. Why does the interviewer come up with the questions she does? Are they "good" questions?

SOME POSSIBILITIES FOR WRITING

1. Attempt to answer one of the questions in the poem.
2. Write this same scene from the point of view of Mr. Smith.
3. Choose one of the Critical Thinking Points from above and develop your original responses further.

Further Suggestions for Writing—
"Been There, Done That"

1. Write an essay titled "Looking Forward/Looking Back," no matter where you are in your college career.

2. Compare and contrast the life you know as a college student to the life you might have had if you had made some other choice.

3. Compare and contrast some aspect of your school—for example, graduation requirements, football, dating—now to how it was twenty or forty years ago or more.

4. Education, or what it means to be educated, means different things to different people. Choose two or three people from your life—parents, teachers, siblings, friends—for whom education means something quite different from what it means to you and examine some of these differences.

5. Human nature is constantly puzzling. Explore your thoughts on some apparently contradictory aspect of human behavior that you find particularly on a college campus: for instance, students pay tuition but often choose to miss class; most college students are legally adults but are often treated like children.

6. Does your school offer distance education courses? Argue for or against these courses.

7. Argue for or against a topic such as speech codes at your university, the Greek System at your school, intramural athletics, or exploitation of student athletes.

8. Argue that college should or should not prepare students for specific careers.

9. Argue that universities do too much or too little for students.

10. Argue that too much has been made of technology at your university.

11. Argue that student athletes at major universities are or are not exploited.

12. Many people feel student organizations that endorse political and/or religious beliefs should not be supported by student fees. Argue for or against that proposition.

13. Write a paper titled "A History of Affirmative Action Policies on College Campuses."

14. What do you make of the fact that college grades do not seem to correlate very well with success after graduation? What might be some of the causes and/or implications of this lack of correlation?

15. Evaluate your high school's ability to prepare a student for college.

16. Compare and contrast the university system in the United States to that in some other country.

17. Compare and contrast two-year institutions and four-year colleges or universities.

18. Interview someone you know who has a "job" and someone who has a "career." Compare the two concepts of work using their specific examples.

What are some generalizations you can make about the differences between a job and a career?

19. Working in groups, read and discuss the mission statement and rationale for general studies requirements in your college catalogue. What values do these statements express? Do you agree with them? Why or why not? Do you feel that a person who enrolls in your college has an obligation to endorse and uphold these values? Compare your reactions with those of the other groups in your class.

20. Why do students care what other students think? Write an essay called "Peer Pressure Among College Students."

21. Research shows that current college graduates will change careers about six times throughout a lifetime. Visit your campus Career Center to gather information about at least three potential careers for yourself. What about your life now makes you believe that each of these careers might be appropriate for you? What education and/or skills do you need to acquire for each profession?

22. Why do some students drop out of college?

23. Read or reread Samuel H. Scudder's "Take This Fish and Look at It," in Chapter 2, and compare it to Walt Whitman's "When I Heard the Learn'd Astronomer." What theories of education and knowledge do the two pieces share? How are they different?

24. Imagine a dialogue between the characters in "The Art of Regret" and "The Eighty-Yard Run." What might they talk about? What might they say? What support do you have for your position?

25. Imagine a dialogue between the narrators of "Signed, Grateful" and "Passion." What might they talk about? What might they say? What support do you have for your position?

26. Read *Shakespeare, Einstein, and the Bottom Line: The Marketing of Higher Education* by David L. Kirp (2003) and/or *Brainwashed: How Universities Indoctrinate America's Youth* by Ben Shapiro (2004) and/or *The Uses of the University* by Clark Kerr (2001) and/or any other broad examination of higher education. What insights and/or new awareness have you come to concerning your own education after considering these points of view?

27. Choose at least three films from the list at the end of this chapter. What do they seem to say about life after college? What support do you have for your position?

28. Choose one of your responses to "Some possibilities for writing" in this chapter and do further research on some aspect of the topic. Write about how and why this new information would have improved your previous effort.

29. Find the original text from which one of the selections in this chapter was taken. What led you to choose the text you did? How does reading more from the text affect your original reading? Is there more you would like to know about the text, its subject, or its author? Where might you find this further information?

Selected Films—"Been There, Done That"

Amongst Friends (1993, USA). Three wealthy suburban childhood friends turn to crime as young adults. Written and directed by 26-year-old Rob Weiss. Drama/ Crime. 86 min. R.

A Beautiful Mind (2001, USA). A biopic of the meteoric rise of John Forbes Nash Jr., a math prodigy who was able to solve problems that baffled the greatest of minds. He overcame years of suffering from schizophrenia to win the Nobel Prize. Drama. 135 min. PG-13.

The Big Chill (1983, USA). An ensemble cast of baby boomers reunite for a long weekend after the suicide of an old college friend. Drama. 103 min. R.

Carnal Knowledge (1971, USA). A gritty look at the seedy sex lives of two college pals (Jack Nicholson and Art Garfunkel) through the filter of their partners (among them Candice Bergen and Ann-Margret). Drama. 96 min. R.

Class of '63 (1973, USA). An old flame reignites at a class reunion. Drama. 74 min. N/R.

Fight Club (1999, USA). A 30-something-year-old man disillusioned by what his life has become encounters an exciting stranger who introduces him to a new way of life. Drama/Thriller. 139 min. R.

Flatliners (1990, USA). Medical students begin to explore the realm of near-death experiences, hoping for insights. They begin having flashes of walking nightmares from their childhood, reflecting sins they had committed or had had committed against them. Thriller. 113 min. R.

Forrest Gump (1994, USA). Chronicles Forrest Gump's accidental experiences with some of the most important people and events in the United States from the late 1950s through the 1970s including meeting with Elvis Presley, President Kennedy, Lyndon Johnson, and Richard Nixon; fighting in Vietnam; and so on. Comedy/Drama. 132 min. PG-13.

Four Friends (1981, USA). Three men who love the same woman find their entwined lives fractured by college, drug abuse, and the Vietnam War. Drama. 115 min. R.

Girl, Interrupted (1999, USA). Feeling adrift since graduation, Susanna "accidentally" overdoses on pills and booze and is accused of trying to commit suicide. Based on Susanna Kayson's autobiographical account of her stay in a mental hospital in the 1960s. Drama. 127 min. R.

The Graduate (1967, USA). Director Mike Nichols's watershed portrait of an aimless college graduate (Dustin Hoffman) whose progression from sex to love finally defines him. Drama/Comedy. 105 min. R.

Grosse Pointe Blank (1997, USA). Martin Blank is a professional assassin who is sent on a mission to a small Detroit suburb, Grosse Pointe, where, by coincidence, his ten-year high school reunion party is taking place at the same time. Comedy/ Romance. 107 min. R.

The Heidi Chronicles (1995, USA). Adapted by Wendy Wasserman from her Pulitzer Prize–winning play, the film follows a woman from prep school to Vassar

College and on through her adult life and loves. Made for cable. Drama. 94 min. N/R.

How to Make an American Quilt (1995, USA). Finn is a graduate student finishing a master's thesis and preparing for marriage when she returns to her grandmother's home for the summer and records her elders' tales of romance and sorrow as they construct a quilt. Drama. 109 min. PG-13.

Kicking and Screaming (1995, USA). Four recent college graduates don't want to face the realities of life on the outside. Comedy. 96 min. R.

Marie (1985, USA). The true story of a single mother (divorced after her husband battered her) who works her way through school and finally rises to the head of the Tennessee parole board. Sissy Spacek stars. 113 min. PG-13.

No Sleep 'til Madison (2002, USA). One by one, 30-year-old Owen Fenby's friends are deserting his annual pilgrimage to the Wisconsin State High School Hockey Tournament, forcing him to confront some harsh truths about his hockey obsession. Comedy. 85 min. N/R.

Old School (2003, USA). Three men are disenchanted with life and try to recapture their college days. Comedy. 90 min. R.

Philadelphia (1993, USA). When a man with AIDS is fired by a conservative law firm because of his condition, he hires a homophobic small-time lawyer as the only willing advocate for a wrongful dismissal suit. Drama. 125 min. PG-13.

Poetic Justice (1993, USA). Pop star Janet Jackson plays a creative young woman who gives up her dream of college after her boyfriend is murdered. She becomes a hair stylist but continues writing poetry (penned for the film by Maya Angelou). The sobering cinematography shows post-1992-riot South Central L.A. Drama. 109 min. R.

Reality Bites (1994, USA). A bright young cast (Winona Ryder, Ethan Hawke, Ben Stiller, Janeane Garofalo) stumbles into the real world after college. Romantic drama. 94 min. PG-13.

Riding in Cars with Boys (2001, USA). Beverly Donofrio's best-selling memoir spans 20 years, from Bev's pregnancy at 15 in 1963, through parenthood on welfare with a heroin-addicted husband, and some resentment as an adult as her teenaged son takes priority over her ultimate goal of finishing college and publishing her memoir. Drama/Comedy. 132 min. PG-13.

Romy and Michele's High School Reunion (1997, USA). Lisa Kudrow and Mira Sorvino play ditzy best friends who attend their ten-year high school reunion, but first they completely remake their styles and identities in order to impress the people who tormented them in school. Comedy. 92 min. R.

Secondhand Lions (2003, USA). A story that looks back at a shy, young boy sent by his irresponsible mother to spend the summer with his wealthy, eccentric uncles in Texas. Comedy/Drama. 113 minutes. PG-13.

She's Having a Baby (1988, USA). After a dismal try at grad school, Peter Pan–ish writer Kevin Bacon jests his way into an ad agency job, while he deals haphazardly with marriage, fidelity, and planning parenthood. Comedy. 106 min. PG-13.

St. Elmo's Fire (1985, USA). A loose-knit group of college friends finds that each of them bears a unique burden in facing adulthood. Drama. 108 min. R.

Tao of Steve (2000, USA). Underachieving, overweight kindergarten teacher Dex rediscovers a woman at his ten-year college reunion who forces him to reexamine his Zen-like system of seduction. Comedy. 87 min. R.

When Harry Met Sally (1989, USA). After graduating from college, Sally (Meg Ryan) carpools with her friend's boyfriend, Harry (Billy Crystal), to New York City. They meet by chance several times over the years and form a bond. Romantic comedy. 96 min. R.

For Critical Thinking Points on these films, see Appendix (p. 281).

Appendix

Thinking and Writing About Film

AS YOU WATCH

1. How is film, as a genre, different from written genres such as poetry, essays, novels, and short stories? Are you more likely to "interpret" a film or one of the other genres? Why?

2. Some literary scholars believe that the book has been replaced by film. Do you believe this is true? Why or why not? What might have contributed to scholars having such a belief?

3. How is film more accessible than books to a general audience? Is this positive or negative? In what ways?

4. What stereotypes are apparent in this film? In what ways, if any, does this film attempt to break out of stereotypes?

5. Do any characters and/or scenes in this film remind you of yourself or your experiences? Why?

AFTER YOU'VE WATCHED

1. Which character in the film can you identify with the most? Which can you identify with the least? Why?

2. In your opinion, does this film offer a realistic depiction of high school or college? Why or why not?

3. In what ways is this film a reflection of its time? If the film takes place before its release date, was the time it was made reflected in the script?

4. What specifically in the film makes this a "coming of age" movie? Could it fall into another category? Can you create a category for this film?

5. Do you believe this film promotes a positive or negative image of students or teachers, men or women? How? Why?

SOME POSSIBILITIES FOR WRITING

1. Films often cite the original text in the credits. Is this film based on a play, novel, or short story? If so, read the original and decide what has been added and/or deleted in the transition from print to film. Speculate why those aspects were added and/or deleted. Which did you prefer, the written or film version? Why?

2. Choose at least two characters from the film and imagine a page of original dialogue between them. Extend an existing scene in the film, or create your own.

3. Read at least three reviews of this film and compare and contrast them. Which do you agree/disagree with? Why?

4. Imagine you have been asked to film "A Day in the Life of a Freshman" on your campus. What elements of your life would you include? If you have access to a video camera (many university libraries rent them), film some of your scenes.

5. Choose one piece in this collection and write a proposal to a film studio about why this piece would make an excellent film.

6. Watch at least three films from three different decades, and write a response about how each depicts high school and/or college students or teachers. What do these films seem to be saying about education/learning? In what ways are these films a depiction of the times in which the stories take place and/or the times in which they were made?